STUDY AND REVISE

AS/A2 Level

Physics

First published 2000
exclusively for WHSmith by

Hodder and Stoughton Educational
338 Euston Road
LONDON NW1 3BH

A CIP record for this book is available from the British Library

Text: Laureen Gibson and Sharon Blair-Burke
Mind Maps: The Buzan Centres

ISBN 0-340-78003-7

10 9 8 7 6 5

Year 2005 2004

Typeset by Tech-Set Ltd, Gateshead, Tyne and Wear.

Printed and bound in Great Britain for Hodder & Stoughton Educational by
The Bath Press Ltd.

CONTENTS

You are now in the most important educational stage of your life and are soon to take exams that may have a major impact on your future career and goals. As one A Level student put it: 'It's crunch time!'

At this crucial stage of your life, the thing you need even more than subject knowledge is the knowledge of **how** to remember, **how** to read faster, **how** to comprehend, **how** to study, **how** to take notes and **how** to organise your thoughts. You need to know how to **think**; you need a basic introduction on how to use that super computer inside your head – your brain.

The next few pages contain a goldmine of information on how you can achieve success, both at school and in your A Level exams, as well as in your professional or university career. These pages will give you information on memory, thinking skills, speed reading and study that will enable you to be successful in all your academic pursuits. You will learn:

1 How to remember more *while* you are learning.

2 How to remember more *after* you have finished a class or a study period.

3 How to use special techniques to improve your memory.

4 How to use a revolutionary note-taking technique called Mind Maps that will double your memory and help you to write essays and answer exam questions.

5 How to read everything faster, while at the same time improving comprehension and concentration.

6 How to zap your revision.

How to understand, improve and master your memory

Your memory really is like a muscle. Don't exercise it and it will grow weaker; do exercise it and it will grow incredibly more powerful. There are really only four main things you need to understand about your memory in order to increase its power dramatically:

1 Recall during learning – you must take breaks!

When you are studying, your memory can concentrate, understand and remember well for between 20 and 45 minutes at a time. Then it needs a break. If you carry on for longer than this without one, your memory starts to break down. If you study for hours non-stop, you will remember only a fraction of what you have been trying to learn and you will have wasted valuable revision time.

So, ideally, *study for less than an hour*, then take a five- to ten-minute break. During this break, listen to music, go for a walk, do some exercise or just daydream. (Daydreaming is a necessary brainpower booster – geniuses do it regularly.)

During the break your brain will be sorting out what it has been learning and you will go back to your study with the new information safely stored and organised in your memory banks.

Make sure you take breaks at regular intervals as you work through your *Revise AS and A2 Level* book.

2 Recall after learning – surfing the waves of your memory

What do you think begins to happen to your memory straight after you have finished learning something? Does it immediately start forgetting? No! Your brain actually *increases* its power and carries on remembering. For a short time after your study session, your brain integrates the information making a more complete picture of everything it has just learnt. Only then does the rapid decline in memory begin, and as much as 80% of what you have learnt can be forgotten in a day.

However, if you catch the top of the wave of your memory, and briefly review back what you have been revising at the correct time, the memory is stamped in far more strongly and stays at the crest of the wave for much longer. To maximise your brain's power to remember, take a few minutes and use a Mind Map to review what you have learnt at the end of a day. Then review it at the end of a week, again at the end of a month and, finally, a week before the exams. That way you'll surf-ride your memory wave all the way to your exam, success, and beyond!

3 The memory principle of association

The muscle of your memory becomes stronger when it can **associate** – when it can link things together.

Think about your best friend and all the things your mind automatically links with that person. Think about your favourite hobby and all the associations your mind has when you think about (remember) that hobby.

When you are studying, use this memory principle to make associations between the elements in your subjects and to thus improve both your memory and your chances of success.

4 The memory principle of imagination

The muscle of your memory will improve significantly if you can produce big **images** in your mind. Rather than just memorising the name of an historical character, **imagine** that character as if you were a video producer filming that person's life.

Your new success formula: Mind Maps®

You have noticed that when people go on holidays or travels they take maps. Why? To give them a general picture of where they are going, to help them locate places of special interest and importance, to help them find things more easily and to help them remember distances, locations and so on.

It is exactly the same with your mind and with study.

If you have a 'map of the territory' of what you have to learn, then everything is easier. In learning and study, the Mind Map is that special tool.

As well as helping you with all areas of study, the Mind Map actually *mirrors the way your brain works*. Your Mind Maps can be used for taking notes from your study books, taking notes in class, preparing your homework, presenting your homework, reviewing your tests, checking your and your friends'

knowledge in any subject, and for *helping you understand anything you learn*.

As you will see, Mind Maps use, throughout, Imagination and Association. As such, they automatically strengthen your memory muscle every time you use them. Throughout this *Study and Revise AS and A2 Level* book you will find Mind Maps that summarise the most important areas of the subject you are studying. Study them, add some colour, personalise them, and then have a go at drawing your own – you will remember them far better! Put them on your walls and in your files for a quick and easy review of the topic.

Using Mind Maps

Mind Maps are a versatile tool – use them for taking notes in class or from books, for solving problems, for brainstorming with friends, and for reviewing and revising for exams – their uses are infinite! You will find them invaluable for planning essays for coursework and exams. Number your main branches in the order in which you want to use them and off you go – the main headings for your essay are done *and* all your ideas are logically organised.

How to draw a Mind Map

1 Start in the middle of the page with the paper turned sideways. This gives your brain more radiant freedom for its thoughts.

2 Always start by drawing a picture or symbol. Why? because **a picture is worth a thousand words to your brain**. Try to use at least three colours, as colour helps your memory even more.

3 Let your thoughts flow, and write or draw your ideas on coloured branching lines connected to your central image. These key symbols and words are the headings for your topic.

4 Next, add facts and ideas by drawing more, smaller, branches on to the appropriate main branches, just like a tree.

5 Always print each word clearly on its line. Use only one word per line.

6 To link ideas and thoughts on different branches, use arrows, colours, underlining and boxes.

How to read a Mind Map

1 Begin in the centre, the focus of your topic.

2 The words/images attached to the centre are like chapter headings; read them next.

3 Always read out from the centre, in every direction (even on the left-hand side, where you will have to read from right to left; instead of the usual left to right).

Super speed reading and study

What happens to your comprehension as your reading speed rises? 'It goes down.' Wrong! It seems incredible, but it has been proved that the faster you read, the more you comprehend and remember.

So here are some tips to help you to practise reading faster – you'll cover the ground much more quickly, remember more *and* have more time for revision and leisure activities.

How to make study easy for your brain

When you are going somewhere, is it easier to know beforehand where you are going, or not? Obviously it is easier if you do know. It is the same for your brain and a book. When you get a new book, there are seven things you can do to help your brain get to 'know the territory' faster.

1 Scan through the whole book in less than 20 minutes, as you would do if you were in a shop thinking whether or not to buy it. This gives your brain control.

2 Think about what you already know about the subject. You'll often find out it's a lot more than you thought. A good way of doing this is to draw a quick Mind Map on everything you know after you have skimmed through it.

3 Ask who, what, why, where, when and how questions about what is in the book. Questions help your brain 'fish' the knowledge out.

4 Ask your friends what they know about the subject. This helps them review the knowledge in their own brains and helps your brain get new knowledge about what you are studying.

5 Have another quick speed through the book, this time looking for any diagrams, pictures and illustrations, and also at the beginnings and ends of chapters. Most information is contained in the beginnings and ends.

6 Build up a Mind Map as you study the book. This helps your brain organise and hold (remember) information as you study.

7 If you come across any difficult parts in your book, mark them and move on. Your brain *will* be able to solve the problems when you come back to them a little bit later, much like saving the difficult bits of a jigsaw puzzle for later. When you have finished the book, quickly review it one more time and then discuss it with friends. This will lodge it permanently in your memory banks.

Super speed reading

1 First read the whole text (whether it's a lengthy book or an exam paper) very quickly, to give your brain an overall idea of what's ahead and get it working. (It's like sending out a scout to look at the territory you have to cover – it's much easier when you know what to expect.) Then read the text again for more detailed information.

2 Have the text a reasonable distance away from your eyes. In this way your eye/brain system will be able to see more at a glance and will naturally begin to read faster.

3 Take in groups of words at a time. Rather than reading 'slowly and carefully', read faster, more enthusiastically. Your comprehension will rocket!

4 Take in phrases rather than single words while you read.

5 Use a guide. Your eyes are designed to follow movement, so a thin pencil underneath the lines you are reading, moved smoothly along, will 'pull' your eyes to faster speeds.

Helpful hints for exam revision

To avoid exam panic, cram at the start of your course, not the end. It takes the same amount of time, so you may as well use it where it is best placed!

Use Mind Maps throughout your course and build a Master Mind Map for each subject – a giant Mind Map that summarises everything you know about the subject.

Use memory techniques, such as mnemonics (verses or systems for remembering things like dates and events or lists).

Get together with one or two friends to revise, compare Mind Maps and discuss topics.

And finally ...

- *Have fun while you learn* – studies show that those people who enjoy what they are doing understand and remember it more and generally do better.

- *Use your teachers* as resource centres. Ask them for help with specific topics and with more general advice on how you can improve your all-round performance.

- *Personalise your* **Study and Revise AS and A2 Level** book by underlining and highlighting, by adding notes and pictures. Allow your brain to have a conversation with it!

Your amazing brain and its amazing cells

Your brain is like a super computer. The world's best computers have only a few thousand or hundred thousand computer chips. Your brain has 'computer chips' too; they are called brain cells. Unlike the computer, you do not have only a few thousand computer chips – the number of brain cells in your head is a *million million*! This means you are a genius just waiting to discover yourself! All you have to do is learn how to get those brain cells working together, and you'll not only become more smart, you'll have more free time to pursue your other fun activities.

The more you understand your amazing brain, the more it will repay and amaze you!

Ao Introduction

Enter the world of A-Level Physics

Many students ignore introductions to Physics text books in their eagerness to go straight to the answer to overdue homework problems. . . . **BIG MISTAKE!!!** (*especially if you have paid for the book*). Introductions tell you how to maximise the benefits of the contents.

So slow down and spend 5 minutes reading *how to get the best* from this book

This is a revision guide **not** a detailed text book. Please go and get. . .

- Your usual text book
- Your class notes
- Past exam papers
- Your syllabus

Using all of the above is essential when you want to revise *thoroughly*.

What does this book offer you?

1 Simple, to the point, **notes**. With common mistakes and misunderstandings highlighted and corrected.

2 We teach through **questions** as often as possible. Doing questions is the only true test of whether you understand and can apply a concept. That is why so many students *don't* revise by tackling questions, THEY ARE AFRAID they can't do them . . . mad isn't it?

3 We give **answers** to every problem set. The purpose of this book is to *show you* how to work logically through problems using the theory. However, we urge you. . .

. . . after you have read the question, read it **again**

Using any hints given, you **must** attempt to answer *before* peeking at the solution. Ideally COVER UP THE ANSWER automatically as you read each question.

When you look at the solution . . . **learn from it**, and you will eventually gain confidence

4

At different points in the text, the **faces** warn you, help you and make comments. Look out for them.

5 **Experiments** have been included that you may be asked to describe in a written paper. Where possible, given in a simple diagram, with a list of what you measure and how to determine the results.

6 We have drawn some **Mind Maps** for you. They are good fun, satisfying to do and invaluable as an at-a-glance revision tool. To get true value from them, however, you MUST draw your own!!

7 Some sections (e.g. Mechanics and Motion) principally give problem practice, other sections need help in understanding the ideas, or with developing the concepts and theory.

8 In writing this text book we have not forgotten those students who really struggle with Physics.

It's all here for you . . . . GOOD LUCK!!!

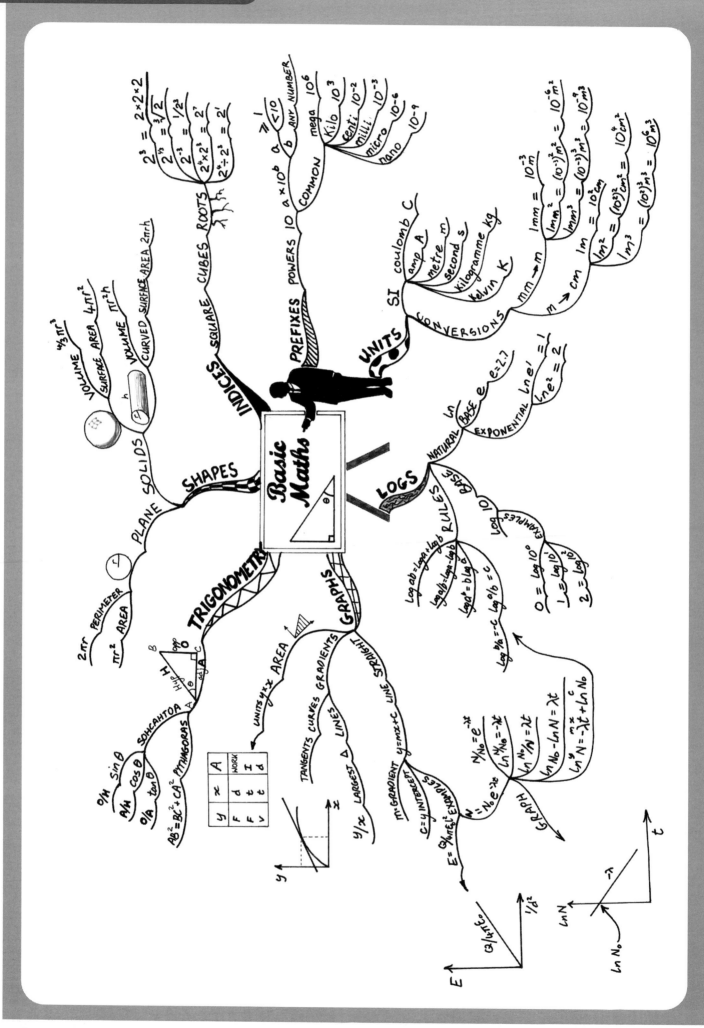

A1 Basic maths

Mathematics is an essential tool to physicists. The majority of exam questions require you to feel comfortable with using a lot of GCSE Maths, and to push it a little bit further. Try not to be scared of fiddling, juggling (screaming and starting again) with numbers and equations; this will really help you 'see' what the question is getting at.

Indices

This table works with most calculators.

notation	examples	calculator: press in order
x^a	$2^3 = 2 \times 2 \times 2 = 8$	2 x^y 3
$x^{1/a} = \sqrt[a]{x}$	$2^{1/3} = \sqrt[3]{2} = 1.26$	2 $x^{1/y}$ 3
$x^{-a} = \dfrac{1}{x^a}$	$2^{-3} = \frac{1}{2^3} = 0.125$	2 x^y 3 +/−
$x^a \times x^b = x^{(a+b)}$	$5^4 \times 5^3 = 5^7 = 78125$	5 x^y 4 × 5 x^y 3
$x^a \div x^b = x^{(a-b)}$	$5^4 \div 5^3 = 5^1 = 5$	5 x^y 4 ÷ 5 x^y 3
$(x^a)^b = x^{ab}$	$(5^2)^3 = 5^6 = 15625$	(5 x^y 2) x^y 3

Prefices (powers of 10)

multiple	prefix	symbol
$\times 10^{-1}$	deci	d
$\times 10^{-2}$	centi	c
$\times 10^{-3}$	milli	m
$\times 10^{-6}$	micro	μ
$\times 10^{-9}$	nano	n
$\times 10^{-12}$	pico	p
$\times 10^{3}$	kilo	k
$\times 10^{6}$	mega	M
$\times 10^{9}$	giga	G
$\times 10^{12}$	tera	T

 "The exam was 10^{12} bull. Don't 10^9le, how would you feel if your Physics teacher was 10^{-1}mated by a 10^3 whale before he finished teaching the course", cried the 10^{-2}mental pupil

- It is seen as good practice to express numbers in the following way, using **standard form**

$$0.02 = 2 \times 10^{-2}$$ when the decimal goes right, the power is −ve

$$0.375 = 3.75 \times 10^{-1}$$

$$1300 = 1.3 \times 10^3$$ when the decimal goes left, the power is +ve

no. between 1 and 10 | power of 10

 Don't mix up indices and prefixes. So many students do the following

$2000 = 2^3$ **NO** $2000 = 2 \times 10^3$ **YES** $(2^3 = 2 \times 2 \times 2)$

$0.006 = 6^{-3}$ **NO** $0.006 = 6 \times 10^{-3}$ **YES** $\left(6^{-3} = \dfrac{1}{6^3}\right)$

Converting units

Questions

Convert the following to SI units

1

a 3 ms **b** 48 μs **c** 0.43 g **d** 4×10^3 mm

Answers

a $3\,\text{ms} = 3 \times 10^{-3}$ s
b $48\,\mu\text{s} = 48 \times 10^{-6} = 4.8 \times 10^{-5}$ s
c $0.43\,\text{g} = 0.43 \times 10^{-3}\,\text{kg} = 4.3 \times 10^{-4}$ kg

 Don't forget a gram is a $\frac{1}{1000}$ th of 1 kg

d $4 \times 10^3\,\text{mm} = 4 \times 10^3 \times 10^{-3}\,\text{m} = 4$ m

 Watch out for those sneaky questions that don't give SI units where needed (under stress in an exam it is such a common mistake)

Trigonometry

- $\cos 0° = 1$
  $\sin 0° = 0$
- $\sin a = \dfrac{\text{opposite}}{\text{hypoteneuse}}$ $\left(\mathbf{s} = \dfrac{\mathbf{o}}{\mathbf{h}}\right)$
- $\cos a = \dfrac{\text{adjacent}}{\text{hypoteneuse}}$ $\left(\mathbf{c} = \dfrac{\mathbf{a}}{\mathbf{h}}\right)$
- $\tan a = \dfrac{\text{opposite}}{\text{adjacent}}$ $\left(\mathbf{t} = \dfrac{\mathbf{o}}{\mathbf{a}}\right)$

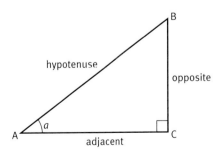

 Remember the mnemonic SOHCAHTOA

- **Pythagoras' Theorem** is often useful to remember

From the triangle above $\mathbf{AB^2 = AC^2 + CB^2}$

Logs

- **Logs to base 10**

Logarithms are systems used to express large, unwieldy numbers in a *simple* way (pick yourself off the floor and continue to read please!)

Try these on your calculator

number	press	equals
Log 1 or $\log 10^0$	1 log	0
Log 10 or $\log 10^1$	10 log	1
Log 100 or $\log 10^2$	100 log	2

 Some calculators require log to be pressed before the number

Do you notice a pattern? ......

Log 10ⁿ = n

So $\log 100000 = \log 10^5 = 5$

Log is based on the number 10

- **Logs to base e (ln)**

Natural logs, ln, on your calculator are based on a special number given the symbol **e**

e = 2.718

so, similarly, $\ln 2.718^1 = 1$

$\ln 2.718^2 = 2 \ldots$ etc

- The rules of log (or ln) are as follows

1 $\log(ab) = \log a + \log b$
2 $\log(a/b) = \log a - \log b$
3 $\log a^b = b \log a$
4 $\log a/b = -c$ then $\log b/a = c$
5 $a = 10^b$ then $b = \log a$

You can prove any of these to yourself by replacing **a** and **b** with numbers and trying these functions in your calculator

Now let's use these lovely logs

Question

2 A sample of radioactive material contains 10^{18} atoms. It has a half-life $(t_{1/2})$ of 2 days. How long will it take for 10^3 atoms to remain?

Answer

$N = N_0 \, e^{-\lambda t}$, $\lambda = \ln 2/t_{1/2}$
N = number of particles at time t,
N_0 = number of particles at time $t = 0$

$$\frac{N}{N_0} = e^{-\lambda t}$$

Using Rule 4 $\ln \dfrac{N}{N_0} = -\lambda t$

Using Rule 5 $\ln \dfrac{N_0}{N} = \lambda t$

$$\ln \frac{10^{18}}{10^3} = \frac{\ln 2}{172800} \times t \quad (2 \text{ days} = 172800\,\text{s})$$

$$\ln 10^{15} = 4 \times 10^{-6}\, t \left(\frac{10^{18}}{10^3} = 10^{18-3} = 10^{15} \right)$$

Using Rule 3 $15 \ln 10 = 4 \times 10^{-6}\, t$

$$t = 8634694\,\text{s} = 100 \text{ days}$$

Graphs

Whether you interpret or plot graphs, you must be able to grasp the following

- **Equations for graphs**

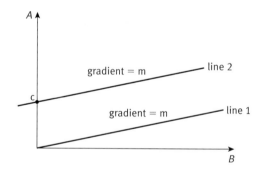

ALL straight-line graphs have an equation of the form

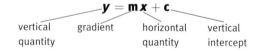

y = m x + c

vertical quantity   gradient   horizontal quantity   vertical intercept

... where y and x are the two variables. They depend on each other

Usually x is the variable you set (independent) And y is the variable you measure as a result (dependent)

From the graph
eqn of line 1 $A = mB + 0$
eqn of line 2 $A = mB + c$

Examples

1 $V = RI$

$y = mx + c$

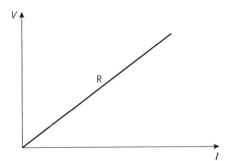

2 $N = N_0 e^{-\lambda t}$

The index notation makes you think otherwise, but you have two variables, N and t, the rest of the terms are constant so rearrange

$\dfrac{N}{N_0} = e^{-\lambda t}$ ∴ $\ln \dfrac{N_0}{N} = \lambda t$ (see earlier)

Using Rule 2 of logs $\ln N_0 - \ln N = \lambda T$

∴ $\ln N = -\lambda t + \ln N_0$

$(y = mx + c)$

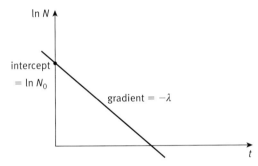

3 The distance a ball falls from rest can be found using the equation of motion $s = ut + \frac{1}{2}gt^2$

$u = 0$ ∴ $s = \frac{1}{2}gt^2$ (notice your second variable is t^2 not t)

$y = mx + c$

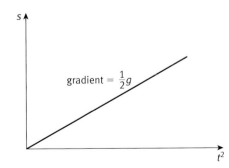

4 $E = \dfrac{Q}{4\pi\varepsilon d^2}$ E and d are the two variables

$E = \dfrac{Q}{4\pi\varepsilon}\dfrac{1}{d^2}$

$(y = m \quad x + c)$

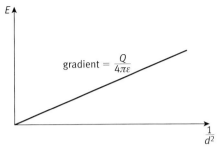

5 A steel wire of length 5 m and mass 8 g has a series of weights hung from it. Its extension is shown here. Given that the speed of sound in a solid can be determined by the equation

$v = \sqrt{\dfrac{E}{\rho}}$,   where E = the Young modulus ρ = density

use the graph to estimate the speed of sound in steel

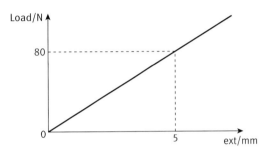

$\text{Gradient} = \dfrac{\text{Load}}{\text{Extension}} = \dfrac{F}{e}$

$E = \dfrac{Fl}{Ae}$ $\rho = \dfrac{M}{V} = \dfrac{M}{Al}$

∴ $v = \sqrt{\dfrac{Fl}{Ae} \div \dfrac{M}{Al}}$

∴ $v = \sqrt{\dfrac{Fl}{Ae} \times \dfrac{Al}{M}}$ ∴ $v = \sqrt{\dfrac{F}{e} \cdot \dfrac{l^2}{M}}$

Gradient from the graph, the rest is given in the question.

Tangents and gradients

- A **gradient** is a measure of the *steepness* of a line or curve, ie the steepest part of a curve has the biggest gradient

- A **tangent** shows the gradient on a curve at a specific instant. The gradient of a *curve* varies. Remember, always make your tangent as **big** as possible. When measuring it this will **reduce errors**

- The units of the gradient are the units of the

y variable $\div x$ variable

Question

3

a Find the maximum acceleration from the graph

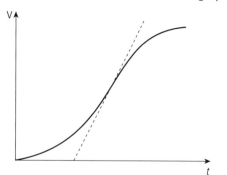

b. What are the units of the gradient?

Answers

a Draw the steepest tangent and measure the gradient of it

b $\dfrac{\text{units of } v}{\text{units of } t}$ = units of acceleration

Areas under graphs

The area **under** a curve represents the quantity that you get from multiplying the **y** quantity × the **x** quantity

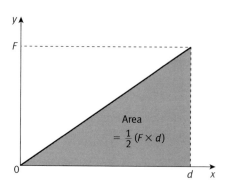

eg $F \times d$ = work done, so the shaded area has the units of work done, but numerically is equal to $\frac{1}{2}(F \times d)$ because the force is varying between O and F

The units of the area are the units of **y** × units of **x**

Question

4 What does the area under the graph of **x** against **y** represent in the following cases?

Answer

y	x	quantity/area
force	distance	work done
force	time	impulse
speed	time	distance
current	time	charge
force	extension	energy stored in a spring

- If you are asked to **estimate** the area under a curve, eg the work done, then **count the squares**

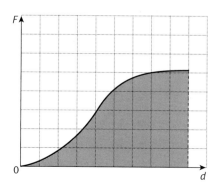

Playtime

If you take 4 circles of felt (or any soft material) of the same radius, they can be stitched together to form a sphere (make your seam infinitely narrow of course!!!)

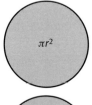

Sphere surface area = $4\pi r^2$

Perimeter, area, volume

shape	area	volume	curved surface area	perimeter
circle	πr^2			$2\pi r$
sphere		$\frac{4}{3}\pi r^3$	$4\pi r^2$	
cylinder		$\pi r^2 h$	$2\pi r h$	

Converting units

Many mistakes are made by students converting the units of areas and volumes to SI units

eg, $21\,\text{mm}^3$

Start by writing out a sequence

$1\,\text{mm} = 10^{-3}\,\text{m}$
$1\,\text{mm}^2 = (10^{-3})^2\,\text{m}^2 = 10^{-6}\,\text{m}^2$
$1\,\text{mm}^3 = (10^{-3})^3\,\text{m}^3 = 10^{-9}\,\text{m}^3$

so $\quad 21\,\text{mm}^3 = 21 \times 10^{-9}\,\text{m}^3$

 If you think logically, of course $21\,\text{mm}^3$ is going to be a tiny fraction of a cubic metre

eg, $3\,\text{cm}^3$
$1\,\text{cm} = 10^{-2}\,\text{m}$
$1\,\text{cm}^2 = (10^{-2})^2\,\text{m}^2$
$1\,\text{cm}^3 = (10^{-2})^3\,\text{m}^3$

so $\quad 3\,\text{cm}^3 = 3 \times 10^{-6}\,\text{m}^3$

Question

5 A metal wire contains 6×10^{22} electrons/cm^3 and has a cross-sectional area of $1.5\,\text{mm}^2$. The electrons have a drift velocity, v, of $1.5\,\text{mm s}^{-1}$.

Calculate the current in amps in the wire.
($e = 1.6 \times 10^{-19}\,\text{C}$)

You are now entering converting units heaven!

Answer

$I = nAve \qquad n = 6 \times 10^{22}$ per $1\,\text{cm}^3$

$\therefore\ n = 6 \times 10^{22}$ per $1 \times 10^{-6}\,\text{m}^3$

$\qquad = \dfrac{6 \times 10^{22}\,e}{1 \times 10^{-6}\,\text{m}^3} = 6 \times 10^{28}$ electrons/m^3

$A = 1.5\,\text{mm}^2 = 1.5 \times 10^{-6}\,\text{m}^2$

$V = 1.5\,\text{mm s}^{-1} = 1.5 \times 10^{-3}\,\text{m s}^{-1}$

$I = (6 \times 10^{28})\,(1.5 \times 10^{-6})\,(1.5 \times 10^{-3})\,(1.6 \times 10^{-19})$

Gather your powers of 10

$\therefore\ I = 21.6 \times 10^{0}$

$\therefore\ I = 21.6\,\text{A}$

Changing the subject

Questions

6 Make the bold letter the subject in each equation

i) $v = \boldsymbol{f}\lambda$

ii) $\frac{1}{2}m\boldsymbol{v}^2 = mgh$

iii) $\dfrac{P_1 V_1}{T_1} = \dfrac{P_2 V_2}{\boldsymbol{T_2}}$

iv) $s = ut + \frac{1}{2}\boldsymbol{a}t^2$

v) $y = m\boldsymbol{x} + c$

Answers

i) $\dfrac{v}{\lambda} = \boldsymbol{f}$

ii) $\boldsymbol{v}^2 = \dfrac{2mgh}{m} = 2gh$
$\therefore\ \boldsymbol{v} = \sqrt{2gh}$

iii) $P_1 V_1 \boldsymbol{T_2} = P_2 V_2 T_1$
$\therefore\ \boldsymbol{T_2} = \dfrac{P_2 V_2 T_1}{P_1 V_1}$

iv) $s - ut = \frac{1}{2}\boldsymbol{a}t^2$
$\dfrac{2(s - ut)}{t^2} = \boldsymbol{a}$

v) $y - c = m\boldsymbol{x}$
$\dfrac{y - c}{m} = \boldsymbol{x}$

Proportionality

You may be asked about the relationship between terms in an equation

eg, $\quad$ pressure $P = \dfrac{F}{A}$

P is **directly proportional** to F when **A** is constant

$\qquad P \propto F$

ie, as P rises so will F

$\qquad$ as P falls so will F

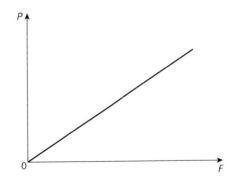

P is **inversely proportional** to A

$$\boldsymbol{P} \propto \dfrac{\boldsymbol{1}}{\boldsymbol{A}}$$

ie, as P rises A will fall

$\qquad$ as P falls A will rise

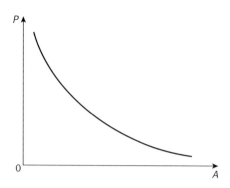

Questions

7 A Young's slits arrangement is set up. A fringe pattern is produced. What effect on the fringe spacing (y) will the following actions have?

  a Increasing the wavelength of the light source (λ)

  b Decreasing the slit separation (a)

Answers

Using the equation for Young's slits $y = \dfrac{\lambda D}{a}$

a $y \propto \lambda$ so if $\lambda \Uparrow$ then $y \Uparrow$

b $y \propto \dfrac{1}{a}$ so if $a \Downarrow$ then $y \Uparrow$

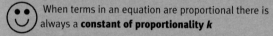 When terms in an equation are proportional there is always a **constant of proportionality k**

eg, $y \propto x$ so $y = kx$

     $y \propto \dfrac{1}{x}$ so $y = \dfrac{k}{x}$

A2 Physical quantities

There are 7 basic quantities

basic quantity	unit	symbol
mass	kilogramme	kg
length	metre	m
time	second	s
current	amp	A
temperature	kelvin	K
amount of substance	mole	mol
luminous intensity	candela	cd

- A physical quantity must be represented as a product of a number and a unit

  eg, $7\,m\,s^{-2}$, $0.8\,\mu A$, $100\,K$

- Combinations of these 7 basic quantities can form **derived physical quantities**, for example

quantity	SI units	name (if any)
acceleration	$m\,s^{-2}$	
force	$kg\,m\,s^{-2}$	newton (N)
momentum	$kg\,m\,s^{-1}$	
charge	$A\,s$	coulomb (C)
resistance	$kg\,m^2\,s^{-3}\,A^{-2}$	ohm (Ω)
frequency	s^{-1}	hertz (Hz)

Questions

1 The final step of a calculation is:

$$\sqrt{\frac{(7 \times 10^{-1}\,N)\,(4 \times 10^{-4}\,m)}{2 \times 10^{-2}\,kg}}$$

What is the answer a unit of?

a acceleration **b** force **c** mass/second

d speed **e** momentum

Answers

Ignore the numbers, but remember the units are square rooted

$$\sqrt{\frac{N\,m}{kg}} = \sqrt{\frac{kg\,m\,s^{-2}\,m}{kg}} = \sqrt{m^2\,s^{-2}} = m\,s^{-1} = \text{speed}$$

Question

2 Define the volt, and state its unit in terms of base quantities

Answer

Use $W = QV$ $\therefore$ $\text{volt} = \dfrac{\text{joule}}{\text{coulomb}}$

$\therefore$ $\text{volt} = \dfrac{kg\,m^2\,s^{-2}}{A\,s} = kg\,m^2\,A^{-1}\,s^{-3}$

Homogeneity

This is a term we apply to equations that mean 'sameness'. Consider these equations:

a $10\,m = 15\,m - 5\,s$ ⎫

b $7\,kg = 4\,kg + 3\,\Omega$ ⎭ These are clearly wrong as you cannot add or subtract quantities with different dimensions

These equations are **not homogeneous** with respect to units

If an equation is correct, each term in it must have the same dimensions as every other

c $14\,A = 13\,A - 1\,A$

This equation **is homogeneous** with respect to units but clearly the numbers are wrong

d $2a = \dfrac{v - u}{t}$ $m\,s^{-2} = \dfrac{m\,s^{-1} - m\,s^{-1}}{s}$

Here, velocity units minus velocity units gives velocity units

$$m\,s^{-2} = \frac{m\,s^{-1}}{s} = m\,s^{-2}$$

 don't treat units like numbers

This equation **is homogeneous** with respect to units but...

If the units are the same on each side, the equation is only *possibly* correct. This method does not check numerical factors

Question

3 Show this equation is homogeneous with respect to units
$$P = h\rho g$$

Answer

$P = \dfrac{\text{Force}}{\text{Area}} = h\rho g$

$\dfrac{N}{A} = m\,\dfrac{kg}{m^3}\,m\,s^{-2}$

$\dfrac{kg\,m\,s^{-2}}{m^2} = kg\,m^{-1}\,s^{-2}$

$kg\,m^{-1}\,s^{-2} = kg\,m^{-1}\,s^{-2}$

Question

4 The relationship between 5 physical quantities
A, B, C, D, E is

$AB = C + DE$

If D has the units $m\,s^{-1}$ and E has the unit s,
what are the units of C?

Answer

the same as DE . . . . . . m

A3 Practical hints

Comforting preamble

Many students dread the practical exams more than any of the other exams

Why? Perhaps because in many ways you cannot revise for it, you have literally got to think on your feet and the time restraint is never felt as keenly as it is in this exam

Never fear, there are lots of ways you can smooth your passage through this demanding ordeal. You need to learn the tricks of the trade!!

Measuring instruments

There are three basic pieces of practical equipment you need to feel comfortable with using: the micrometer screw gauge, the vernier callipers, the oscilloscope

The vernier callipers

This uses a vernier scale
They measure small lengths, eg, the diameter of a slotted weight, to the nearest **0.1 mm**
Check that, when the jaws meet, the zeros coincide

 Show you have checked this on your exam paper

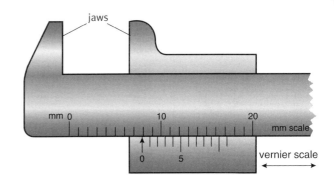

1. Move the jaws to grip the object firmly
2. Note the highest number reached on the mm-scale before the ↑ on the vernier scale
3. Note where divisions on each scale coincide, then read off the vernier scale

Example

Using the vernier diagram above as an example

The highest number reached on the mm-scale before the ↑ on the vernier scale is 7 mm.

The divisions coincide on the 6th line after the zero on the vernier

The length is then 7.6 mm

The micrometer screw gauge (MSG)

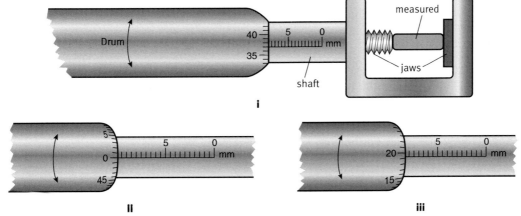

Used for measuring very small lengths, eg, thickness of a paperclip, to the nearest **0.01 mm**

One revolution of the drum is 0.50 mm making it travel across one division on the shaft

Always check that, when the jaws are together, the reading is zero

 Show that you have checked for this on an exam paper

 Always measure an object in 3 different places if you can, and take the average

i the shaft is between 7.5 and 8 mm
the drum is on 37 = 0.37 mm
so the reading is 7.5 + 0.37 = 7.87 mm
ii the shaft is on 10 mm
the drum is on 0 = 0 mm
so the reading is 10.00 mm

Your significant figures reflect the accuracy of the instrument

iii the shaft is between 8 and 8.5 mm
the drum is on 19 = 0.19 mm
so the reading is 8 + 0.19 = 8.19 mm

The oscilloscope (CRO)

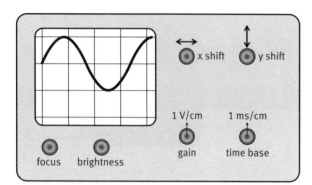

In an exam it is usually made extremely clear which controls you are to use, so don't start fiddling with anything else

This device can be used to measure voltages and to display wave patterns

The focus brings the trace into sharp relief

The brightness alters the intensity of the trace

 Altering the focus affects the brightness and vice versa

The X shift moves the whole trace laterally, from side to side. Use it to centralise the trace on the screen

The Y shift moves the whole trace vertically up and down. Use it to place the 'x axis' of the trace on the central horizontal grid line on the screen

The gain changes the 'y axis' scale on the grid, eg, from 1 V/cm to 5 V/cm

 Be careful as the grid lines could be 0.5 cm apart!

The time base changes the 'x axis' scale on the grid, eg, from $1 \, \text{ms cm}^{-1}$ to $10 \, \text{ms cm}^{-1}$ (ms = millisecond = 10^{-3} s)

 Be careful as the grid lines could be 0.5 cm apart!

This question is an adaptation of the type of problem you could be dealing with in the exam ... stick at it

Question

1 An ac supply is connected to a light bulb, and it lights with the same intensity as when it is connected to a 24 V battery

   i The battery is connected to an oscilloscope and the gain is altered so the trace is deflected by 1 cm. The battery is then disconnected, fig **i**

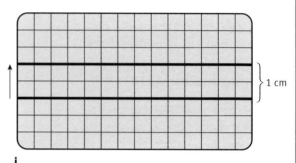

i

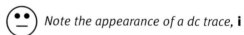

ii

   ii The ac supply is then connected to the oscilloscope, without the gain being adjusted. Calculate the total vertical length of this trace on the screen, fig **ii**

   ☺ *Need equation from ac theory section...*

   $V_0 = \sqrt{2} \times V_{RMS}$

   ☺ *Note the appearance of a dc trace, **i***

Answer

Step 1   With the battery connected, 24 V → 1 cm
The question implies that with the ac supply

$V_{RMS} = 24 \, \text{V}$ ∴ $V_0 = \sqrt{2} \times 24 = 34 \, \text{V}$

So when the ac supply is connected, the **centre** of the screen to the **peak** of the sine curve represents 34 V

Step 2   24 V ⟶⟶⟶ 1 cm

              1 V ⟶⟶⟶ $\frac{1}{24}$ cm

              34 V ⟶⟶⟶ $\frac{34}{24}$ cm = 1.4 cm

Remember the question asks for the total length and there is a peak of V_0 above and below

              Total length = 2 × 1.4 = 2.8 cm

Resist temptation to remove any tapes from the terminals, etc. during a practical exam!

Errors and uncertainty

To illustrate briefly how we deal with uncertainties in measurements consider 2 quantities, a and b

$a = 0.30\,\text{mm} \pm 0.01\,\text{mm}$

$b = 0.25\,\text{mm} \pm 0.02\,\text{mm}$

* **Adding** and **subtracting** quantities ...... **add** uncertainties

$a + b = 0.55 \pm 0.03\,\text{mm}$

$a - b = 0.05 \pm \mathbf{0.03}\,\text{mm}!!$

Uncertainties **always increase** when adding or subtracting quantities

* **Multiplying** and **dividing** quantities ...... **add** % uncertainties

You must first find the % **uncertainty** for a and b

% error of $a = \dfrac{0.01}{0.30} \times 100 = 3.33\%$

% error of $b = \dfrac{0.02}{0.25} \times 100 = 8\%$

so $\quad a \times b = 0.30 \times 0.25 = 0.075 (\pm 11.33\%)$

so $\quad \dfrac{a}{b} = \dfrac{0.3}{0.25} = 1.2 (\pm 11.33\%)$

Whether $\times$ or $\div$ you **add % uncertainty**

* **Index of quantities** ...... **Multiply** % uncertainty by the index

Again use the % error for a and b

$a^2 = 0.3^2 (\pm 2 \times 3.33\%) = 0.09\,(\pm 6.66\%)$

$b^{\frac{1}{2}} = 0.25^{\frac{1}{2}} = \sqrt{0.25} = 0.5 \pm (\frac{1}{2} \times 8\%) = 0.5 \pm (4\%)$

You **multiply the % uncertainty** by the index

Lets put them all together now...

2 Using a and b above, calculate the value and uncertainty of

$$\frac{ab^{\frac{1}{3}}}{a^2}$$

Answer

$\dfrac{ab^{\frac{1}{3}}}{a^2} = \dfrac{0.3 \times 0.25^{\frac{1}{3}}}{0.3^2} = 2.10\,\text{mm}$ is the value

$\left(3.33 + \frac{1}{3} \times 8\right) + 2 \times 3.33 = 12.7\%$ is the uncertainty

Gems of advice

* Increasing the distance to be measured with the same instrument, *reduces* the error

You measure two lengths with a metre ruler,

$A = 800\,\text{mm}$, and $B = 80\,\text{mm}$.

Let's assume the uncertainty in your reading is 1 mm The % uncertainty in both these lengths is

% of $A \Rightarrow \frac{1}{80} \times 100 = 1.25\%$

% of $B \Rightarrow \frac{1}{800} \times 100 = 0.125\%$ smaller uncertainty!!

Measuring thickness of foil/paper ... fold it as many times as possible before using an MSG (micrometer screw guage). Then divide the reading by the number of layers.

Measuring thickness of a microscope slide ... measure a few stacked together with an MSG and divide as before.

Timing oscillations ... time 20 oscillations and divide the total time by 20 for T. (Time period)

* You are meant to find **all equipment provided useful** to you. Examiners will want to see evidence of that in your answers ... so state it/ draw it/include it in your precautions

Set squares are usually provided so you can check a metre ruler is vertical (fig **i**), or to avoid parallel error

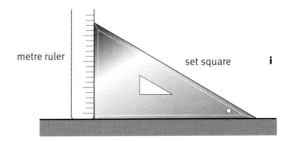

metre ruler   set square   **i**

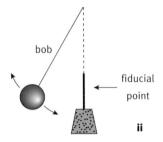

bob

fiducial point

ii

A cork and pin are usually provided for making a steady marker for whole oscillations (fiducial points) (fig **ii**)

- **Oscillations** should be

  1 Small

  2 Repeated when possible

  3 Used with a fiducial point

  4 Timed in 20's and divided to find time period

pendulum length/m	time for 20 osc/s	average time 20 osc/s	time, T, of 1 osc/s
0.25	8.32, 8.06, 8.44	8.27	0.41
0.30	9.00, 9.25, 9.05	9.10	0.46

- **Tabulating results**, see example table above

  1 If you repeated readings, tabulate them

  2 Put mathematical steps in the table eg, T, $1/T$

3 State units in column heading

4 If you are drawing a graph, you need at least 6 or 7 **readings**, apart from the zero if included

- **Graphs**

  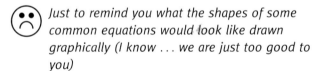 ← how points on graph should be marked

  1 Don't join obvious curves with straight lines between points, use smooth freehand!!

  2 Errors in your readings are sometimes obvious, let your curve bypass the error

  3 Use the information in the question carefully when deciding if a curve passes through 0,0

  4 Choose a sensible scale to use as much of the graph paper as is reasonable
  You may need to read intercepts, so check the question fully before you choose your scale
  Don't use multiples of 3 in your scale ... difficult to use ... leads to mistakes

  5 Label axes clearly, state units

  6 Whether measuring the gradient of a straight line or a tangent to a curve, make your triangle a large one

  7 A negative gradient may require a negative sign in calculations

Just to remind you what the shapes of some common equations would look like drawn graphically (I know ... we are just too good to you)

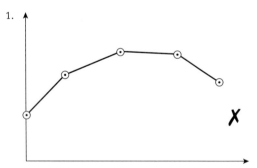

1.   X

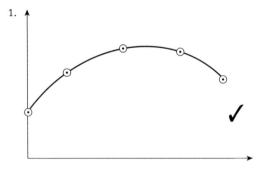

1.   ✓

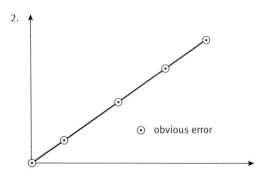

2.   ⊙ obvious error

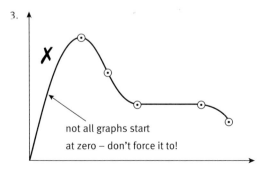

3.   X

not all graphs start at zero – don't force it to!

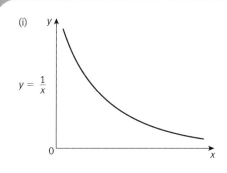

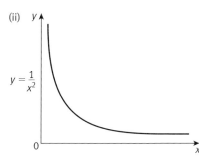

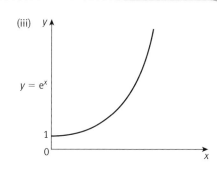

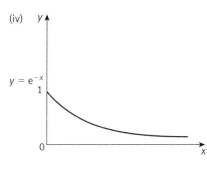

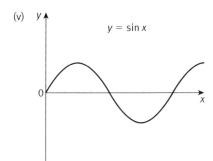

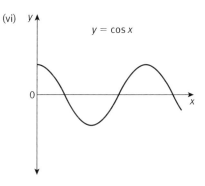

- **Units** often need to be converted to SI units
  Remember to give **units to all your answers**

- **Precision**
  1 Your measurements should reflect the precision of your instrument
  eg, if you measure the thickness of a metre rule with an MSG, your values should be to the nearest 0.01 mm, so 3.3 mm is <u>wrong</u>, 3.30 mm is <u>right</u>

  2 Repeat measurements and average the data. The thickness of a metre rule should be measured in 3 places and these measurements written for the examiner to see

  3 Use your common sense when stating uncertainties, they are likely to be
  ± 0.01 mm with an MSG
  ± 0.1 mm with vernier callipers
  ± 1.0 mm with a ruler

  4 If recording the temperature of a liquid, stir it and keep the thermometer bulb completely submerged

  5 Always read instruments at eye level, squatting down if necessary, eg, mercury thread in a thermometer

  6 Check the zero of instruments such as voltmeters, vernier callipers, etc. If there is an error you must compensate for it in further measurements

  7 When drawing diagrams show distances correctly (see below)

- **Marks**
  The marks shown for each part of a question are an excellent indicator of how many points/steps/ assumptions are needed

- **Don't panic**
  1 Don't give up if you are sure you have messed up the measuring. Correctly using whatever data you have in the subsequent questions can still give you substantial marks ... interpret *your* data!

  2 It's better to ask the invigilator for help, than to seize up or plough on blindly. You will usually only lose a few marks

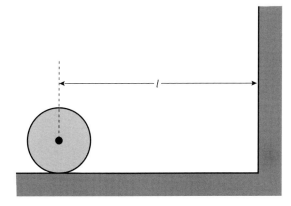

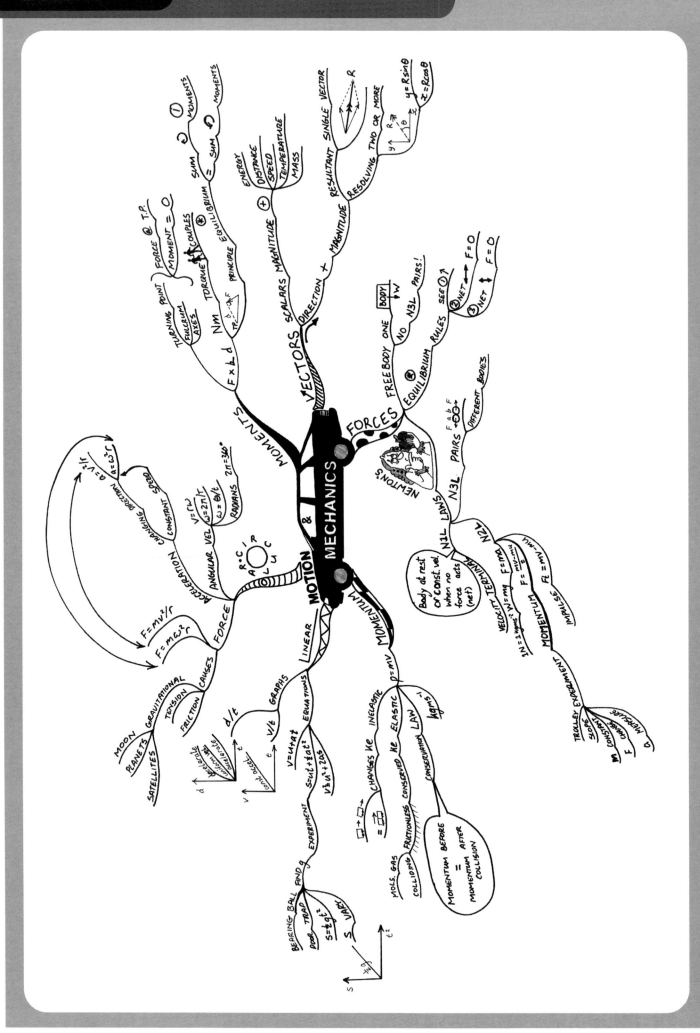

B4 Vectors and moments

Beginner's box

- Vector quantities have magnitude and direction
- Scalar quantities have magnitude only
- Moment = Force × Distance

Force vectors

Here is a fairly full classification of vectors and scalars

scalar	unit	vector	unit
distance	m	displacement	m
speed	$m\,s^{-1}$	velocity	$m\,s^{-1}$
temperature	K	acceleration	$m\,s^{-2}$
mass	kg	force	N
energy	J	moment	N m
charge	C	momentum	$kg\,m\,s^{-1}$
volume	m^3	current	A
density	$kg\,m^{-3}$	flux density	T
power	W		
frequency	Hz		
time	s		
pressure	Pa		
pd	V		
electric potential	V		

- Similar **scalar** quantities are **added**

eg, at one point on its fall a ball has 4 J of PE and 5 J of KE, so its total energy must be 9 J

Adding vectors takes a bit more thought

Resultant of vectors

- The **resultant** of two (or more) vectors is a **single** vector producing the same effect

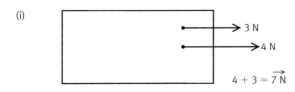

(i)

$$3\,N$$
$$4\,N$$
$$4 + 3 = \overrightarrow{7\,N}$$

Vectors acting in the same direction can be added

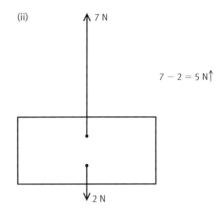

(ii)

$$7\,N$$
$$7 - 2 = 5\,N\uparrow$$
$$2\,N$$

Vectors acting in the opposite direction are subtracted

- Vector direction is important (eg, in momentum questions). You may wish to assign vectors going right as positive and vectors going left as negative

Parallelogram of vectors

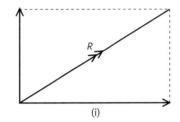

R

(i)

Produce a parallelogram from the two vectors and measure the diagonal

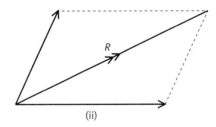

R

(ii)

Question

1 A box is pulled by 4 ropes in different directions with the forces shown

What is the resultant force on the box?

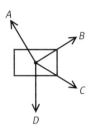

Answer

Step 1   Find a resultant of each pair, R_1, R_2

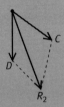

Step 2   Find the resultant of R_1 and $R_2 = R_3$

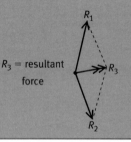

R_3 = resultant force

Resolving vectors

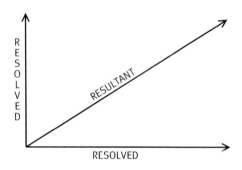

- **Two vectors** (or more) can replace a single vector and still have the same effect. This is called **resolving** a vector into its **components**

Resolving is the 'opposite' of finding the resultant

A stool is pulled by single rope with a force Z across the floor at the angle shown, θ

(i)

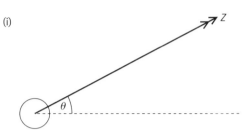

(ii)

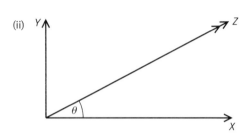

If ropes with forces X and Y replaced Z they could have an identical effect on the stool if Z is their diagonal

How do we find the values of X and Y? Easy – use your GCSE trigonometry

$$\cos \theta = \frac{X}{Z} \quad \therefore \quad \boxed{X = Z \cos \theta}$$

$$\sin \theta = \frac{X}{Z} \quad \therefore \quad \boxed{Y = Z \sin \theta}$$

(i)

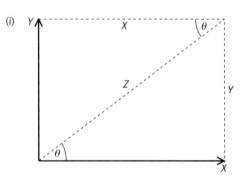

(ii)

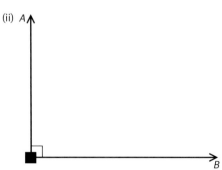

Here are two perpendicular forces A and B. The resolved component of A onto the line of B is zero, because $\cos 90° = 0$

Study and Revise AS and A2 Level Physics

Questions

2

a Jack is pushed in his buggy with a force of 200 N, at 50° to the ground. What is the horizontal component of this force, ignoring friction?

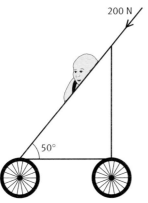

200 N

50°

b Why would it feel lighter to pull Jack? (V. tricky! Think about the vertical components.)

Answers

a $X = 200 \cos 50°$

$\approx 129\,\text{N}$

b **i** When you pull the buggy the vertical component of the force can be subtracted from the weight, giving a smaller net vertical force

ii When you push the buggy the vertical component can be added to the weight, giving a larger net vertical force

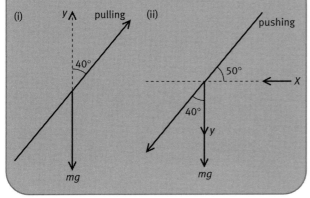

(i) pulling

40°

mg

(ii) pushing

50°

40°

y

mg

Moments

- The **turning effect** of a force is the moment

- Moment = force × perpendicular distance to the turning point (tp)

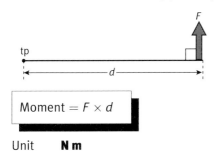

F

tp

d

Moment $= F \times d$

Unit **N m**

- How to find the not so obvious perpendicular distances...

eg, here is an aerial view of a door being pushed at an angle

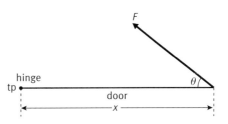

F

hinge
tp

door

θ

x

Extend the line of direction of the force, then draw a line from the tp to meet it at a right angle

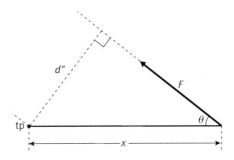

d''

F

tp

θ

x

d'' is the perpendicular distance from the force to the tp

$$\sin \theta = \frac{d''}{x} \quad \therefore d'' = x \sin \theta$$

😐 *Any force at the tp has a moment $= 0$ as its distance from the tp is zero*

Principle of moments

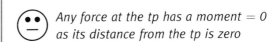

d_1

d_2

F_1

F_2

acw

cw

A moment can be clockwise

$$F_2 \times d_2$$

A moment can be anticlockwise

$$F_1 \times d_1$$

- The principle of moments states

> **When a body is in equilibrium the sum of the clockwise moments is equal to the sum of the anticlockwise moments about any point**

Question

3 This seesaw is in equilibrium

What distance (a in the diag.) is the 2 N force from the pivot? 'Ignore its weight'

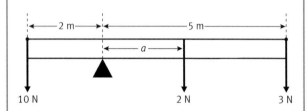

Answer

Sum of anticlockwise (acw) moments = sum of clockwise (cw) moments

$$10 \times 2 = (2 \times a) + (3 \times 5)$$
$$20 = 2a + 15$$
$$\therefore a = 2.5 \, \text{m}$$

This question is trickier, you need to understand...

 *Moments can be taken about **any** convenient tp*

Question

4 A ruler is supported as shown. All distances marked are equal.

Support S is repositioned at a. What will happen to the upward force on the ruler caused by S?

(Hint, draw forces on the diagram, including weight, and sum the moments)

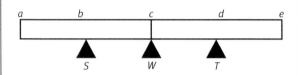

Answer

Take moments in the original position

Step 1
@ S, $W = 2T$
@ T, $W = 2S$ $\therefore S = T$

so upward force from S and T are equal

Step 2
When repositioned

@ S·, $2W = 3T$
@ T, $W = 3S$
$\therefore 6S = 3T$ $\therefore S = 0.5T$

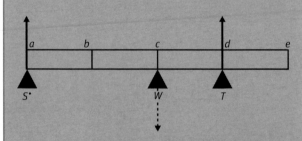

so the upward force on the ruler caused by S *decreases* (is halved)

B5 Forces and equilibrium

There are 4 types of forces we know of at present

Strong nuclear
Electromagnetic (EM)
Weak nuclear
Gravitational

- In Mechanics we deal with gravitational and EM forces

- Gravitational forces are attractive (pulls) and commonly called weight

EM forces can be attractive or repulsive and are commonly called

Friction: between surfaces of 2 bodies so as to oppose relative movement

Contact: when atoms of 2 bodies are close together

Tension: eg, pulled by a stretched string

Compression: eg, push of a rod on an attached body

Other common terms are drag, lift, upthrust, electrostatic and magnetic forces

Freebody force diagrams

These can be unnecessarily confusing
Follow a few simple rules every time you draw one

1 Be clear about the single object you are considering
2 Draw a simple sketch of it
3 Mark the weight on it
4 Mark on the relevant forces where the object touches anything else

eg, a bucket being lifted by a pulley

T the pull of the rope on the bucket

W the pull of the Earth on the bucket

a book resting on a table

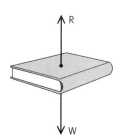

R the push of the table on the book

W the pull of the Earth on the book

 These are NOT Newton 3rd Law pairs (N3L). Remember N3L pairs act on different bodies as in the diagram below

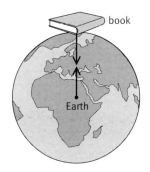

book

Earth

N3L pairs

ie, the book is pulled down by the Earth, the Earth is pulled up by the book. This force is too small to have a noticeable effect on the Earth

Question

1 The evil scientist dropped his rival into a giant flask of boiling oil. He asked his apprentice to state the 3 main forces and the origin of these forces on the body

 Many students miss answering each part *of a question, especially when they have not been labelled i), ii) etc...*

Answer

Weight — caused by the pull of the Earth
Upthrust — caused by the weight of the fluid displaced
Drag — caused by friction on the body from the oil as it drops

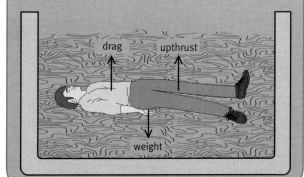

drag   upthrust

weight

Equilibrium

- If an object has forces acting on it but is in equilibrium then

  i The net horizontal force is zero

  ii The net vertical force is zero

  iii Sum of cw moments = sum of acw moments (about any turning point, so it does not rotate)

 If the total (net) forces on a body equal zero ie, equilibrium, then it can either be at rest or at a constant velocity (Newton's 1st Law)

Questions

2 An iron bar is pivoted at X and has a length of 3 m and weighs 600 N

It is held to one side by a force *F* acting at Y where $\theta = 49°$

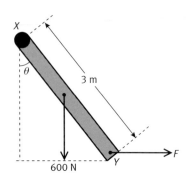

Calculate

a *F*

b The horizontal and vertical forces acting on the bar at X

Answers

a @ X, sum cw moments = sum acw moments

$$600 \times 1.5 \sin 49 = F \times 3 \cos 49$$

$$600 \times 1.13 = F \times 2.0$$

$$F = 345 \, N$$

b As the bar is in equilibrium

veritcal force must equal the weight = 600 N

horizontal force must equal *F* = 336 N

Questions

3 Mr Jones pointed to the diagram on his blackboard with a ruler, thus

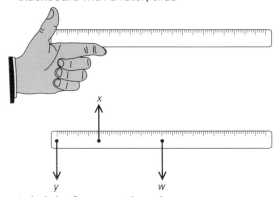

a Label the forces on the ruler

b List the forces in order of increasing magnitude

Remember your freebody rules

Answers

Using moments, in equilibrium

@ W,   Y < X (as Y is further away)

@ X,   W < Y

∴ W < Y < X

This next question brings many of the above principles together and is a bit scary. Persevere with the answer, which is long, as I'm trying to explain each step

Question

4   A ladder, on rough ground, 10 m long and of mass 40 kg leans, on a smooth wall. The ladder base is 6 m from the wall. Calculate the friction F between the ladder and the ground

Answer

If the ground were smooth the ladder would slip to the right, so friction must be to the left

Follow the freebody force diagram rules

W: acts from the centre of the ladder
R: is the push of wall on ladder

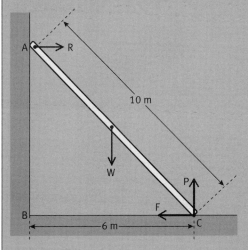

P: is the push of the ground on the ladder
F: friction from rough ground
(smooth wall, no friction)

As this ladder is in equilibrium then every force must have a horizontal/vertical opposite, so…

$$P = W$$
$$\therefore P = 400 \, N$$

Now, we need F but we don't know R, so if we take moments about A we can ignore R

@ A, W and F turn the ladder cw
        P turns the ladder acw

$$\therefore 3W + 8F = 6P$$
$$\therefore 1200 + 8F = 2400$$
$$8F = 1200$$
$$F = 150 \, N$$

Centre of gravity

Question

5   How would you find the centre of gravity of a clamp stand?

Answer

Balance it on a knife edge or suspend it so there is no tilting

• The centre of gravity of a body is the point where all the weight appears to act
  In this example you can draw a single force for the weight through the centre of gravity

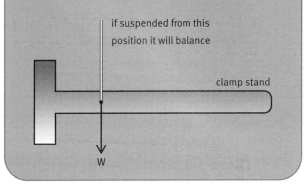

The centre of gravity of a body is not always in the centre, think about weight distribution

B6 Momentum (ρ)

Beginner's box

*   Momentum of an object = mass × velocity

    $$p = m \times v$$

    force = rate of change of momentum

*   *Ft* is called the **Impulse** of the body, a measure of its change in momentum

    $$Ft = mv - mu = \text{Impulse}$$

    Area under Ft graph = impulse

 Many students forget about impulse ... DON'T

Law of Conservation of Momentum

*   When no external forces act on bodies that are interacting, the total momentum remains constant

momentum before interaction	=	momentum after interaction

Examples of interaction: collision, explosion, coupling, firing, embedding, etc.

 You are very likely to be asked to apply the laws of conservation of momentum and energy to situations

Question

1   John, who weighs 80 kg, is standing on an ice rink. He throws his bag of mass 2 kg to the edge with a horizontal velocity of 10 m s^{-1}. With what velocity will he recoil?

Answer

Momentum of John and bag before = zero (both stationary) (i)

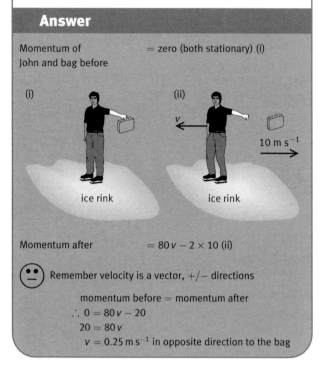

ice rink   ice rink

Momentum after   = $80v - 2 \times 10$ (ii)

 Remember velocity is a vector, +/− directions

momentum before = momentum after
∴ $0 = 80v - 20$
$20 = 80v$
$v = 0.25$ m s^{-1} in opposite direction to the bag

Elastic and inelastic collisions

*   In an **elastic** collision **KE is conserved**

eg, A magnetic puck colliding with the magnetic field of another puck on a friction-free surface

*   In an **inelastic** collision the **KE is changed** into other energy forms

eg, Any collision where two objects stick together

Questions

2 In a traffic accident an 800 kg car, travelling at 20 m s^{-1}, collided with a stationary lorry, mass 3200 kg, and remained attached

a What is the initial speed after collision of the car and the lorry?

b Using calculations, demonstrate whether the crash is elastic or inelastic

Answers

a Momentum before = momentum after
$$800 \times 20 = 4000 \times v$$
so the speed of the lorry and car after collision is
$$v = 4 \, \text{m s}^{-1}$$

b KE before $\quad \frac{1}{2}mv^2 = \frac{1}{2}800 \times 20^2 = 160\,000\,\text{J}$

KE after $\quad \frac{1}{2}mv^2 = \frac{1}{2}4000 \times 4^2 = 32\,000\,\text{J}$

∴ KE lost is 128,000 J
so the collision must be inelastic and the KE will be transferred to other forms of energy, eg, compression of car, sound, heat, etc

 EXPERIMENT

How would you demonstrate the Conservation of Momentum?

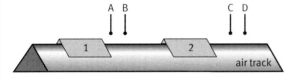

- Glider 1 and 2 of same mass, 200 g
- Glider 1 is given a gentle push and passes by light gates A and B — time recorded as t_1
- It attaches (via magnet) to glider 2, which is initially stationary. Both move past light gates C and D — time recorded as t_2
- Distances AB and CD measured
- $v_1 - AB/t_1$, $v_2 = CD/t_2$
- Experiment repeated each time adding 50 g to glider 1

Before			After		
moving mass	velocity v_1	p	moving mass	velocity v_2	p

If the momentum before and after remain constant then the Law of Conservation of Momentum has been demonstrated

B7 Newton's Laws of Motion

For over 300 years these laws have formed the basis of mechanical physics. Einstein's theory of relativity modifies these laws only when objects being considered are approaching the speed of light

Newton's 1st Law (N1L)	A body will stay at rest or continue at a uniform velocity unless external forces act on it

A ball falling through air experiences three forces,

Weight, *W*
Upthrust, *U*
Drag, *D*

Now, when...

weight > upthrust + drag   the ball accelerates down

weight = upthrust + drag   the net force on the ball is zero so it continues at the velocity it had reached when the forces balanced (**terminal velocity**)

☹ *It does NOT come to rest in mid-air!*

Newton's 2nd Law (N2L)	The rate of change of momentum of a body is proportional to the force acting on it. It moves in the direction of that force

$$F = \frac{mv - mu}{t}$$

$$= \frac{m(v - u)}{t}$$

so $\boxed{F = ma}$

The newton

Force is measured in newtons (N). The equation $F = ma$ can be used to define the newton

$$1\,\mathrm{N} = 1\,\mathrm{kg\,m\,s^{-2}}$$

so   **1 N is that force which accelerates a mass of 1 kg by $1\,\mathrm{m\,s^{-2}}$**

1 N is about the weight of an apple

Newton's 3rd Law (N3L)	If a body *A* exerts a force on body *B*, then body *B* exerts an equal and opposite force of the same kind on body *A*

😐 *An N3L pair acts on different bodies*

(i)

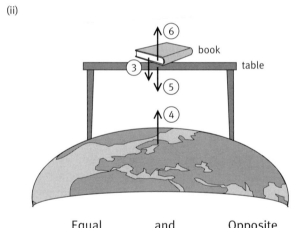

(ii)

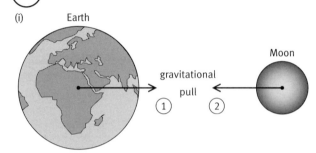

Equal	and	Opposite
① pull of Moon on Earth		② pull of Earth on Moon
③ pull of Earth on book		④ pull of book on Earth
⑤ push of book on table		⑥ push of table on book

pairs

Questions

1   A caravan of mass 1000 kg is pulled by a force of 3500 N and experiences a constant frictional force of 500 N

    a   Draw a freebody force diagram of the caravan showing the magnitude of the forces (look back at the rules!)

b Calculate the magnitude and direction of the resultant force on the caravan

c How far will it move from rest in 20 s? (eqns of motion)

Answers

a

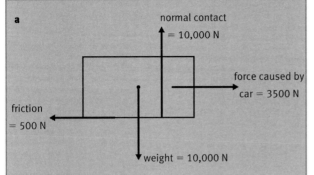

normal contact = 10,000 N

force caused by car = 3500 N

friction = 500 N

weight = 10,000 N

b Net horizontal force = 3500 − 500 = 3000 N

c N2L $F = ma$

$3000 = 10\,000 \times a$

$\therefore a = 0.3\,\text{m s}^{-2}$

$t = 20\,\text{s}, \quad a = 0.3\,\text{m s}^{-2}, \quad u = 0$

$s = ut + \frac{1}{2}at^2$

$= 0.15 \times 400$

$= 60\,\text{m}$

Question

2 An object of mass 50 kg accelerates down a slope angled at 50° to the horizontal. Neglecting friction, calculate its acceleration

Answer

First draw a clear diagram of the situation, marking all the forces acting on the ball

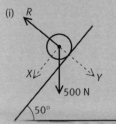

(i)

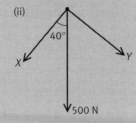

(ii)

Step 1 You must resolve the weight into its component of force acting down the slope. It is this that is causing the acceleration of the object along the slope

$500 \cos 40° = X$

$\therefore \quad X \approx 383\,\text{N}$

Step 2 using N2L $F = ma$

$383 = 50 \times a$

$\therefore \quad a = 7.66\,\text{m s}^{-2}$

 Force Y must be equal to the normal reaction otherwise the ball would not stay on the slope ... again Y and the normal reaction are not N3L pairs because they are acting on the same object

B8 Linear motion

Beginner's box

- speed $= \dfrac{\text{distance}}{\text{time}}$ m s^{-1}

- acceleration $= \dfrac{\text{change in velocity}}{\text{time}}$ m s^{-2}

Basics

- **Distance** is a **scalar** quality (magnitude only)

  Displacement is a **vector** quantity (magnitude and direction) giving the length and direction of one point from another

eg, Alfred Ant walks 3 cm north, 4 cm east

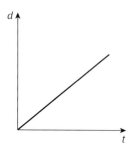

4 cm

3 cm

θ

D

Distance walked is 7 cm
Displacement, D is
5 cm at $\theta°$, E of N

- **Speed** is a **scalar** quantity

  Velocity is a **vector** quantity

😊 *Remember this idea with circular motion!!*

$$\text{velocity} = \frac{\text{displacement}}{\text{time}} \quad (\text{m s}^{-1})$$

- Acceleration is a vector quantity

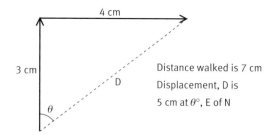

$$\text{acceleration} = \frac{\text{change in velocity}}{\text{time}} \quad (\text{m s}^{-2})$$

Displacement/Time graphs

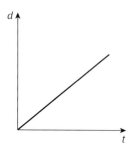

d

t

gradient shows uniform velocity

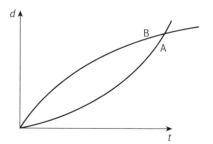

d

t

B
A

gradient shows changing velocity
A = acceleration
B = deceleration

Velocity/Time graphs

- gradient shows constant acceleration

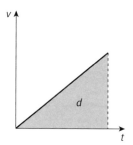

v

d

t

- area under any shape of v/t graph always represents the distance travelled

$$\tfrac{1}{2}v \times t = d$$

Question

1 Darren the Dog is chasing Colin the Cat around the garden. Describe Colin's motion in the sections shown

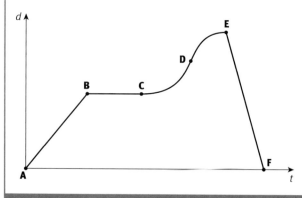

d

A
B
C
D
E
F

t

Answer

A–B	uniform velocity away from rest (Colin confident)
B–C	stationary (Colin stops to tease Darren)
C–D	non-uniform acceleration (Colin not so cocky now)
D–E	non-uniform deceleration (Colin sees Darren is on a chain)
E–F	uniform velocity back to start (Colin very smug)

Equations of motion

- A body moving with a constant acceleration can be analysed using these equations (remember a constant acceleration of zero is a constant velocity)

1 $v = u + at$	u = initial velocity
	v = final velocity
2 $s = ut + \frac{1}{2}at^2$	t = time taken
	s = displacement
3 $v^2 = u^2 + 2as$	a = acceleration

- In questions about objects moving up and down we replace a by g

- A combination of two or three equations may be needed to solve problems, for example

  Given v, u and s you may need to find t ...
  Use eq. 3 to find a, then you can use eq. 1 to find t!

- In the question below a rising object has an acceleration of $-g$.
  You have to understand the directions of s, v and a

The positive direction is usually up (to the right), so

1 velocity down (to the left) is negative

2 displacement below start position (to the left) is negative

3 acceleration down (to the left) has $a = -g$

So why does an object thrown upwards have $a = -g$?

Because its is NOT accelerating but decelerating at a rate of $9.8\,\text{m s}^{-1}$ every second assuming air resistance is negligible (<u>Warning</u> ... Physics can make your brain hurt!)

Questions

2 The bride threw her bouquet vertically upwards (poor shot ... overexcited) at $3\,\text{m s}^{-1}$. Her chief bridesmaid wants to know

a How long will the bouquet take to return to the ground?

b How far is the descent?

Assume $g = 10\,\text{m s}^{-2}$, air resistance is negligible and the bridesmaid is a very competitive physicist!

 Start to note all the different types of assumptions for each topic; you are often asked to state them in exam questions

Answers

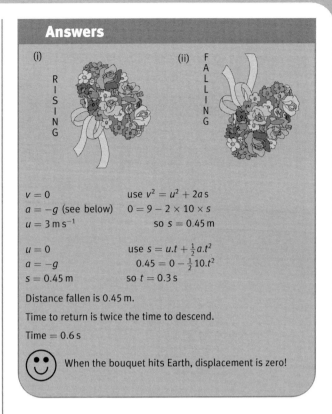

(i) RISING   (ii) FALLING

$v = 0$	use $v^2 = u^2 + 2as$
$a = -g$ (see below)	$0 = 9 - 2 \times 10 \times s$
$u = 3\,\text{m s}^{-1}$	so $s = 0.45\,\text{m}$

$u = 0$	use $s = u.t + \frac{1}{2}a.t^2$
$a = -g$	$0.45 = 0 - \frac{1}{2}10.t^2$
$s = 0.45\,\text{m}$	so $t = 0.3\,\text{s}$

Distance fallen is $0.45\,\text{m}$.

Time to return is twice the time to descend.

Time = $0.6\,\text{s}$

When the bouquet hits Earth, displacement is zero!

Acceleration due to gravity

At GCSE you may have been asked:

'A book and feather are dropped from the same height above Earth. Which of the following is true?

A. both hit at the same time
B. book lands first
C. feather lands first

Hopefully you would say ... B ... because the feather would experience greater **air resistance**, so reducing its acceleration

But in the strange and wonderful world of A-level Physics we often ignore minor irritations such as air resistance

In which case then ... A is correct. Both objects are in free fall

- A mass dropped above the Earth will fall with the **acceleration of free fall** (g) when air resistance is negligible. It varies but is approximately $9.81\,\text{m s}^{-2}$

- In free fall ALL bodies accelerate at g, irrespective of their differing masses. A body of greater momentum, however, will hit the ground with greater force ($F = mg$)

  So, even in a vacuum, gasping to breathe, you would rather be hit by a feather than a book!

- g can also be called **gravitational field strength**, the units being N kg^{-1} $\left(\text{from } g = \dfrac{F}{m}\right)$

Question

3 Going back to the feather and book, what would happen to them on the Moon?

Answer

There is no atmosphere on the Moon, so they hit the surface simultaneously

 EXPERIMENT TO MEASURE g

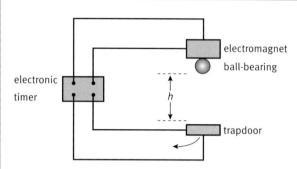

electromagnet

ball-bearing

electronic timer

h

trapdoor

- Timer started. This cuts off current to electromagnet and ball drops
- When ball hits trapdoor, timer stops automatically
- h is varied giving different values of t

Assume ... no residual magnetism in electromagnet when switched off, so ball drops immediately

$h/$m	$t/$s

Use

$$s = u.t + \tfrac{1}{2}a.t^2$$
$$s = h$$
$$a = g$$
$$u = 0$$

so

$$h = \tfrac{1}{2}g.t^2$$

 This can be put in the form of a straight-line graph:

$$y = \quad m.x \ + \ c$$
$$\quad \uparrow \quad \uparrow \ \uparrow \quad \uparrow$$

so

$$h = \tfrac{1}{2}g.\ t^2 + 0$$

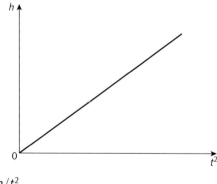

plot h/t^2

$$\text{gradient} = \tfrac{1}{2}g$$

$$g = 2 \times \text{gradient}$$

Questions

4 A javelin thrower starts her run and stops on the line, throwing the winning shot. Here is a graph of her horizontal speed

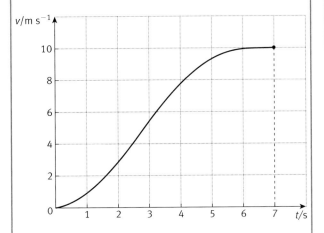

Use the graph to:

a estimate the distance she ran

b estimate her maximum acceleration

 Show the examiner you have used the graph;

think gradients, think tangents, think large triangles; and

think units (v is in $\mathrm{m\,s^{-1}}$, t is in s)

Answers

a distance = area under the curve
count the squares (nearly 21)
$\qquad = 42\,\mathrm{m}\,(\pm 3\,\mathrm{m})$

b draw a long tangent with steepest gradient

$a = \dfrac{v-u}{t} \simeq \dfrac{10-0}{3.5}$

so $\quad a = 2.9\,\mathrm{m\,s^{-2}}$

Questions

5 A Canadian ice-hockey player struck the puck. It took 2000 ms to move 840 cm from rest. The puck accelerated for the whole distance, with uniform acceleration.

Calculate the speed of the puck after 2000 ms

 Do you need to change any units?

 Don't calculate average speed for (a), they want final speed

Answers

$u = 0 \quad t = 2000\,\mathrm{ms} = 2\,\mathrm{s} \quad s = 840\,\mathrm{cm} = 8.4\,\mathrm{m}$

use $s = ut + \frac{1}{2}at^2$ to find a $\quad 8.4 = 0 + 2a$
$\qquad\qquad\qquad\qquad\qquad\qquad a = 4.2\,\mathrm{m\,s^{-2}}$

then substitute a into $v = at$ $\quad v = 0 + 4.2 \times 2$
$\qquad\qquad\qquad\qquad\qquad\qquad v = 8.4\,\mathrm{m\,s^{-1}}$

Projectiles

Here we are considering objects, dropping or being thrown at an angle to the vertical

(i)
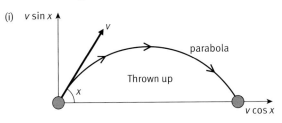

(ii)
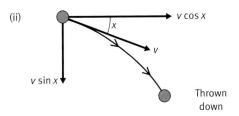

1 A projectile can move in a **parabolic** way

2 The horizontal and vertical components of motion are considered separately

3 The vertical component is the result of the effects of the acceleration caused by gravity

4 If it takes time t to reach maximum height in (i) the total time of flight is 2t

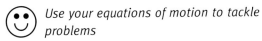 *Use your equations of motion to tackle problems*

The best way to understand projectile problems is to practise a variety of them. As each situation arises you will get a better feel for the rules

Questions

6 A missile is projected with a velocity of $150\,\mathrm{m\,s^{-1}}$ at an angle of $40°$ above the horizontal. Calculate

a the time taken to reach its maximum height

b the time the missile is in the air

c the horizontal distance it travels

Assume $g = 10\,\mathrm{m\,s^{-2}}$

Answers

a As we are considering height, look at vertical motion should be $v\sin x = 150\sin 40° = 96.4\,\mathrm{m\,s^{-1}}$

Using equations of motion
$u = 96.4\,\mathrm{m\,s^{-1}}$,
$v = 0$ (at maximum height ball is stationary momentarily before changing direction)
$a = -g$ (ball moving against gravity)

$$v = u + at$$
$$0 = 96.4 - 10t$$
$$t = 9.64\,\mathrm{s}$$

b Total time of flight is $2t = 2 \times 9.64 = 19.28\,\mathrm{s}$

c As we are considering distance horizontally then
$u = v\cos x = 150\cos 40° = 114.9\,\mathrm{m\,s^{-1}}$
$t = 19.28\,\mathrm{s}$
$g = 0$ (no vertical considerations in horizontal motion!)
$s = ut + \frac{1}{2}gt^2 = 114.9 \times 19.28 + 0 = 2215\,\mathrm{m}$

Question

7 Three identical balls have the trajectories shown in the diagram below. Neglecting air resistance, which ball will reach the ground first?

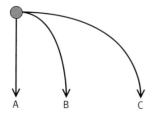

Answer

Trick question, they will all reach the ground simultaneously.
They all experience the same acceleration g
They all travel the same vertical distance s
They all start from rest, $u = 0$
So considering vertical motion
Using $s = ut + \frac{1}{2}at^2$ then t must be constant for each ball

B9 Circular motion

You will only be considering objects moving at a steady speed in a circular fashion. A change in speed changes the radius of rotation, which can force you to have to get messy with maths. We are considering cars on tracks, weights twirled on strings, etc

A body's rate of rotation is called its **angular speed** ω, where

$$\omega = \frac{\theta}{t}$$

$$\frac{\theta}{t} = \frac{\text{angle turned through}}{\text{time taken}}$$

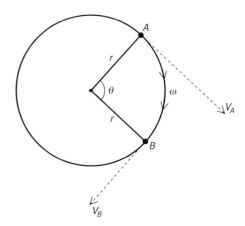

- It is usual in circular motion to measure θ not in degrees, but in **radians** (rad) (why make life easy for you?)
  1 radian $= 57.3°$ **2π radians $= 360°$**

So ω is measured in radians per second

eg,   Express the following in π radians
     $120°$, $240°$, $90°$

2π radians is $360°$ so...

$$120° = \tfrac{1}{3} \times 360° \quad \therefore \quad 120° = \frac{2\pi}{3}\ \text{radians}$$

$$240° = 2 \times 120° \quad \therefore \quad 240° = \frac{4\pi}{3}\ \text{radians}$$

$$90° = \tfrac{1}{4} \times 360° \quad \therefore \quad 90° = \frac{2\pi}{4}\ \text{radians}$$

- The time to complete one revolution is the **Time Period, T**

$$\omega = \frac{\theta}{t}, \quad \text{but when } t = T \quad \theta = 360° = 2\pi$$

$$\therefore \quad \omega = \frac{2\pi}{T} \qquad \therefore \quad T = \frac{2\pi}{\omega}$$

- The number of revolutions per second is the **frequency of rotation, f**

  using the definition of T

  If 1 oscillation takes T seconds

  Then $\frac{1}{T}$ oscillations takes 1 second

  So

$$f = \frac{1}{T}$$

- In the circle shown the instantaneous linear velocity at A and B is V_A and V_B. Imagine the string breaks when the stone reaches A, it will carry on in a straight line with velocity V_A

  It can be shown

$$\omega = \frac{v}{r} \quad \text{or} \quad v = r\omega$$

where r = radius of circle
          v = uniform speed around circle

Centripetal acceleration

- A body moving at a uniform speed in a circle has a centripetal acceleration

A classic question on many exams asks

'If a body moving in a circle has a uniform speed, how can it be accelerating?'
(Refer to the circle diagram shown) The magnitude of velocities V_A and V_B may be the same, but they are in different directions, so there is a change in velocity, hence an acceleration

- It can be shown that

centripetal acceleration $a = \frac{v^2}{r}$

               or $a = \omega^2 r$

(units $\mathrm{m\,s^{-2}}$)

Question

1 The blades on a propeller make 50 revolutions per second. The diameter of the circle the blades describe is 4 m. Find

a the angular speed ω

b The linear speed of the tip of the blade

c The centripetal acceleration of the tip of the blade

d How would the acceleration vary from the centre of the blades to the tip?

 Do not try to use $a = \frac{v^2}{r}$ to answer (d) as v is not constant

Answers

a $\omega = \frac{\theta}{t} = \frac{50 \times 2\pi}{1} = 3.4\,\mathrm{rad\,s^{-1}}$

b $v = r\omega = 2 \times 100\pi = 628\,\mathrm{m\,s^{-1}}$

c $a = r\omega^2 = 2 \times 10000\pi^2 = 1.97 \times 10^5\,\mathrm{m\,s^{-2}}$

d centre $\Longrightarrow$ tip, using $a = r\omega$, r gets bigger, ω stays the same, so a gets bigger also

Centripetal force

- A centripetal force must exist as there is a centripetal acceleration (N2L)

- $F = ma, \quad a = r\omega^2 \quad a = \frac{v^2}{r}$

  So

$$F = \frac{mv^2}{r} = mr\omega^2$$

 If you were asked to name the type of force causing a satellite to orbit the moon, never say centripetal force. You must describe the force which causes the centripetal force

type of circular motion	force causing it
satellite orbiting moon	gravitational force exerted by moon
stone twirled horizontally on a string	tension force in string
rally car on a track	frictional force on tyres from the road
banking aeroplane	push of air
electrons circling a nucleus	electric force of attraction exerted by proton in nucleus

Questions

2 A conker of mass 0.05 kg is twirled on a string vertically at a constant speed. Its circular path is of radius 60 cm and its angular speed is 15 rad s^{-1}

a Find the tension in the string in the 3 positions shown

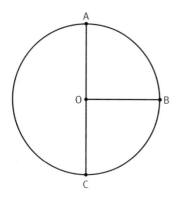

b Why is the string more likely to break in position C?

(Keeping the angular speed constant is actually impossible, but don't let that stop you enjoying yourself answering this lovely question)

 Remember that the centripetal force is the result of other forces acting

Question

3 A child is pushed higher and higher on a swing. Eventually she feels herself coming off the surface of the chair slightly. Give a reason for this

Answer

As the chain of the swing approaches a horizontal position, the tension can be lost in the chain, which means the centripetal force is zero

Answers

a A $\therefore$ $mr w^2 = T + mg$

$\therefore$ $T = 0.05 \times 0.6 \times (15)^2 - 0.50$

$\therefore$ $T = 6.25$ N

B as mg is perpendicular to T its resolved component along the line of T is zero

$\therefore$ $mr w^2 = T$

$\therefore$ $T = 0.05 \times 0.6 \times (15)^2$

$\therefore$ $T = 6.75$ N

C $mr w^2 = T - mg$

$T = 6.75 + 0.50$

$T = 7.25$ N

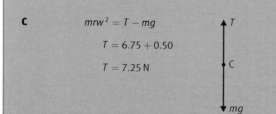

b Because there is the greatest tension here caused by the resultant forces at C

B10 Work, energy and power

- Work is done when an applied force moves its point of application in the direction of the force.

  Work = force × distance moved
  In direction of force

  $$W = Fs$$ (units N m or J)

 If the object does not move in the direction of the force then you must remember to resolve the force onto the object's line of direction.

eg, Consider the work done, (WD) pulling this sledge a distance of 150 m

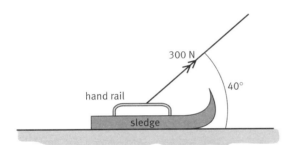
300 N
40°
hand rail
sledge

$$WD = Fs$$
$$= 300 \cos 40° \times 150$$
$$= 3.44 \times 10^4 \text{ J}$$

- Energy transfers allow work to be done. We describe energy by using the following terms

Light	Electrical
Chemical	Potential – gravitational
Nuclear	electrostatic
Thermal (internal)	elastic
Sound	

  Energy transfer = Work Done

- Kinetic energy (KE) is energy a body has as a result of its motion

Kinetic energy $= \frac{1}{2} \times$ object mass $\times$ speed^2

$$KE = \frac{1}{2}mv^2$$

- Gravitational potential energy (PE) is energy a body has because of its position above Earth's surface

Change in potential energy = mass × g × height moved

$$PE = mgh$$

 Assume g is constant near the Earth's surface

- The **Law of Conservation of Energy** states (GCSE!)

'Energy cannot be created or destroyed but only changed from one form into another'

ie, **the total energy of an isolated system is constant**

eg, Ignoring air resistance, a ball thrown up gains PE and loses KE, so

gain in PE = loss in KE

This graph indicates a transfer between PE and KE as the ball rises and falls

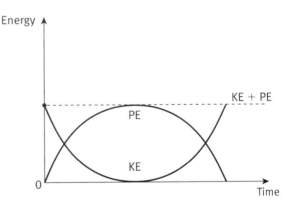
Energy
KE + PE
PE
KE
0
Time

If, at any point, you add the values of the KE and PE on the graph, you would find

KE + PE = constant

- **Power** is the rate at which work is done or energy transferred

$$\textbf{Average Power} = \frac{\textbf{Work Done}}{\textbf{Time}} \text{ (Energy transferred)}$$

$$P = \frac{Fs}{t}$$

$$\therefore \quad P = Fv$$

units in **watts** or **J s^{-1}**

Questions

1 A gun fires a bullet of mass 100 g horizontally. This graph shows the variation of the force on the bullet with distance from rest

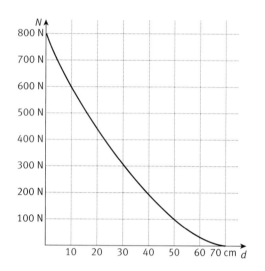

a Estimate the work done on the bullet

 Here estimate means use the graph

b With what acceleration does the bullet leave the gun?

Answers

a One square = 1000 N cm = 10 N m

Count the number of whole squares and make an approximation of the rest

number of squares $\sim 20\frac{1}{2}$

work done = (20.5 × 1000) N cm

$\qquad$ = 20500 N cm

$\qquad$ = 205 J

b $m = 0.1$ kg $\quad F = ma = 800$ N

thus $\quad a = 800 \div 0.1 = 8000$ m s^{-2}

Questions

2 Here is a perfectly spherical boulder rolling down a perfectly straight hill (as they do). Its mass is 40 kg and it reaches a speed of 5.4 m s^{-1} from rest at the bottom

a What is the work it does against friction?

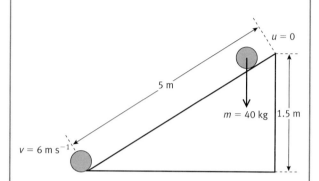

b How do you know when a slope is friction compensated?

Answers

a PE = mgh = 40 × 10 × 1.5 = 600 J

 It might be tempting to state this as the answer but this value assumes no friction, and the question wants you to account for this.

As v and u have been given, think about the KE

$$\text{KE gained} = \tfrac{1}{2}mv^2 - \tfrac{1}{2}mu^2$$
$$= 0.5 \times 40 \times 5.4^2 = 583 \text{ J}$$

∴ Work done against friction = 600 − 583 = 17 J

b The speed down the slope is constant

Question

3 A cross-country runner, mass 50 kg, moves up a hill raising his height by 7 m in 30 s. What power does he develop in raising his mass?

Answer

$$P = \frac{mgh}{t}$$

$$= \frac{50 \times 10 \times 7}{30} \approx 116.7 \, \text{W}$$

C11 Energy for temperature changes

Temperature

- This is a measure of the degree of 'hotness' of a substance measured on a chosen scale, eg, the length of mercury in a capillary bore

   *Remember it's a fundamental **scalar** quantity when measured in kelvin (K)*

- If two bodies at different temperatures are placed in **thermal contact**, heat will flow from the body at a higher temperature to that at a lower temperature

- Heat flow will cease when the bodies are at the same temperature. We call this **thermal equilibrium**

  So when your cup of tea goes cold because you were so absorbed in revising, it has reached thermal equilibrium (same temperature) with the room

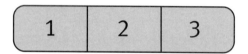

- Zeroth law of thermodynamics ... if bodies 1 and 3 are each in thermal equilibrium with body 2, then 1 and 3 must also be in thermal equilibrium with each other

   Put simply, they are all at the same temperature

Temperature scale

Question

1 You are given an uncalibrated (no scale marked) mercury thermometer. Using simple laboratory equipment, how would you calibrate it?

Answer

Step 1 Place the thermometer fully in a beaker of crushed melting ice, wait a couple of minutes and mark where the mercury level is (X_0) using a very fine permanent marker pen, without lifting the bulb out of the ice (tricky)

Step 2 Place the thermometer in the steam from a beaker of boiling water for a couple of minutes until the mercury stops rising, and again mark where the mercury level is (X_{100})

Step 3 Use a millimetre ruler to measure the distance

$$X_{100} - X_0$$

Hopefully you realise that this length represents the temperatures from 0° to 100°C

Divide the length into 10, where each division represents 10°C

 This is only a rough calibration. Your water may not be pure, which can lead to errors locating the melting and boiling points of water. Your temperature divisions will only be as accurate as your instrument

- From the above question it is clear that

$$100°C \quad \propto \quad X_{100} - X_0$$

As we have assumed there is a linear relationship between a 1°C increase in temperature and the rise of mercury, then for **any temperature** θ

$$\theta°C \quad \propto \quad X_\theta - X_0$$

As the constant of proportionality is the same

$$\frac{\theta}{100} = \frac{X_\theta - X_0}{X_{100} - X_0}$$

This is the **empirical** scale of temperature for the thermometer.

Absolute zero

- Absolute zero is the temperature at which the energy of molecular motion of matter is at a minimum

  (Even at absolute zero the oscillations never become zero)

Absolute zero = − 273.16°C = 0K

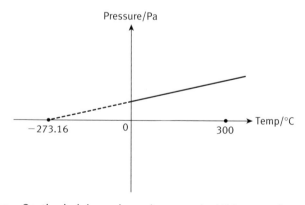 *When a fixed volume of gas cools, its pressure decreases. Experimental readings cease when the gas liquefies, but you can extrapolate the graph back to zero pressure: the temperature at that point is absolute zero! The closest value to have been reached is 0.00001K*

- On the kelvin scale an increase in 1K is very close to an increase of 1°C

θ/°C	T/K
−273	0
0	273
100	373

- So

$$T/K = \theta/°C + 273$$

Thermometers

thermometer	how it works	approximate temperature range (°C)	advantages	disadvantages
mercury-in-glass	mercury expands with an increase in temperature, it rises up the capillary bore	−39 to 500	direct reading, portable, easy to use, inexpensive	not very accurate eg, non-uniformity of bore, fragile, contains toxic Hg
thermocouple	two different metals, A and B, eg, copper and iron, are joined at two junctions. The difference in temperature between the junctions provides a small EMF. *Note: a galvanometer will register the presence of an EMF*	−248 to 1477	measures rapidly fluctuating temperature, inexpensive, reads wide range of temps, junction can measure temperature of a tiny spot	constant volume gas more accurate
constant volume gas thermometer	a fixed mass of gas, eg, helium, in a bulb at a constant volume. As temperature changes, the pressure of the gas changes to produce a change in height, h. X is the constant volume level	−270 to 1500	very accurate, very sensitive, reads wide range of temps, a **standard** by which others are calibrated	bulb is cumbersome, not direct reading, responds slowly, complex to use

Question

3 The length of mercury in a thermometer is 4 cm at the melting point of ice and 18 cm at the boiling point of water. If the thermometer is placed in a beaker of water and maintained at $\theta°$C, the length of mercury becomes 14 cm. What is the temperature $\theta°$C?

Answer

$$X_\theta = 14\,\text{cm}, \quad X_0 = 4\,\text{cm}, \quad X_{100} = 18\,\text{cm}$$

$$\frac{\theta}{100} = \frac{X_\theta - X_0}{X_{100} - X_0}$$

$$\frac{\theta}{100} = \frac{14 - 4}{18 - 4} = \frac{10}{14} = 0.71$$

$$\therefore \quad \theta = 71°\text{C}$$

Question

4 Consider a mercury-in-glass thermometer

a Why is the capillary bore so thin?

b Why is the glass surrounding the bore so much thicker?

c Why is the bulb glass so thin?

Answers

a To produce a measurable change in the length of the mercury column as it rises with even a small temperature change

b To protect the fragile bore and to slightly magnify the width of the column of mercury

c So it quickly reaches thermal equilibrium with the temperature of the substance it is measuring

Question

5 A thermocouple has its cold junction in ice-water at 0°C. When the hot junction is in boiling water, 100°C, the EMF is 1.95 mV. The temperature of the hot junction changes, and the EMF is now 1.42 mV. Estimate the new temperature. What assumption have you made?

Answer

$$X_0 = 0\,\text{mV}, \quad X_\theta = 1.42\,\text{mV}, \quad X_{100} = 1.95\,\text{mV}$$

$$\frac{\theta}{100} = \frac{X_\theta - X_0}{X_{100} - X_0} = \frac{1.42 - 0}{1.95 - 0} = 0.73$$

so the new temperature is 73°C

Assumption: that when both junctions are in ice the meter reads 0 mV. Also that there is a proportional rise in EMF with temperature rise

C12 Internal energy and thermodynamics

- All molecules of matter move and so have kinetic energy. There are forces of attraction between the molecules, despite them moving apart, so they also have potential energy

internal energy (U) = total KE + total PE of molecules

- The higher the temperature of a substance the greater the KE of the molecules

  Thus a cold object has less internal energy than an identical object at a higher temperature

- When comparing the 3 states of matter, the PE of the molecules compares as follows

  gas > liquid > solid

  because of the amount of separation between the molecules and the temperature

Heating and working

When energy is flowing or in the process of being transferred it is called heating or working

- A temperature difference between two bodies causes heat energy to flow from the hotter body to the colder one

  The increased energy in the once colder body is NOT an increase in its heat but an increase in its internal energy

  eg, a spoon placed in a hot drink does not gain heat but gains internal energy

- When a force moves its point of application from one place to another, the transferred energy is called work

 Temperature differences do not cause the transfer, but temperature changes may result

eg, a rubber belt moves round a roller underneath the metal dome in a Van de Graaff generator. The internal energy of the roller increases (temperature ↑), not because heat has been transferred to it, but because work has been done on it by friction

Question

1 A battery is connected to a small electrical heater, the temperature of the heater increases. Which of the following statements is correct?

a The electrons in the wire gain heat from the battery and in turn pass that heat to the heater

b The battery does work on the electrons in the wire, which, in turn, do work on the heater

Answer

Hope you know it's (b)

First law of thermodynamics

To **increase** the internal energy (ΔU) of a gas you can

Increase the heat supplied **to** it (ΔQ)

Do work **on** it, ie, compress it (ΔW)

 Compression transfers energy to the gas, like squashing a spring

So the first law can be stated as

$$\Delta U = \Delta Q + \Delta W$$

 Potentially tricky bit here. Read carefully, then re-read

Notice the words, **increase, to, on**, highlighted above. In text books or exam questions you could be presented with the same law but stated in a different way. This should not be a problem if you understand the law.

Rearranging the above

$$\Delta U - \Delta W = \Delta Q$$

If $+\Delta W$ is work done **on** the gas

then $-\Delta W$ is work done **by** the gas on the surroundings (expansion!)...

So the way the first law is expressed depends on the definition of ΔW, the work done

Question

2 A filament bulb of power 24 W has been switched on for the evening. Apply the first law of thermodynamics to a 3-second period during its operation

State the value of each term in the equation, with an explanation

 Watch out for your interpretation of ΔQ

 Remember Power = Energy/Time

Answer

$\Delta U = \Delta Q + \Delta W$

$\Delta U = 0$, because the bulb has been on for a while, and its temperature stays constant (no increase)

$\Delta Q = -72$ J (energy = power × time = $24 \times 3 = 72$ J) heat is transferred from the filament to the surroundings

$\Delta W = +72$ J

work is done on the bulb by the power source

 Check your equation balances

Question

3 Phred the physicist bought a bag of chips and placed them in his food flask for the journey home. He fascinated people on the bus by telling them how you could apply the first law of thermodynamics (1LTD) to his chips

The flask was a very good insulator
His chips stayed at 38°C

Decide whether each term in the equation $\Delta U = \Delta Q + \Delta W$ is positive, negative or zero, explaining why

Answer

$\Delta U = 0$, because the temperature of the chips is steady

$\Delta Q = 0$, because heat is not being transferred to or from the chips

$\Delta W = 0$, because no work is being done on or by the chips

 Check your equation balances

The heat engine

- A heat engine changes thermal energy into work Useful engines work continuously in cycles, eg, the steam engine, petrol and diesel engines

- The **Second Law of Thermodynamics** (2LTD) states

> Heat engines, operating in a cycle, cannot convert 100% of the thermal energy they possess into work

- ie, they cannot be 100% efficient. For example, as a result of burning petrol in a car the piston in the engine does work, but about 70% of the thermal energy is transferred as heat to the atmosphere. So the engine is only 30% efficient (see below)

- The **thermal efficiency** of a heat engine, ξ, is

$$\therefore \quad \xi = \frac{\text{useful work output}}{\text{energy input}}$$

 ξ has no unit, it is a ratio

- To calculate the efficiency as a percentage multiply ξ by 100.

- It can be shown that if T_1 and T_2 are the kelvin temperatures of the hot source and the cold sink, respectively, we can also say

$$\xi = \frac{T_1 - T_2}{T_1} = 1 - \frac{T_2}{T_1}$$

 Remember I said kelvin temperatures

- **Maximum thermal efficiency** occurs when T_2/T_1 is as low as possible, thus

  T_1 (hot source) needs to be as high as possible
  T_2 (cold sink) needs to be as low as possible

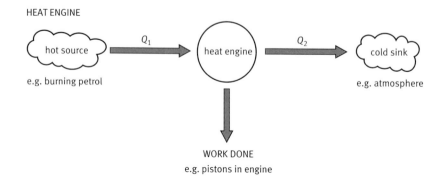

HEAT ENGINE

hot source — Q_1 → heat engine — Q_2 → cold sink

e.g. burning petrol   e.g. atmosphere

WORK DONE
e.g. pistons in engine

In real heat engines there are also other losses, eg, because of frictional effects, incomplete combustion of fuel, unnecessary movement of parts of the engine

Questions

4 The steam in a steam engine has a temperature of 127°C. It condenses at 77°C

a What is the maximum thermal efficiency?

b How could the efficiency be increased and why might this change not be possible?

c What would the condensing temperature have to be to create 100% efficiency?

Answers

a $\xi = \dfrac{T_1 - T_2}{T_1} = \dfrac{400 - 350}{400} = 0.125 = 12.5\%$

 Who forgot to convert to kelvin???

b You could increase the steam temperature

The materials in the engine may not be able to withstand higher temperatures

c Absolute zero, $\dfrac{400 - 0}{400} = 1 = 100\%$. Remember this value

has not yet been reached in practice

The heat pump

- A heat engine working in reverse is called a **heat pump**. Work is done on the pump so that it can transfer heat from a cold sink to a higher temperature reservoir

Examples might make this clearer for you

1 A heat pump could be used to heat a building if there were a river or stream running nearby. Thermal energy can be extracted from the cold river (yes, making it even colder) by an electric pump and transferred to the heating system of the building

 Unfortunately the colder it is outside the less well the pump works, because it is trying to extract thermal energy from an even colder river. So the heat pump works best in the summer

2 A refrigerator uses a special liquid (coolant) that, by extracting thermal energy from the food, evaporates. An electric pump removes and condenses this vapour, transferring latent heat to the surroundings via fins at the back of the fridge

They are hot ... don't touch

Questions

5 Consider the figure below

a What relationship is there between the energy transfers shown on the diagram?

b Why is the electricity supply necessary to pump the energy outside?

c Why are cooling fins inside a freezer compartment at the top and not at the bottom?

Answers

a The total energy flowing into the heat pump = the total energy flowing out (the law of conservation of energy)

b In transferring heat from a cold area to a hotter area you are working against the temperature gradient, so work has to be put into the system

c The air at the top of the compartment will be hotter than below because of convection

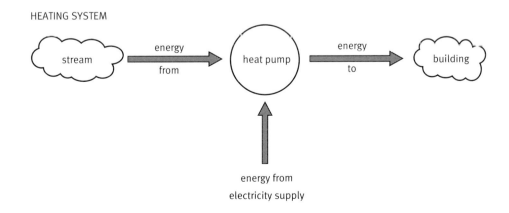

C13 Heat transfer

Beginner's box

- Heat is transferred by four methods: conduction, convection, radiation, and evaporation
- A good conductor is a poor insulator

Conduction

At GCSE you were probably taught that conduction was the method of heat transfer in solids only. In fact it takes place in **solids, liquids and gases**, but in different ways.

- **Metals:** Very fast moving free electrons gain energy at the hotter area of the metal and diffuse quickly to the colder area, carrying energy with them

   This process also occurs in liquid metals

   These electrons are also responsible for electrical conduction, so a good electrical conductor is always a good thermal conductor

- **Non-metal solids and liquids:** The atoms in the hotter regions vibrate energetically and transfer some of their energy to neighbouring molecules in the colder regions. This is a much slower process than electron conduction

  Thus electrical insulators tend to be poor thermal conductors

- **Gases:** Gas molecules collide frequently, and those with greater KE transfer some of their energy to molecules with less KE. Energy is redistributed from warmer areas to cooler areas until, eventually, all regions contain molecules of equal energy, on average

  Gases are worse thermal conductors than liquids

Convection

Heat can be transferred through liquids and gases more quickly by convection

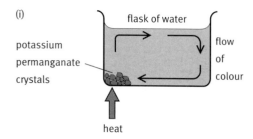

(i)
flask of water
potassium permanganate crystals
flow of colour
heat

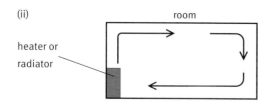

(ii)
room
heater or radiator

In both the situations above, the heated water/air expands, becoming less dense and, thus, rises. Cooler water/air falls to replace it and, in turn, is heated and rises, and so on, creating a convection current.

The hotter/less dense water/air rising could be considered as driving the convection current, pushing the colder/denser water/air

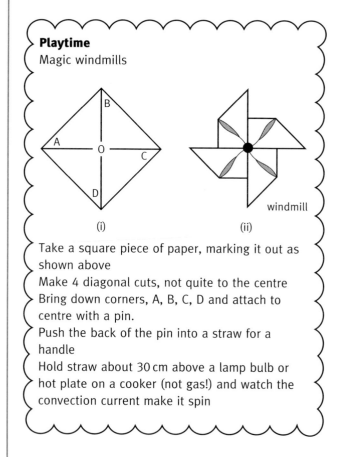

Playtime
Magic windmills

(i)   (ii)   windmill

Take a square piece of paper, marking it out as shown above
Make 4 diagonal cuts, not quite to the centre
Bring down corners, A, B, C, D and attach to centre with a pin.
Push the back of the pin into a straw for a handle
Hold straw about 30 cm above a lamp bulb or hot plate on a cooker (not gas!) and watch the convection current make it spin

Radiation

Thermal radiation is emitted by objects: the higher their temperature, the more radiation they emit. The radiation is electromagnetic in nature

- Thermal radiation occurs mainly at infrared wavelengths, but visible and ultraviolet wavelengths are involved at higher temperatures

- It has the same properties as all other electromagnetic waves

  — can travel through a vacuum
  — its speed in a vacuum is $3 \times 10^8 \, \text{m s}^{-1}$

— transverse wave
— not affected by magnetic/electrical fields
— obeys the Inverse Square Law
— can be reflected

- Objects that **absorb** radiation undergo a heating effect. Objects can also **reflect** radiation. Different surfaces on a body produce different effects

	dull black	shiny black	white	silver
emitter	best	→	→	worst
absorber	best	→	→	worst
reflector	worst	→	→	best

 *A **black body** absorbs all the radiation incident on it, and reflects none, like a heat 'sponge' soaking up all the radiation*

Evaporation

A liquid evaporates when the molecules at the surface with a greater KE overcome any forces of attraction and are able to escape. As the more energetic ones escape, the average KE of the molecules left in the liquid drops, so its temperature is reduced

Get out of your outside swimming pool on a windy day to drink your pina colada, and you'll soon feel evaporation cooling!

 A common misconception is that only boiling liquids evaporate. Not true. Think about how we dry clothes. Clouds are caused by the evaporation of water from the Earth's surface, eg, the oceans. Try leaving a saucer of water to one side for a day or two near sunlight. It will evaporate

- You can increase the rate of evaporation by

method	effect
passing a current of air over the liquid	assists the escape of molecules
increasing the liquid surface area	more room for molecules with higher KE to escape
heating the liquid	increases the amount of molecules with enough KE to escape

Heating matter

Heat capacity (*C*)

The heat capacity of an object is a measure of how much energy it will need to raise its temperature by 1 K

$$C = \frac{\Delta Q}{\Delta \theta}$$

ΔQ = thermal energy
$\Delta \theta$ = temperature rise
C is measured in $J\,K^{-1}$

Specific heat capacity (*c*)

This can be a more useful value because it tells you how much energy **1 kg** of a material needs to raise its temperature by 1 K

$$c = \frac{\Delta Q}{m \Delta \theta}$$

m = mass of substance in
Unit is $J\,K^{-1}\,kg^{-1}$

The two equations can be combined

$$c = \frac{C}{m} \qquad \therefore \quad C = mc$$

 The specific heat capacity (shc) of a substance can change if the conditions it is under change, eg, air at a constant pressure has one value, air at a constant volume has another

Question

1 A sample of material from an archaeology dig is to be identified. Calculate its specific heat capacity if it has a mass of 0.5 kg, and it takes 3000 J to raise its temperature from 12°C to 27°C

Answer

$\Delta \theta = 27 - 12 = 15°C$. This is the same as a change of 15 K

$$c = \frac{\Delta Q}{m \Delta \theta} = \frac{3000}{0.5 \times 15} = 400\,J\,K^{-1}\,kg^{-1}$$

Question

2 A shower has the water heated by a 9 kW electric heater, from 15 to 40°C. If the shc of water is 4200 J K⁻¹ kg⁻¹, and 1 litre of water has a mass of 1 kg, what is the flow rate of the water in litres per minute?

 Convert units to SI!

Answer

Step 1

$P = 9000\,\text{W}, \quad t = 60\,\text{s}$

$Pt = \Delta Q \quad \therefore \quad \Delta Q = 9000 \times 60 = 5.4 \times 10^5\,\text{J per minute}$

Step 2

$c = \dfrac{\Delta Q}{m\Delta\theta} \qquad m = \dfrac{\Delta Q}{c\Delta\theta}$

$ = \dfrac{5.4 \times 10^5}{4200 \times 25} = 5.14\,\text{kg}$

Flow rate = 5.14 litres min⁻¹

 Remember to give the answer exactly as the question asks for it

Questions

3 Phred the physicist wants to cook his potatoes. He adds 2 kg of water to his aluminium pan, of mass 0.5 kg, and puts it on a low flame on the cooker. He records the temperature as the water heats up

shc water = 4200 J K⁻¹ kg⁻¹
shc aluminium = 900 J K⁻¹ kg⁻¹

time (min)	temp (°C)
0.0	20.0
2.5	31.0
5.0	38.5
7.5	44.0
10.0	47.5
12.5	50.0
15.0	52.0
20.0	54.0
25.0	55.0

a Plot a graph of the results

b What is the heat capacity of the pan and water?

c What is the rate of temperature rise of the water in the first 2.5 min?

d At what rate is energy absorbed by the water and pan? (Note that there are energy losses)

e Explain the shape of the curve as heating progresses

Answers

a Notice the time plots are not even ... be careful

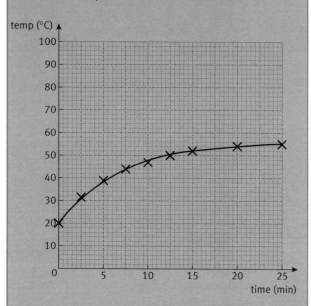

b $C_{\text{pan}} = mc = 0.5 \times 900 = 450\,\text{J K}^{-1}$

$C_{\text{water}} = mc = 2 \times 4200 = 8400\,\text{J K}^{-1}$

$\therefore$ total heat capacity = 8850 J K⁻¹

c gradient $\simeq \dfrac{11\,\text{K}}{150\,\text{s}} = 0.073\,\text{K s}^{-1}$

 Remember to convert your time units and that a difference of 1°C and 1 K is the same

d from **c**, $\dfrac{\Delta\theta}{t} = 0.073$

rate of energy supplied $= \dfrac{\Delta Q}{t} = \dfrac{mc\Delta\theta}{t}$

$C = mc \quad \therefore \quad \dfrac{\Delta Q}{t} = C \times 0.073$

$\phantom{C = mc \quad \therefore \quad \dfrac{\Delta Q}{t}} = 8850 \times 0.073 = 646\,\text{J s}^{-1}$

e As the water gets hotter, the temperature gradient between it and the surroundings increases, which brings about a greater loss of thermal energy per second

EXPERIMENT

How would you measure the shc of a liquid and a solid?

LIQUID, eg, paraffin

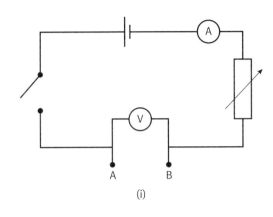

(i)

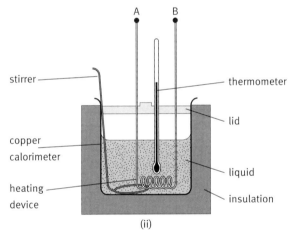

stirrer

copper
calorimeter

heating
device

thermometer

lid

liquid

insulation

(ii)

 Careful when heating paraffin

- Weigh calorimeter (M) without, then with liquid (M + m) to establish mass of liquid ... m

- Take the temperature of the liquid θ_1

- Attach the circuit (i) to the apparatus, switch on heater, start a timer

- Stir, keep ammeter reading steady, using the variable resistor. Note V and I

- After a time, t, record the temp θ_2, the highest reached

- Calculate $\theta_2 - \theta_1 = \Delta\theta$

Energy supplied to heater	=	Energy given to calorimeter	+	Energy given to liquid

$$V I t = Mc_1\Delta\theta + mc_2\Delta\theta$$

If the shc for the calorimeter is known, then c_2, the shc for the liquid, is the only unknown above

 Heating is usually prolonged to establish a temperature rise of a few degrees, so heat loss to the surroundings will occur. In more rigorous experiments a cooling correction is measured (see an advanced Physics text book)

SOLID, eg, aluminium

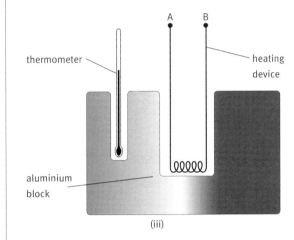

thermometer

heating
device

aluminium
block

(iii)

- Measure the mass of the block, m, and the initial temperature θ_1

- Keep ammeter reading steady, using variable resistor

- Attach and switch on the circuit for a time, t, recording I, V, and the temperature θ_2, the highest reached

Energy supplied to heater = energy given to block

$$V I t = mc\Delta\theta$$

$$c = \frac{V I t}{m\Delta\theta}$$

Here, c, the shc for aluminium, is the only unknown

Questions

4 A 3 kg block of aluminium has two holes in which are inserted a 90 W heater and a thermometer. The heater was switched on for 500 s, and the following readings were obtained

time (s)	temp (°C)
0	11.0
50	11.5
100	12.7
200	15.3
300	17.8
400	20.4
500	22.9
600	23.5
700	23.2

a Plot the graph temp/time

b Calculate the shc for the block

c What was the room temperature, and would a change in that value, during the experiment have an effect on the increase in the observed temperature?

 Two parts to this question . . . don't forget!

d Why is the graph curved at the start and the end?

e Your result for the shc is higher than it should be. Explain why

f What could you do to improve accuracy?

 Even though the temperature continues to rise after the heater is switched off, thermal energy is still being transferred. Use the maximum temperature when calculating θ

Answer

a Plot your own curve

b $c = \dfrac{\Delta Q}{m\Delta\theta}$ where $\begin{aligned} m &= 3\,\text{kg} \\ \Delta\theta &= 12.5\,\text{K} \end{aligned}$

$\Delta Q = V I t = 90 \times 500 = 45000\,\text{J}$

$\therefore \quad c = \dfrac{\Delta Q}{m\Delta\theta} = \dfrac{45000}{3 \times 12.5} \simeq 1200\,\text{J}\,\text{kg}^{-1}\,\text{K}^{-1}$

c The starting temperature, assume the block is in thermal equilibrium with the room . . . 11°C

The observed temperature rise would be greater because some attempt has been made to compensate for heat losses to surroundings.

d Start: heat transfer to thermometer is not immediate, conduction takes time

End: conduction is still happening for a while after the heater is switched off

e There will be heat losses to the surroundings, which means that $\Delta\theta$ is lower than it should be

$c = \dfrac{\Delta Q}{m\Delta\theta}$ so the lower $\Delta\theta$ the higher c is

f Lag the block, lowering the heat losses

Changes of phase

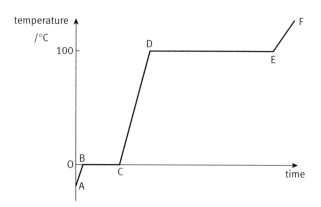

A change of phase is a change from one state of matter to another. The figure represents a solid being heated continuously e.g ice

A → B solid
C → D liquid
E → F gas

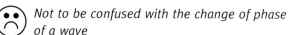 *Not to be confused with the change of phase of a wave*

In these three stages, as thermal energy is being given to the material, the KE of the molecules and the temperature is increasing, and the temperature rises

Why then does the KE of molecules still not go up from B → C and D → E, even though the material is being heated continuously?

It is here that the material uses the energy to change phase; the potential energy between the molecules increases as work is done on them. They move further apart against their attractive forces. This thermal energy is described as **latent heat** (latent because it is hidden)

Latent heat (L)

- **specific latent heat of vaporisation** (L) is the thermal energy needed to change a unit mass of **liquid** to a **vapour** without a change in temperature

- **specific latent heat of fusion** (L) is the thermal energy needed to change a unit mass of **solid** to a **liquid,** *without a change in temperature*

- In both cases

$$L = \frac{\Delta Q}{m}$$

where m = unit mass
ΔQ = thermal energy
units of L are $J\,kg^{-1}$

- You may find the following diagram useful in describing changes in phase

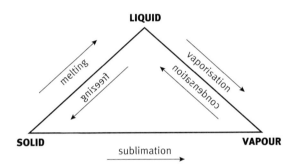

 When a given mass of a substance freezes or melts the same amount of latent thermal energy is involved

 EXPERIMENT

How would you measure the latent heat of vaporisation of a liquid directly?

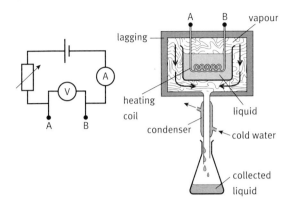

- Let the liquid boil for a few minutes

  Then you know all the electrical energy is being used to provide latent heat

- Note the ammeter and voltmeter readings, using rheostat to keep I constant

- Measure a mass, m, of the collected liquid in a time t

$$Q = mL$$

where
$$Q = V I t$$

$$\frac{V I t}{m} = L$$

 Assume there are no heat losses from the lagging

Question

5 Three ice-lolly holders contain a squash + water mixture. Each has a mass of 0.1 kg, and they are placed in a freezer compartment. They take 24 hours to freeze

How much heat energy will be transferred out of the freezer to freeze the mixture?

$$L_{mixture} = 3.3 \times 10^5 \, J\,kg^{-1}$$

Answer

$$Q = mL = 0.1 \times 3.3 \times 10^5 = 33000 J$$

How many of you would, in an exam situation, forget there are 3 of them?

$$Q_{total} = 3 \times 33000 = 9.9 \times 10^4 \, J$$

This next one is taking no prisoners. Be brave

6 After studying for hours Anna decides to have a tea break. She heats an old kettle containing 1 kg of water, initially at 20°C. It boils in 4 minutes, but in daydreaming over a physics problem, she leaves it boiling for a further 10 minutes! Only 0.65 kg is left

a Calculate the latent heat of vaporisation of water

b Name two sources of error in this calculation (shc water = $4200\,J\,K^{-1}\,kg^{-1}$)

Answers

a $L = \Delta Q/m$, the mass of the water turned to vapour is 0.35 kg, so you need to calculate the energy supplied in that last 10 min

Step 1 The energy received by the water in the first 4 min is
$$Q = mc\Delta\theta$$
$$= 1 \times 4200 \times 80 \quad (\Delta\theta = 100 - 20)$$
$$= 336000\,J$$

so energy/min $= \dfrac{336000}{4} = 84000\,J$

Step 2 The energy from the kettle in the last 10 min $= 840000\,J$

so $L = \dfrac{\Delta Q}{m} = \dfrac{840000}{0.35} = 2.4 \times 10^6\,J\,kg^{-1}$

b Heat losses through the sides of the kettle, and assuming that the energy supply was constant (remember Anna has also filled the kitchen with steam)

Thermal conductivity and *U*-values

How well a solid conducts heat is decided by a few factors

Using a rod as an example...

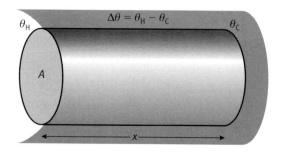

1 The difference in temperature from one end to the other (temperature change) ... $\Delta\theta$

2 The length from the hot to the cold end ... x

3 The cross-sectional area of the solid ... A

4 The thermal conductivity of the material ... *k*

5 The insulation around it (lagging)

These factors can be expressed as an equation

$$\frac{\Delta Q}{t} = \frac{-kA\,\Delta\theta}{x}$$

- $\Delta Q/t$ is the rate of flow of heat

- $\dfrac{\Delta\theta}{x}$ is the temperature gradient

- the minus shows that as the distance along the bar (x) increases the temperature decreases (notice the gradients in the graphs overleaf are negative)

Question

7 What are the units of *k*?

Answer

$$k = \frac{x\Delta Q}{At\Delta\theta}$$

units are $= \dfrac{m\,J}{m^2\,s\,K} \quad (J\,s^{-1} = W)$

$$= W\,K^{-1}\,m^{-1}$$

 Notice we are dealing in kelvins again, but **changes in K are numerically equal to changes in °C**

Steady-state conditions

- When the temperatures at all points in a material are steady

If a bar of metal has one end maintained at a constant high temperature and the other at a constant low temperature, eventually each part of the bar will reach a temperature at which it will remain ... the bar is said to be in **steady state**

- Steady state can be achieved in <u>both</u> lagged and unlagged bars. The lagging simply affects the final temperature at each point, ie, the temperature gradient is affected by lagging

 As each part of the bar is maintaining a different temperature it is **not in thermal equilibrium** *and cannot ever be whilst both ends are kept at different temperatures*

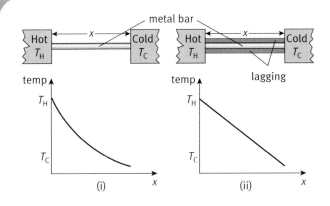

(i)   (ii)

- (i) Unlagged bar

  Notice from the graph that the temperature drops more quickly near the hot end of the bar. As there is a bigger temperature difference with the surroundings there is more heat loss. The temperature gradient is not constant

- (ii) Lagged bar

  Here, with perfect insulation around the bar, no heat is lost to the surroundings and the temperature drop (the temperature gradient) along the bar is constant

 In both cases steady state conditions prevail, but __not__ thermal equilibrium

Question

8 A metal rod, length 70 cm, CSA of 3.0 cm², has a temperature difference of 5 K between its ends

Calculate the rate of heat flow along the rod assuming it is perfectly lagged and has a thermal conductivity of 0.5 kW m⁻¹ K⁻¹

 Convert your units

Answer

$$\frac{\Delta Q}{t} = \frac{-kA\Delta\theta}{x}$$

$A = 3 \times 10^{-4}\,\text{m}^2$ (see page 7 on converting units
$x = 0.7\,\text{m}$ if you are unsure here)
$k = 500\,\text{W m}^{-1}\,\text{K}^{-1}$

$$\therefore \frac{\Delta Q}{t} = \frac{500 \times 3 \times 10^{-4} \times 5}{0.7} = 1.1\,\text{W}$$

Question

9 A cavity wall has two layers of bricks with a layer of air in between. Each layer has the same thickness, and the conductivity of the air is less than that of the brick. The inside surface of the cavity wall is warmer than the outside. Steady state conditions prevail. Assume there are no heat losses to the surroundings

i) sketch how the temperature, θ, varies with the distance, x, from the inside surface of the wall.

ii) sketch how the rate of flow of heat, P, varies with the distance, x, from the inside surface of the wall

Answer

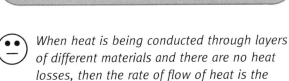

(i)   x   (ii)   x

 When heat is being conducted through layers of different materials and there are no heat losses, then the rate of flow of heat is the same value through each material
$$\frac{\Delta Q}{t} = constant$$

U-values

A U-value is a simpler way of looking at the thermal conductivity of a material

- U-value $= \dfrac{\text{rate of flow of heat}}{\text{area} \times \text{temperature change}}$

$$\frac{\Delta Q}{t} = U \times A \times \Delta\theta$$

The units of the U-value are $W\,m^{-2}\,K^{-1}$

- In U-value calculations, layers of material, e.g glass and air, are regarded as composite materials, so $\Delta\theta$ is the temperature difference across the whole structure. See how much easier the next question is compared with the last one and keep your fingers crossed for this type in your exam!!

Question

1 The rate of heat flow through a double glazing unit is 60 W when the temperature difference across it is 12.5 K. The area of the unit is $1.4\,m^2$. What is its *U*-value?

Answer

U-value $= \dfrac{\text{rate of flow of heat}}{\text{area} \times \text{temperature change}}$

$= \dfrac{60}{1.4 \times 12.5} = 3.4\,W\,m^{-2}\,K^{-1}$

C14 Behaviour of gases

Beginner's box

$$\frac{p_1 V_1}{T_1} = \frac{p_2 V_2}{T_2}$$

where p = pressure,
        V = volume and
        T = temperature of
             gases 1 and 2

Brownian motion

In 1827 a botanist, Robert Brown, was observing pollen particles in water through a microscope, as you do, and noticed their vigorous, random motion. This motion later became known as Brownian motion. Smoke particles illuminated by a light source under a microscope exhibit similar movement

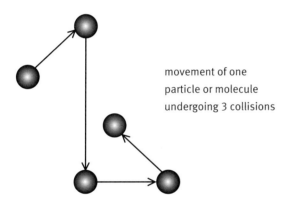

movement of one
particle or molecule
undergoing 3 collisions

Both these observations demonstrate that although we cannot see water/air molecules, they must be colliding with the larger pollen/smoke particles to cause such movement

As the figure shows, every molecule must also move randomly

*   at different speeds (length of displacement caused by collision)

*   in different directions (direction of displacement)

The gas laws

Experiments on the pressures (p), temperatures (T) and volumes (V) of gases have resulted in three gas laws

*   Boyle's Law states

> **pV = constant**
>
> for a fixed mass of gas
> at a constant temperature

 EXPERIMENT

Describe an experiment to verify Boyle's Law

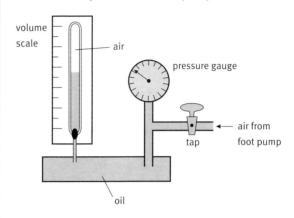

*   Open the tap, note values of V and p

*   Compress the foot pump and close tap

*   Wait until volume constant, read V and p

*   Repeat the above for range of values of V and p

*   Plot p against 1/V

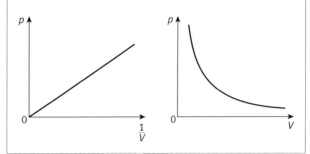

*   Charles' Law states

> **$\dfrac{V}{T}$ = constant**
>
> for a fixed mass of gas
> at a constant pressure

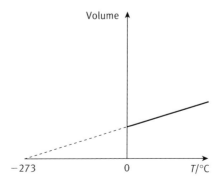

A graph of pressure against volume would look like this!

Caution: the graph only goes through the origin when kelvin temperatures are used
kelvin temp = °C + 273

refer to A Level textbook for Charles Law experiment

- The <u>Pressure Law</u> states

$$\frac{p}{T} = \textbf{constant}$$

for a fixed mass of gas at a constant *volume*

 EXPERIMENT

Describe an experiment to prove the Pressure Law

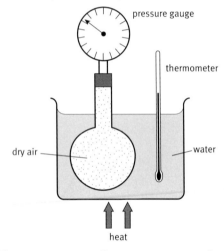

pressure gauge

thermometer

dry air

water

heat

- When pressure reading constant, record *p* and *T*
- Heat water
- Stir water and record *p* and *T* when *p* constant
- Repeat for different values of *T*
- Note atmospheric pressure P_A
- Plot graph of (P_A) against *T*

    Need to measure atmos. press. on a barometer and add to the pressure readings. Watch the pressure units

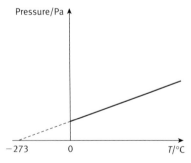

Pressure/Pa

−273   0   *T*/°C

 Caution: the graph only goes through the origin when kelvin temperatures are used

- The **ideal gas equation** brings together these three laws

$$pV = nRT$$

p = gas pressure ($N\,m^{-2}$)
V = gas volume (m^3)
n = number of moles of gas (mol)
R = universal molar gas constant
$\quad = 8.31\,J\,K^{-1}\,mol^{-1}$
T = gas temperature (kelvin)

 The Mole really frightens you doesn't it?? It's a friendly, shy creature, just misunderstood

A mole of any substance has 6×10^{23} atoms in it
So a mole of lead has 6×10^{23} atoms in it
And a mole of hydrogen has 6×10^{23} atoms in it
Of course a mole of lead has more mass than a mole of hydrogen

Gases, ideal and real

- On a macroscopic scale (can be felt or measured with instruments) an **ideal gas** is defined as a gas that satisfies the equation

$$pV = nRT$$

- On a microscopic scale (cannot be measured directly) an ideal gas is defined by the six assumptions that form the basis of Kinetic Theory (see next page)

- An ideal gas does not exist. It is a theoretical model

- **Real gases** behave in a very similar way to ideal gases at low pressures and at temperatures well above their liquefying point

C15 Kinetic theory of gases

This theory combines the ideas of a macroscopic ideal gas with that of its microscopic molecular properties

 Before we begin, this is a long derivation that we've tried to make brief, whilst clear. Check your syllabus to see if you have to learn this … but be warned, many will expect you to <u>understand</u> it and may question you on parts of the derivation. Sneaky, sadistic … never!

Consider a cubic container of a gas having N molecules:

each of mass m
a third moving in each of 3 directions u, v, and w
between each pair of faces of the container

There are a number of assumptions to consider before the theory can be explained

1   Molecules move randomly in all directions
2   All collisions are elastic, all momentum and KE is conserved
3   The intermolecular forces are negligible
4   Total volume of molecules is negligible compared with that of the container
5   The time taken during a collision is negligible compared to time between collisions
6   Molecules have a constant velocity (u, v, w) between collisions and obey Newton's Laws of Motion

 That's why it is called a theory … most theories assume reality is suspended. A physicist drew a circle on the board and said to her students … 'assume this is the shape of a cow…'

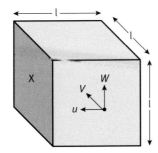

- A molecule moving towards X has momentum mu_1
  After impact it has momentum $-mu_1$ (elastic collision)

  Change in momentum $= mu_1 - (-mu_1) = 2mu_1$

- A molecule moves with constant velocity so will hit face X every t seconds, $t =$ distance/speed,

  each impact is every $\quad t = \dfrac{2l}{u_1} \quad$ seconds apart

- rate of change of momentum

$$= \frac{\text{momentum}}{\text{time}} = \frac{2mu_1}{\dfrac{2l}{u_1}} = 2mu_1 \times \frac{u_1}{2l} = \frac{mu_1^2}{l}$$

using N2L, $\therefore \quad F = \dfrac{mu_1^2}{l}$

The pressure on X is $= F/A$

where the area of a face is l^2

so   pressure $= \dfrac{mu_1^2}{l^3}$ of one molecule

so   pressure $= \dfrac{Nmu_1^2}{l^3}$ of N molecules

- u_1^2 is the square speed in one direction of one molecule
  The average square speed of all the molecules in that direction is called the **mean square speed** $\overline{u^2}$ or $<u^2>$

Now u represents the speed of one-third of the molecules, let the mean square speed of all the molecules be $\overline{c^2}$ or $<c^2>$

where $\frac{1}{3}\overline{c^2} = \overline{u^2}$

- So pressure $p = \frac{1}{3}\dfrac{Nm\overline{c^2}}{l^3}$

density $(\rho) = \dfrac{\text{total mass}}{\text{volume}} = \dfrac{Nm}{l^3} = \dfrac{M}{V}$

so $\quad p = \dfrac{1}{3}\rho\overline{c^2}$

So the pressure of a gas depends on the speed of its molecules

 $\overline{c^2}$ *is the mean of the square speed*
$\overline{c}^2$ *is the square of the mean speed*
– don't mix them up!!

if $c_1 = 4$, $c_2 = 5$, $c_3 = 6$ then

$$\overline{c^2} = \frac{16 + 25 + 36}{3} = 25.67$$

$$\overline{c}^2 = \left(\frac{4 + 5 + 6}{3}\right)^2 = 25.00$$

 RMS speed = root mean square speed

$$= \sqrt{\overline{c^2}} \text{ or } = \sqrt{<c^2>}$$

Temperature and kinetic theory

Here we are going to link temperature with the microscopic quantities of molecules

$$p = \frac{1}{3}\rho\overline{c^2} = \frac{1}{3}\frac{M}{V}\overline{c^2}$$

$$\therefore \quad pV = \frac{1}{3}M\overline{c^2}$$

We can manipulate this equation to look at the average KE of a molecule

$$pV = \frac{2}{3}N\left(\frac{1}{2}m\overline{c^2}\right)$$

Remember $pV = nRT$

n = number of moles of a gas
R = universal gas constant
T = temperature of gas in Kelvins

So $\quad \frac{2}{3}N\left(\frac{1}{2}m\overline{c^2}\right) = nRT$

$$\frac{1}{2}m\overline{c^2} = \frac{3}{2}\frac{nR}{N}T$$

Now $\quad N_A = \frac{N}{n} = \frac{\text{total no. of molecules}}{\text{total no. of moles}}$

This is the number of molecules per mole, which defines Avagadro's number (N_A), so

$$\frac{1}{2}m\overline{c^2} = \frac{3}{2}\frac{R}{N_A}T$$

R/N_A = Boltzmann's constant, $k = 1.38 \times 10^{-23}\,\text{J K}^{-1}$

So the average KE of a molecule is given by

$$\boxed{\frac{1}{2}m\overline{c^2} = \frac{3}{2}\,kT}$$

So the speed of the molecule of a gas depends on the temperature of the gas

- The following question looks at the **variation of the speed of molecules** in an ideal gas

Question

1 The equation $\frac{1}{2}m\overline{c^2} = \frac{3}{2}kT$ implies that at zero kelvin the KE of a molecule is zero (it is stationary). Comment on this

Answer

This equation is dealing with an ideal gas where there is only KE of the molecules; the molecules in a real gas also have PE and are not stationary at zero kelvin

Zero kelvin = absolute zero and has not been reached experimentally

Questions

2 A cylinder has a volume of 0.09 m³, and contains an ideal gas (X) at a temperature of 300 K and a pressure of 80 kPa. Calculate

a the mass of the gas X in the cylinder

b the number of gas molecules in the cylinder

c the rms speed of the gas molecules
$R = 8.3\,\text{J K}^{-1}\,\text{mol}^{-1}$, $N_A = 6.0 \times 10^{23}$,
mass of 1 mole of gas X = 0.034 kg

Answers

a $pV = nRT$

$80 \times 10^3 \times 0.09 = n \times 8.3 \times 300$

$\qquad\qquad n = 2.89 = $ no. of moles

so mass $= 2.89 \times 0.034 = 0.098\,\text{kg}$

b there are 6.0×10^{23} molecules in 1 mole, so in 2.89 moles

$2.893 \times 6.0 \times 10^{23} = 1.7 \times 10^{24}$ molecules

c $p = \frac{1}{3}\rho\overline{c^2}$ $\rho = \frac{M}{V}$

$\overline{c^2} = \frac{3pV}{M} = \frac{3 \times 80000 \times 0.09}{0.098} = 220408$

so $\sqrt{\overline{c^2}} = 470\,\text{m s}^{-1}$

Question

3 At 127°C nitrogen molecules have an RMS speed of 600 ms⁻¹. What will be their rms speed at 1127°C?

Answer

$\frac{1}{2}m\overline{c^2} = \frac{3}{2}kT$ holds for nitrogen at any temperature

At 127°C, $\frac{1}{2}m\overline{c_1^2} = \frac{3}{2}kT_1$

same gas so k and m remain constant

At 1127°C $\frac{1}{2}m\overline{c_2^2} = \frac{3}{2}kT_2$

thus $\frac{\overline{c_1^2}}{\overline{c_2^2}} = \frac{T_1}{T_2}$, but we are using rms speeds

$$\sqrt{\frac{\overline{c_1^2}}{\overline{c_2^2}}} = \sqrt{\frac{T_1}{T_2}},$$

 Convert T into kelvins!!! °C + 273 = K

$$\frac{600}{\sqrt{\overline{c_2^2}}} = \sqrt{\frac{400}{1400}}$$

rearranging rms at 1127°C is 1122.5 m s⁻¹

D16 Electrons, charge and current

Electrons

- The electrical transfer of energy in a metallic conductor is brought about by the movement of negative charges called **electrons**

- Electrons, individually, all carry the same amount of charge **e** where

$$\mathbf{e} = -1.6 \times 10^{-19} \text{ coulombs (C)}$$

 A proton carries $+1.6 \times 10^{-19}$ C

- At one time it was thought the flow of electricity was from positive (+ve) to negative (−ve). We know now that electrons in a metal flow to the positive. However, by convention we still draw current flow on diagrams going from +ve to −ve!!! ???? !!!!

- +ve to −ve   **conventional** current flow
  −ve to +ve   **actual** negative electron flow

Charge

- The **coulomb** is defined as

  the quantity of electrical charge carried past a given point in a circuit when a steady current of 1 amp flows for 1 second

$$Q = It$$

Q = charge (coulombs)
I = current (amps or coulombs/s)
t = time

Question

1 A metal wire carries 1 A (1 coulomb every second). How many electrons pass any point in a time of 1 second?

Answer

$$Q = It \quad Q = 1 \times 1 = 1\,C$$
$$e = 1.6 \times 10^{-19}\,C$$

so in 1 C there are $\dfrac{1}{1.6 \times 10^{-19}}$ electrons

$$= 6.25 \times 10^{18} \text{ electrons per second}$$

Drift velocity of an electron

Electrons have a random speed at room temperature of about 10^5 m s^{-1}. Because they move as much in one direction as another this does not constitute a current. When a pd is applied across a conductor the electrons are then given a very slow steady velocity called the **drift velocity**. The drift velocity can be derived as follows

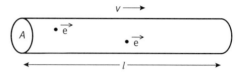

Here is length, l, of a conductor with a cross-sectional area (CSA) A having n electrons per unit volume, each carrying a charge e

The volume of the conductor $V = A \times l$

The no. of e's in this volume is $n \times A \times l$

The total charge of these e's is $n \times A \times l \times e$

 '*nAle*'

A battery placed across the ends of the conductor causes the electrons to drift with a velocity v travelling the length, l, in a time, t

now $I = \dfrac{Q}{t} = \dfrac{nAle}{t}$

but $v = \dfrac{l}{t} \quad \therefore \quad t = \dfrac{l}{v}$

so now $I = \dfrac{nAle}{\frac{l}{v}}$

$$I = nAve$$

 '*nAve*'

$$\therefore \quad v = \dfrac{I}{nAe}$$

- Typical values of drift velocities are

conductor	drift speed of electrons
copper	2×10^{-5} m s^{-1}
tungsten	0.25 m s^{-1}
silicon	80 m s^{-1}

Question

2 If the drift speed of an electron is $2 \times 10^{-5}\,\mathrm{m\,s^{-1}}$ then why would a light come on almost at the instant you press the switch?

Answer

When the light is switched on, electrons at all points around the circuit instantly start their drift

Questions

3 A heating element carries a current of 5 A

a How much charge passes a given point each minute?

b How many electrons pass this point in a minute?

Answers

a $I = 5\,\mathrm{A}$ $t = 60\,\mathrm{s}$ $Q = It$

$\therefore\ Q = 5 \times 60 = 300\,\mathrm{C}$

b One electron has $1.6 \times 10^{-19}\,\mathrm{C}$

so there are $\dfrac{300}{1.6 \times 10^{-19}}$ electrons passing that point

$= 1.875 \times 10^{21}$ electrons

Now for a question that will really challenge your mathematical skills . . . each part helps you with the next . . . be careful

Questions

4 62 kg of copper contains 6×10^{26} atoms
Copper has a density of $9 \times 10^3\,\mathrm{kg\,m^{-3}}$

 1 mole of copper has 6×10^{23} atoms

a How many electrons will there be in a cubic metre of copper? (1 atom has 1 free electron)

b A copper wire is 0.5 m long, with a CSA of $2 \times 10^{-6}\,\mathrm{m^2}$. How many electrons will it contain?

c What is the total charge on the free electrons per metre of the wire?

d What is the drift velocity of the electrons?

Answers

a $\text{density} = \dfrac{\text{mass}}{\text{volume}}$

$9 \times 10^3 = \dfrac{62}{\text{volume}}$

$\therefore\ \text{volume} = \dfrac{62}{9 \times 10^3} = 6.89 \times 10^{-3}\,\mathrm{m^3}$

so $6.89 \times 10^{-3}\,\mathrm{m^3}$ has 6×10^{26} electrons

so $1\,\mathrm{m^3}$ has $\dfrac{6 \times 10^{26}}{6.89 \times 10^{-3}}$ electrons

$n = 8.7 \times 10^{28}$ electrons

b $l = 0.5\,\mathrm{m}$ $A = 2 \times 10^{-6}\,\mathrm{,m^2}$

$\therefore$ the volume $= Al = 1 \times 10^{-6}\,\mathrm{m^3}$

from **a**

$1\,\mathrm{m^3}$ has 8.7×10^{28} electrons

volume of copper wire $= 0.5 \times 2 \times 10^{-6}$

$= 1 \times 10^{-6}\,\mathrm{m^3}$

so $1 \times 10^{-6}\,\mathrm{m^3}$ has $1 \times 10^{-6} \times 8.7 \times 10^{28}$ electrons

$= 8.7 \times 10^{22}$ electrons in the wire

c In 1m of the wire there are

$2 \times 8.7 \times 10^{22}$ electrons

so the total charge

$= 17.4 \times 10^{22} \times 1.6 \times 10^{-19}$

$= 2.8 \times 10^4\,\mathrm{C}$

d $v = \dfrac{I}{nAe} = \dfrac{3}{8.7 \times 10^{28} \times 2 \times 10^{-6} \times 1.6 \times 10^{-19}}$

$= 1.08 \times 10^{-4}\,\mathrm{m\,s^{-1}}$

- **Kirchhoff's Law**

The sum of the currents flowing into a junction is equal to the sum of the currents flowing out of that junction

$$I_1 + I_2 = I_3 + I_4$$

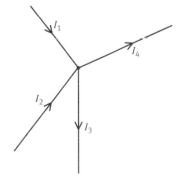

Ammeters

- Ammeters are placed in series with the components in a circuit

- They have a negligible resistance, so as not to affect the value of the current they are trying to measure

-

meter	symbol
ammeter	(A)
milliammeter	(mA)
microammeter	(μA)

D17 Resistance and Ohm's Law

- When the same voltage is applied across conductors of different materials, sizes and temperatures, different currents are created. The quantity in the conductor that causes this difference is called **resistance**

- resistance $= \dfrac{\text{voltage}}{\text{current}}$ $\qquad R = \dfrac{V}{I}$

$$V = IR$$

 *The **V**atican **I**s **R**eligious*

The unit of resistance is the Volt per ampere which is called the **ohm** (Ω)

 Georg Ohm, Bavarian, 1769–1854

- **Resistors in series**

As you know from GCSE, resistors in **series are added**. As a proof consider this diagram

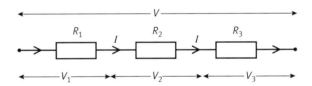

The total voltage V is divided between the resistors,

$$V = V_1 + V_2 + V_3$$

The same current passes through each resistor. For the whole circuit

$V = IR$ and $V_1 = IR_1$, $V_2 = IR_2$, $V_3 = IR_3$

$$\therefore \quad IR = I(R_1 + R_2 + R_3)$$

$$R = R_1 + R_2 + R_3$$

- **Resistors in parallel**

Consider this diagram

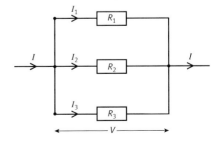

At a junction in a circuit, the current divides into I_1, I_2, I_3 going through resistors R_1, R_2, R_3

The voltage across each branch is the same, so

$I = I_1 + I_2 + I_3$ from Kirchhoff's Law

$I = \dfrac{V}{R}$ and $I_1 = \dfrac{V}{R_1}$, $I_2 = \dfrac{V}{R_2}$, $I_3 = \dfrac{V}{R_3}$

$$\frac{1}{R} = \frac{1}{R_1} + \frac{1}{R_2} + \frac{1}{R_3}$$

 Resistors in parallel MADE SIMPLE!

1. $\dfrac{1}{R_T} = \dfrac{1}{R} + \dfrac{1}{R} = \dfrac{2}{R}$ $\quad \therefore \quad R_T = \dfrac{R}{2}$

If there were three branches each of equal resistance then $R_T = \dfrac{R}{3}$ etc ...

2 *Notice that the resistance of a parallel arrangement always comes out lower than an individual resistance.*
Imagine that branches of resistors are like football turnstiles or supermarket checkout tills. The more there are of them, the more people get through (ie, more current) because the overall resistance is lower

Question

1 A portion of a circuit is shown below. Calculate its total resistance

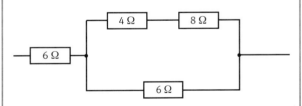

Answer

Step 1 Add the top branch $4\,\Omega + 8\,\Omega = 12\,\Omega$

Step 2 Add the top and bottom branches
$$\frac{1}{R} = \frac{1}{12} + \frac{1}{6} = \frac{1+2}{12} = \frac{1}{4}$$
so $R = 4\,\Omega$

Step 3 $4\,\Omega + 6\,\Omega = 10\,\Omega$

Question

2 A circuit has been set up as shown below

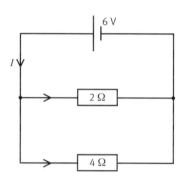

a What is the pd across each resistor?

b Calculate the value of I.

Answer

a The pd across each is the same ... 6 V

b Calculate the total resistance

$$\frac{1}{R} = \frac{1}{2} + \frac{1}{4} = \frac{3}{4} \quad \therefore \quad R = \frac{4}{3}\,\Omega$$

Then use $I = \dfrac{V}{R} = \dfrac{6}{4/3} = 4.5\,A$

Questions

3 Consider these circuits

Circuit 1

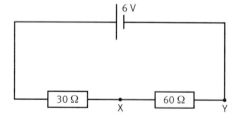

Circuit 2

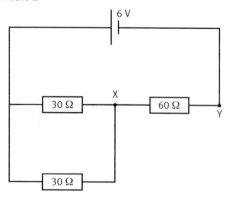

a What is the voltage across XY in circuit 1?

b What is the voltage across XY in circuit 2?

Answers

a Total $R = 30 + 60 = 90\,\Omega$ in circuit 1

$$\therefore \quad I = \frac{V}{R} = \frac{6}{90} = 0.067\,A$$

$\therefore$ the voltage across XY is $I \times 60$

$$0.067 \times 60 \approx 4\,V$$

b In circuit 2 the new resistance must be calculated for the parallel branch $R = 15\,\Omega$ $\left(\text{remember that little parallel rule I showed you earlier that } R_T = \dfrac{R}{2}\right)$

total $R = 15 + 60 = 75\,\Omega$

$$\therefore \quad I = \frac{6}{75} = 0.08\,A$$

$\therefore$ the voltage across XY is now $0.08 \times 60 = 4.8\,V$

Question

4 This question is a real brain teaser. It should lubricate your grey cells ready for all those exam-type questions. If you can get this on your first attempt go and reward yourself with a chocolate bar (full-fat)

In this circuit all the resistors have the same value, x. Calculate the total resistance in terms of x.

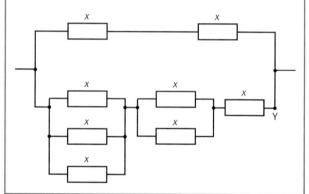

Answer

Step 1
Add series resistors in top row

$$x + x = 2x$$

Step 2
Combine 3 parallel resistors

$$\frac{1}{R} = \frac{1}{x} + \frac{1}{x} + \frac{1}{x} = \frac{3}{x} \quad \therefore \quad R = \frac{x}{3}$$

Combine 2 parallel resistors

$$\frac{1}{R} = \frac{1}{x} + \frac{1}{x} = \frac{2}{x} \quad \therefore \quad R = \frac{x}{2}$$

Step 3
Now add resistance in bottom row

$$\frac{x}{3} + \frac{x}{2} + x = \frac{2x + 3x + 6x}{6}$$

$$= \frac{11x}{6}$$

Step 4
Combine top + bottom rows

$$\frac{1}{R} = \frac{6}{11x} + \frac{1}{2x} = \frac{12 + 11}{22x}$$

$$= \frac{23}{22x}$$

$$\therefore \quad R = \frac{22x}{23} = 0.96x$$

- **Ohm's Law**

The current in a conductor is directly proportional to the voltage, *if* the physical conditions (eg, temperature) stay the same

 Always quote this statement for the law, NOT the V = IR equation

- Here are I/V characteristic curves for some devices. Note that it is conventional to put I on the vertical axis.

1

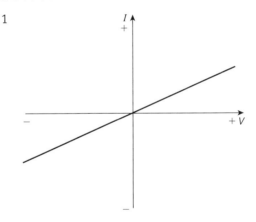

e.g. metal wire at const. temp

2

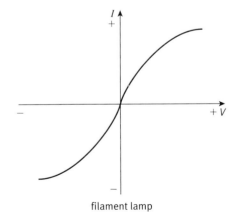

filament lamp

3

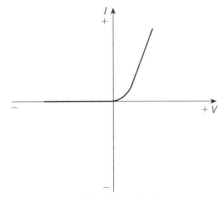

semiconductor diode

4

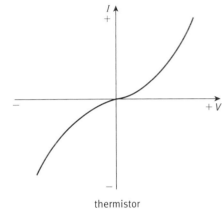

thermistor

1. **Ohmic conductors**, eg, ohmic resistor or metal wire kept at a constant temperature, obey Ohm's Law and produce straight-line graphs going through the origin

2. **Wire filament light bulb**, the resistance of a wire increases as the temperature rises

3. **Semiconductor diode**, the resistance is very large (infinite) in one direction but much less in the other

4. **Non-ohmic conductors**, eg, filament bulb, thermistor, diode, do not obey Ohm's Law and produce curves, or straight-line graphs that do not go through the origin

BIG warning here . . . ALL conductors obey the relationship V = IR, ohmic and non-ohmic at any instant

To find the resistance of a conductor at any particular value of current (or voltage), find the value of the potential difference V and the current I at this point.

Then $R = \dfrac{V}{I}$

 EXPERIMENT

How would you establish if a series of devices were ohmic or non-ohmic conductors?

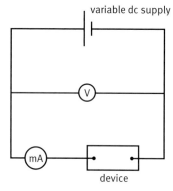

variable dc supply

Set up the circuit shown

- For each device measure a series of values for the voltage and corresponding current (7 values for a graph if possible)

- Reverse the voltage and repeat

- Plot your results on an I/V graph

If the graph is a straight line through the origin the device is ohmic

---

Resistivity (ϱ)

- Experiment shows that the resistance of a uniform conductor, eg a wire, is directly proportional to its length and inversely proportional to its cross-sectional area (CSA)

ie, $R \propto \dfrac{l}{A}$

The constant of proportionality is called the resistivity of a material

$$R = \varrho \dfrac{l}{A}$$

$\therefore \quad \varrho = \dfrac{RA}{l} = \dfrac{\Omega\,\text{m}^2}{\text{m}} = \Omega\,\text{m}$

- The units of resistivity are $\Omega\,\text{m}$

 WHY do we not simply talk about the resistance of a material?

The resistance of a material is not constant, it depends on its dimensions. The resistivity of a material is always constant, so is a better quantity to use to compare different materials

 EXPERIMENT

How would you determine the resistivity of a uniform length of carbon fibre of circular cross-section?

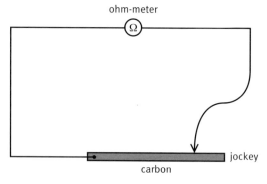

ohm-meter

jockey

carbon

- Measure the diameter of the carbon with a micrometer screw gauge, in *3 places* and average (d)

- Set up the circuit above (the meter provides the current and instantly measures the resistance for you . . . handy!)

- Obtain 7 values for the resistance across different lengths of the carbon

---

- Plot a graph of R against l

The slope will hopefully be a straight line through the origin whose gradient will be $\dfrac{R}{l}$

the CSA of the carbon, $A = \dfrac{\pi d^2}{4}$

so using

$$R = \varrho\frac{l}{A} \quad \therefore \quad \varrho = \frac{RA}{l} = \text{gradient} \times \frac{\pi d^2}{4}$$

Questions

5 Calculate the resistance of 2 cm³ of copper wire when

a It has the shape of a wire of diameter 0.04 cm

b It has the shape of a flat plate 5 mm thick. The current passes through the plate at right angles to its faces

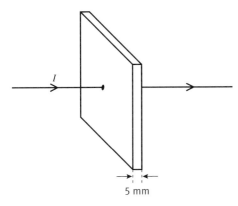

5 mm

The resistivity of copper is $1.7 \times 10^{-8}\ \Omega\,\text{m}$

 Watch your units

Answers

a Volume of a cylinder (the wire) = CSA × length

$$2\,\text{cm}^3 = 2 \times 10^{-6}\,\text{m}^3 \quad \text{Vol} = A \times l$$
$$\text{diameter} = 0.04\,\text{cm} = 4 \times 10^{-4}\,\text{m}$$

$$\therefore \quad 2 \times 10^{-6} = \frac{\pi(4 \times 10^{-4})^2}{4} \times l$$

$$\therefore \quad l = 15.92\,\text{m}$$

$$R = \frac{\varrho l}{A}$$

$$= \frac{1.7 \times 10^{-8} \times 15.92}{\text{CSA}}$$

$$= 2.15\,\Omega$$

b Again, volume = CSA × length

$$2 \times 10^{-6} = A \times (5 \times 10^{-3})$$

$$\therefore \quad A = 4 \times 10^{-4}\,\text{m}^2$$

using $R = \dfrac{\varrho l}{A}$

$$R = 2.125 \times 10^{-7}\,\Omega\,\text{m}$$

- These answers bring up an important point about the **area of the conductor**. Note, in the answers above the resistance of the conductor is smaller when the current goes through the large flattened plate

The bigger the area of cross section the smaller the resistance of a conductor (other things being equal)

 Why? — Put simply, a large area of conductor offers more pathways to the current, and thus less resistance

 Alternatively, remember those checkout tills and turnstiles. A bigger area is like lots of resistor branches giving an overall low resistance

Question

6 Explain why, in a circuit that contains an electric fire and the connecting cables, only the element gets significantly hot.

Answer

Use $R = \varrho\dfrac{l}{A}$

The cable is in series with the element, so the same current flows through both

The element has a small CSA and is very long (coiled like a bulb filament), and a high resistivity so it has a large resistance

$\therefore$ $I^2 R$ is large, thus a lot of heat is emitted

The cable has many strands in parallel, thus a large CSA, and a low resistivity, so it has a small resistance

$\therefore$ $I^2 R$ is small and little heat is emitted in comparison

D18 emf, pd and electrical power

Beginner's box

- Electrical power can be measured in kilowatt hours (kWh) where $1 \text{ kWh} = 3600000 \text{ J}$

- The **emf** (electromotive force) of a circuit is usually provided by the source of electrical energy, eg, the battery, dynamo, etc. It is measured in volts

$$E = \frac{W}{Q}$$

E = emf

W = energy converted from some form into electrical energy

$\therefore$ | $W = QE$ |

Q = charge passing through source

- The **pd** (potential difference) is a measure of how much of that electrical energy from the source has been converted into some other form in other parts of the circuit, eg, into heat, light. A voltmeter measures pd

$$V = \frac{W}{Q}$$

V = pd across device

W = electrical energy converted by device

$\therefore$ | $W = QV$ |

Q = charge passing through device

emf and internal resistance (*r*)

- The total electrical energy supplied to a circuit is less than the source possesses. This is because all practical sources of current have an **internal resistance**. Energy is wasted in overcoming this resistance.

- A battery has a typical emf of 1.5 V, but can only provide approximately 1.3 V to an external circuit, eg, a light bulb. 0.2 V is spent across the internal resistance within the source

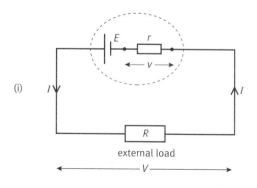

(i)

external load

- From this we can say

| $E = Ir + IR$ |

where

E = emf of the source

Ir = pd across internal resistance $= v$

IR = pd across external load $= V$

so **$E = v + V$**

- An electrical supply connected to an external load is called a **closed circuit** (see circuit i in previous column). As a significant current is being drawn then internal resistance has to be overcome

- An electrical supply that is not connected to an external load is called an **open circuit** (see circuit ii below). If a voltmeter were placed across it, it would measure its emf

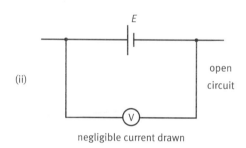

(ii)

open circuit

negligible current drawn

- When the terminals are directly connected (not by a voltmeter, but by wires) the external $R = 0$, so the current is at a maximum. This is called a **short circuit**

 Do not try it at home

- The reading on a voltmeter placed across the terminals of an electrical supply is called the **terminal pd**

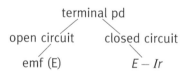

terminal pd

open circuit   closed circuit

emf (E) $E - Ir$

- A car battery needs to have a low internal resistance in order to provide the large current (approx 100 A) for the starter motor

- An EHT supply (5000 V) needs a very large internal resistance (megohms) to limit the current it provides or it could be very dangerous

Voltmeters

- A voltmeter has a very high resistance, thus drawing a negligible current

- A voltmeter is placed across a device. Think of the voltmeter as having invisible fingers touching onto the circuit

Questions

1 A voltmeter across a battery in an open circuit reads 1.5 V, and 1.3 V when attached to a bulb of resistance R. The current through the bulb is 0.2 A.

What is

a The emf of the battery?

b The internal resistance of the battery?

c The value of R?

Answers

a $E = 1.5$ V (just checking you've been paying attention)

b So $E = 1.5$ V, terminal pd $= 1.3$ V, $I = 0.2$ A, internal resistance, r,

$E = Ir + IR$

$1.5 = 0.2 \times r + 1.3$ (remember the external $V = IR$)

$\therefore \quad r = \dfrac{0.2}{0.2} = 1\,\Omega$

c $1.3 = IR = 0.2\,R$

$\therefore \quad R = 6.5\,\Omega$

Questions

2 Consider the following circuit. The ammeter reads 1.6 A when S is open, and 2.0 A when S is closed.
Calculate

a The internal resistance of the battery

b The emf of the battery

Hint: try simultaneous equations, as E is the same in both situations

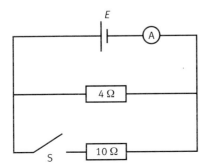

Answers

a $E = IR + Ir$

when S is open $\quad E = 1.6 \times 4 + 1.6r \ldots (1)$

when S is closed the total resistance, R, is found by

$$\frac{1}{R} = \frac{1}{4} + \frac{1}{10} = \frac{7}{20} \quad \text{so} \quad R = \frac{20}{7}\,\Omega$$

so $\quad E = 2 \times \dfrac{20}{7} + 2r \ldots (2)$

$\therefore \quad 6.4 + 1.6r = 5.71 + 2r$ equating (1) and (2)

$\qquad 0.69 = 0.4\,r$

$\qquad r = 1.73\,\Omega$

b Substitute r in either (1) or (2)

$E = 6.4 + 2.76 = 9.16$ V

❄ EXPERIMENT

How would you find the internal resistance of a personal stereo battery?

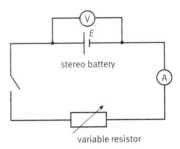

- Set up the circuit shown above

- Record voltmeter reading with the switch open

- This gives E

- Close the switch, adjust the variable resistor so the ammeter reads a minimum current

- Obtain 7 readings of the current and pd over the widest range possible

- Plot V against I

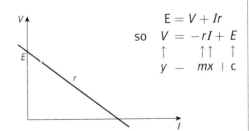

$E = V + Ir$

so $\quad V = -rI + E$

$\qquad \uparrow \qquad \uparrow\uparrow \quad \uparrow$

$\qquad y \quad - \quad mx \mid c$

Thus intercept is E and the gradient is $-r = \left(\dfrac{\Delta V}{\Delta I}\right)$

 Open the switch after each set of readings because when current flows chemical reactions in the cell can cause the emf to drop or the internal resistance to increase

Electrical power

- The rate at which electrical energy is converted into other forms of energy is called the power Remember from previously

    $W = QV$ and $Q = It$

    where W = work done (J)
    $\quad\quad\quad Q$ = charge (C)
    $\quad\quad\quad V$ = voltage (V)
    $\quad\quad\quad I$ = current (A)
    $\quad\quad\quad t$ = time taken (s)

    so $W = ItV$ $\quad \therefore \quad \dfrac{W}{t} = IV$

    $\dfrac{W}{t} = P$ so $\therefore \quad P = VI$

 Power is **V**ery **I**mportant

- As $V = IR$ then $P = IR \times I$ $\therefore$ $P = I^2R$

    As $I = \dfrac{V}{R}$ then $P = V \times \dfrac{V}{R} = \dfrac{V^2}{R}$

    $\therefore$ $\boxed{P = VI = I^2R = \dfrac{V^2}{R}}$

- The unit of power is the watt or joule/s (J s^{-1})

Question

3 Show that the units of power can be written as J s^{-1}, starting from the expression $P = I^2R$

Answer

$$P = I^2R \quad \text{and} \quad R = \dfrac{V}{I}$$

so $P = \dfrac{\text{coulombs}^2}{\text{seconds}^2} \times \dfrac{\text{joules}}{\text{coulomb}} \times \dfrac{\text{seconds}}{\text{coulomb}}$

$\quad\quad = \text{joules second}^{-1}$

- **High voltage transmission** — When there is a current in electrical cables there is a heating effect caused by the resistance, and hence there is a power loss. To reduce this loss the voltage is raised as high as possible, reducing the current necessary, and this decreases the loss in power

 $I^2R \equiv$ *rate of heat loss*

D19 Circuit calculations

These exam-type questions range from ones that are insultingly easy to ones that will reduce you to hysterical sobs, switching on the Teletubbies for a dose of all that is normal and real in the world.

I promise it is worth the effort to review the answers (after you have attempted them on your own) and at least try to understand the solution, even though you might never have thought of tackling it in that way!

Questions

1 Consider the circuit below. E is a source of negligible internal resistance. The pd across the 600 Ω resistor is measured using a voltmeter of resistance 3000 Ω and is found to be 10 V.

a What is the emf of the source?

b What is the pd across the 2000 Ω resistor when the voltmeter is not being used?

 Take note of any points made in italics

 Draw the voltmeter as a resistor in the circuit in parallel with the 600 Ω

Answers

a Step 1 Calculate the total resistance of the parallel branch

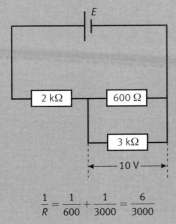

$$\frac{1}{R} = \frac{1}{600} + \frac{1}{3000} = \frac{6}{3000}$$

$\therefore$ $R = 500\,\Omega$

Step 2 The pd across this R is 10 V

So using $V = IR$ $I = \frac{10}{500} = 0.02\,\text{A}$

Step 3 Now we can find the pd across the 2000 Ω resistor

$$V = IR = 0.02 \times 2000 = 40\,\text{V}$$

$\therefore$ the emf $= 40\,\text{V} + 10\,\text{V} = 50\,\text{V}$

b The emf remains constant at 50 V, but we are now not using the voltmeter

The total resistance is 600 Ω + 2000 Ω = 2600 Ω
we can find the current using $V = IR$

$$I = \frac{50}{2600} = 0.019\,\text{A}$$

So now we can find the pd across the 2000 Ω resistor
$V = 0.019 \times 2000 = 38\,\text{V}$

 Not a big difference, having a big resistance in parallel, that is!

Question

2 A resistor of value 40 Ω is made from manganin wire, with a diameter of 0.33 mm and resistivity $4.4 \times 10^{-7}\,\Omega\,\text{m}$. What is the length of this wire?

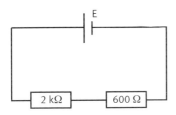 *Watch your units*

Answer

Step 1

$R = \frac{\varrho l}{A}, A = \frac{\pi d^2}{4}$ where $d = 0.33 \times 10^{-3}\,\text{m}$

Step 2

$\therefore$ $l = \frac{RA}{\varrho} = \frac{40}{4.4 \times 10^{-7}} \times \frac{\pi}{4}(0.33 \times 10^{-3})^2$

$\therefore$ $l \simeq 7.8\,\text{m}$

Question

3 The circuit below shows four resistors with a source of emf = 3 V, and internal resistance of 0.5 Ω.

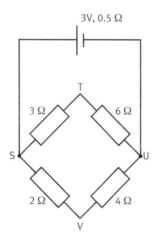

3V, 0.5 Ω

Calculate the current through each resistor

 Think parallel branches

 Treat the internal resistor as just another resistor

Answer

Consider STU as one parallel branch, and SVU as the other

Step 1 Find the total R of the parallel branches

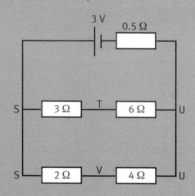

$$\frac{1}{R} = \frac{1}{9} + \frac{1}{6} = \frac{5}{18}$$

$$\therefore \ R = \frac{18}{5}\,\Omega$$

so the total for the circuit is

$$\frac{18}{5} + \frac{1}{2} = \frac{41}{10} = 4.1\,\Omega$$

$\therefore$ using $V = IR$

$$I = \frac{3}{4.1} = 0.732\,A$$

Step 2 So the pd across the internal resistor is

$$V = IR = 0.73 \times 0.5 = 0.366\,V$$

So the pd remaining across the 2 branches

$$3 - 0.366 = 2.634\,V$$

Step 3 The current across the top branch is the same in each resistor, using $V = IR$

$$I = \frac{2.634}{9} = 0.29\,A$$

The current through the bottom branch is

$$I = \frac{2.634}{6} = 0.44\,A$$

The current through the internal resistor = 0.73 A

 Check here that the current in the 2 branches is equal to the current going through the battery

$$0.44 + 0.29 \simeq 0.73\,A$$

Questions

4 A battery of negligible internal resistance is connected in series with a milliammeter and two resistors, of values 10 Ω and 5 Ω. The current reading is 200 mA.

a Draw the circuit diagram

b Is the resistance of the milliammeter very high or negligible? Explain your answer

 Part (b) is asking you two things. So many students lose marks by not answering a question fully ... double check

c Calculate the emf of the battery

Answers

a

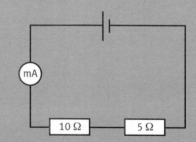

b The resistance of the milliammeter is negligible, otherwise it would affect (reduce) the current of the whole circuit, when its purpose is just to measure

c Total resistance is 15 Ω, $I = 200 \times 10^{-3}\,A$
using $V = IR$

$$emf = 15 \times 200 \times 10^{-3} = 3\,V$$

Questions

5 In the circuit shown, the cell has an emf of 5.0 V, and there is a current of 0.25 A through the motor. The voltmeter reads 4.75 V

a Why are the voltmeter reading and the emf different?

b Calculate the internal resistance of the cell

c Calculate the energy transferred per second by the motor

d What assumption did you make in order to do these calculations?

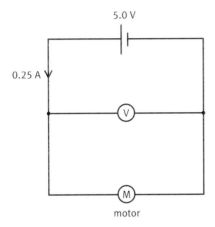

Questions

6 Shown below is a circuit connecting four resistors. The cell has negligible internal resistance

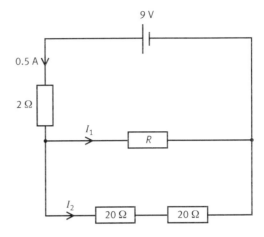

a Calculate I_1 and I_2

b Calculate R

 Don't make the error of thinking there is 9 V across the two branches

Answers

a Current flows through the internal resistance, thus there is a drop in pd across it, leaving less for the rest of the circuit

b The difference in pd is 5 V − 4.75 V = 0.25 V so the pd across the internal resistance is 0.25 V

using $V = IR$, internal resistance $R = \dfrac{0.25}{0.25} = 1.0\,\Omega$

c P = Energy/Time and $P = IV$

so Energy/Time = IV = 0.25 × 4.75 = 1.19 W

d The voltmeter has an infinite (very high!) resistance, and takes a negligible current

Answers

a There is a pd across the 2 Ω resistor that must be subtracted from the cell's emf to know what remains across each parallel branch

Step 1
$V = IR = 0.5 \times 2 = 1\,V$
So there is 9 V − 1 V = 8 V across the parallel branches

Step 2 The total resistance on the bottom branch is
20 Ω + 20 Ω = 40 Ω

$I_2 = \dfrac{8}{40} = 0.2\,A$

 Now use Kirchhoff's Law

$I_1 + I_2 = 0.5\,A$
So $I_1 = 0.3\,A$

b So now you know the current through R is 0.3 A and the pd across it is 8 V
Using $V = IR$

$R = \dfrac{8}{0.3} = 26.7\,\Omega$

Question

7 An electrical circuit has two mystery components in a box, connected to a cell of emf 3 V and a centre-zero ammeter

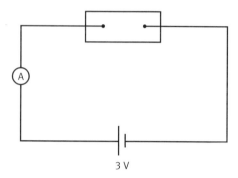

3 V

When the cell is reversed and the current changes direction, the **magnitude** of the current stays the same. From the table below, tick the correct arrangement of the two possible components

1 diode + resistor in series	
2 two diodes in parallel	
3 diode + resistor in parallel	
4 two diodes in series	

Answer

1 There would be no current one way
2 Correct answer. One diode would block one direction, whilst the other would always permit a current
3 One way, the current only goes through the resistor, the other way, it travels through both, thus there is a larger resistance and the magnitude of the current changes
4 The diodes will block the current flow in one direction

Question

8 A wire has a region where its diameter changes from *2d* to *d*, see Figure iii. A current flows through the wire. Calculate the ratio of

$$\frac{\text{drift speed of electron at } X}{\text{drift speed of electron at } Y}$$

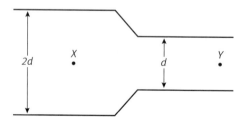

Answer

drift velocity $v = \frac{I}{nAe}$, where

I, the current, remains constant in the wire
n is the number of electrons per unit volume, so also remains constant
e, the electron charge, is a constant value
A, the CSA, changes. Thus the ratio depends on this value
$A = \pi r^2$

$$\frac{\text{drift speed of electron at } X}{\text{drift speed of electron at } Y} = \frac{v_x}{v_y} = \frac{A_y}{A_x}$$

$$\frac{A_y}{A_x} = \frac{\pi \frac{d^2}{4}}{\pi \frac{4d^2}{4}} = \frac{1}{4}$$

Question

9 A lightbulb, 240 V, 100 W, has a tungsten filament. When it is switched on its resistance increases 16 times, as it goes from room temperature to its operating temperature. What is its room temperature resistance?

Answer

$P = IV$
$\therefore$ at operating temp $100 = 240 \times I$
$\therefore I = 0.417\,A$
$R = V/I = 240/0.417 \simeq 576\,\Omega$

So at room temperature its resistance is 16 times less
$576/16 = 36\,\Omega$

Question

10 If the temperature of a metallic conductor increases, its resistance goes up. Which one or more of the following statements accounts for this?

higher drift speed of electrons	
increase in the length of the conductor	
increased amplitude of vibration of the molecules	
reduction in the number of free electrons	

Answer

Increased amplitude of vibration of the molecules in the conductor

Question

11 A battery has an emf of 3 V and internal resistance of 1 Ω, and is connected to a 5 Ω resistor. What is the value of the charge that passes any point in the circuit in 1 minute?

Answer

$E = I(R + r)$

$3 = I(6) \quad \therefore \quad I = 0.5\,\text{A}$

$Q = It = 0.5 \times 60 = 30\,\text{C}$

D20 Sensors and potential dividers

You will come across the use of input and output sensors in exam questions. They are collectively called **transducers**

- A transducer changes electrical signals from one energy form to another

-
input sensor	output sensor
strain gauge	light bulb
light-dependent resistor (LDR)	light-emitting diode (LED)
thermistor	motor
microphone	loudspeaker

- The **thermistor** is a semiconducting device whose resistance falls as its temperature rises

  At higher temperatures the atoms have more KE, which frees more electrons to move from atom to atom

  It can be used as a control device in central heating, to switch the heating off when the room has reached a certain temperature

- The **LDR** is a semiconducting device whose resistance falls as the light intensity on it increases

  It has an extremely high resistance in the dark (several megohms), falling to a few hundred ohms in strong light

  It can be used as a photographic light meter or in a light-activated switching circuit

 LDR/Thermistor
light/heat ⇑   *Resistance* ⇓

Potential dividers

The variation of the resistance of a sensor, or a rheostat, and the resulting changes in pd across them can be put to use in a circuit called a **potential divider**

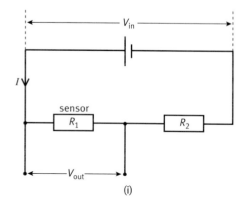

(i)

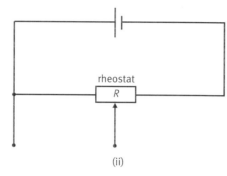

(ii)

i) Any changes in the current or the resistance of R_1 changes the output voltage

ii) The slider or jockey key can be moved across the rheostat to vary the output pd between 0 V and a maximum

For circuit i

$$V_{out} = IR_1 \qquad (1)$$
$$V_{in} = I(R_1 + R_2) \qquad (2)$$

combining (1) and (2)

$$I = \frac{V_{in}}{R_1 + R_2} \quad \text{so} \quad V_{out} = \left(\frac{V_{in}}{R_1 + R_2}\right)R_1$$

$$\therefore \quad \boxed{V_{out} = \left(\frac{R_1}{R_1 + R_2}\right)V_{in}} \qquad (3)$$

$$\therefore \quad \boxed{\frac{V_{out}}{V_{in}} = \left(\frac{R_1}{R_1 + R_2}\right)} \qquad (4)$$

- A practical potential divider is called a **potentiometer**. A television uses potentiometers to alter the volume of the sound and brightness of the picture

☹ *Take your time in following these next two examples*

Example
Potential divider using a thermistor

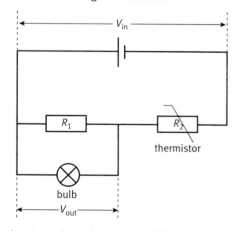

When the thermistor becomes colder, its resistance (R_2) increases, so, using equation (4), the denominator increases, so...

$$\frac{V_{out}}{V_{in}} = \left(\frac{R_1}{R_1 + R_2}\right)$$

$\frac{V_{out}}{V_{in}}$ must decrease, as R_2 increases

As V_{in} remains constant then V_{out} must decrease, so the bulb will get dimmer (or go out)

This circuit could be used in a greenhouse as an indicator of the temperature dropping below a certain value

Example

Potential divider using an LDR

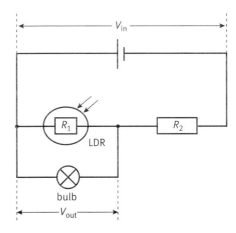

When the light fades the resistance of the LDR (R_1) increases to the order of megohms

 Note that for this circuit to work you must be given such values of R_1 and R_2, so that R_1 gets much much bigger than R_2

Using equation (4)

$$\frac{V_{out}}{V_{in}} = \left(\frac{R_1}{R_1 + R_2}\right)$$

$\frac{V_{out}}{V_{in}}$ must increase, as R_1 increases

As V_{in} is constant, then V_{out} must increase, so the bulb will get brighter.

This circuit could be used as an automatic security light outside a house

Question

1 Connect a battery, ammeter, voltmeter, resistor and an LDR in such a way as to produce a simple lightmeter circuit for a photographer

Explain how this circuit works

Answer

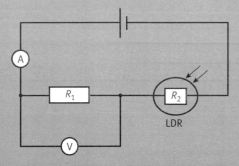

If the light intensity increases, the resistance (R_2) of the LDR decreases

Using equation (4)

$$\frac{V_{out}}{V_{in}} = \left(\frac{R_1}{R_1 + R_2}\right)$$

the ratio $\frac{V_{out}}{V_{in}}$ increases, and V_{in} is constant so V_{out} gets bigger, indicated by the reading on the voltmeter (lightmeter)

So the photographer knows to reduce the aperture or shade the subject

Questions

2 In an experiment to compare the effect of temperature on the resistances of a piece of copper wire and a thermistor, they are placed in turn in the circuit shown below and their resistances measured with an ohmmeter at room temperature and in boiling water

 You may have come across an ohmmeter facility on a multimeter

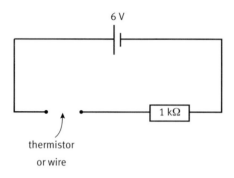

thermistor
or wire

The following results were obtained

	copper wire	thermistor
R at 20°C	1.2 Ω	4000 Ω
R at 100°C	1.4 Ω	60 Ω

a What happens to the pd across the thermistor as it is heated?

b How can your answer in **a** be put to use around the home?

Answers

a As the thermistor is heated, its resistance falls as more electrons are freed, and it takes a smaller share of the available pd

b When a room reaches a desired temperature, the pd across a thermistor providing an output voltage, is low, which could switch the heating off

Questions

3 A potential divider circuit is shown below, connected to a wire ST. The following values were obtained for the current, I, through the wire and the pd, V, across it

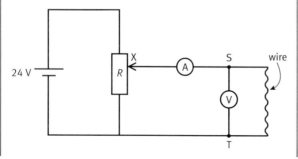

I/amps	V/volts
0.0	0.0
0.4	2.0
0.8	4.0
1.2	6.0
1.6	8.0
1.8	9.2
1.9	11.8

a Plot an I/V curve

 Watch out for the 6th value!

b Explain the shape of the curve

c Why could a value not be read any higher?

d Find the resistance of the wire for lower current values

Answers

a

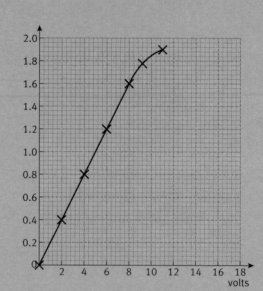

b The wire is showing ohmic properties at low values of current
At 1.6 A the curve flattens out in a non-linear way
The wire is getting hotter as the current increases and resistance increases

c The wire breaks when it gets too hot

 Don't get caught into using values from the table. USE THE GRAPH

D21 Capacitance 1

Beginner's box

- Know that 1 coulomb = Charge passing a point when a current of 1 amp flows for 1 second

- Know that 1 volt = 1 joule of energy is converted for each coulomb of charge (1 joule/coulomb)

- Know that $R = R_1 + R_2$ gives the resultant resistance of 2 resistors in series

- Know that $\dfrac{1}{R} = \dfrac{1}{R_1} + \dfrac{1}{R_2}$ gives the resultant resistance of 2 resistors in parallel

Meaning of capacitance

Every time you take a flash photo you are wanting to release a lot of electrical energy in a very short time. You know that it takes a moment or two for the camera to be ready to take the next flash picture.

Electrical energy is being stored, ready to be released in a flash (!)

A **capacitor** is the **storing device**. It redistributes charge.

It usually consists of 2 parallel conducting plates separated by a very thin layer of insulating material (called a **dielectric**). These plates are often rolled up like a 'Swiss roll'

Uses of capacitors

i. Capacitors can store charge to operate a camera flash, but, also, in large quantities for use in nuclear research

ii. Capacitors are commonly used to smooth rectified current from power supplies or a fluctuating voltage

iii. Capacitors can eliminate sparking in switches

iv. Capacitors are used in timing circuits

v. Because the behaviour of a capacitor in an AC circuit depends on the frequency of the signal, capacitors are an essential part of tuned circuits and act as filters to operate only on certain frequencies. (see Section E27. AC Theory)

Capacitance is the 'charge per voltage' that the capacitor can store

$$\frac{\text{Charge}}{\text{Voltage}} = \text{Capacitance}$$

$$\frac{Q}{V} = C \text{ or}$$

$$\boxed{Q = CV}$$

If Charge Q in coulombs
Voltage V in volts
then **Capacitance C** in **farads**

but 1 farad is an **enormous** capacitance.

so microfarads, $1\,\mu F = 10^{-6}$ farads
or picofarads, $1\,pF = 10^{-12}$ farads

Charging and discharging a capacitor

From above $\qquad \boldsymbol{Q = CV}$

 Thinks ... the queen is, 'C of E' ... (get it?) ... or ... Cable shopping channel is Q.V.C.!

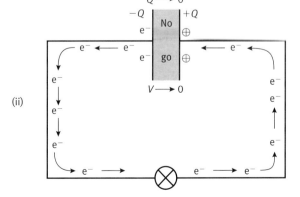

(i) when charged

(ii)

1 In Fig.i the **charging** voltage, V, starts at zero and there is no charge on the plates of the capacitor, $Q = 0$, $V = 0$

2 As the voltage is increased, electrons are repelled from the negative terminal of the battery and begin to build up on the plate of the capacitor, making it negative ($-Q$)

3 At the same time, electrons will be repelled from the other capacitor plate, making that positive ($+Q$)

 *Remember, electrons can't flow in the dielectric **insulator***

- A charge, Q, is collecting on the capacitor and a voltage, V, building across it.

$$Q \propto V$$

$$Q = CV$$

- If microammeters are included on both sides of the capacitor, they will show that:

  (1) the current is in the same direction on the 2 sides of the capacitor (opposite, of course, to the electron flow) and

  (2) there is a surge of current to start with, then this falls as the plates 'fill up' and their charge makes it harder for any more electrons to flow (see E24 Capacitance 2)

  The greater the pd, at the start between the plate and the cell, the greater the current flow.
  As the plate charges, pd between it and the source drops ∴ current drops

- During **discharge** electrons flow, readily at first, back from the negative to the positive plate (the current in the opposite direction) until there are no volts left across the capacitor. Again $Q = 0$, $V = 0$

❄ EXPERIMENT

Charging and **discharging** of a capacitor

- Use a microammeter (centre-zero) to record the current charging a 400 µF capacitor to 12 V and discharging to neutral, or 0 V. The inclusion of a large resistor in series will reduce the current and so slow up the process. 200,000 Ω = 200 kΩ will make it take over a minute

  Diagram (iii) shows a suitable circuit. It includes a 2-way switch so that the capacitor can easily be charged and discharged.

- Practise charging and discharging by connecting the switch to (1) and (2) in turn, to get a 'feel' for the process.

Start using a stop-watch and decide how often you can take readings of the current I, . . . every 10 s, or 5 s if possible

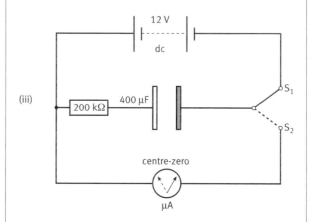

(iii)

Charging: Connect the switch to S_1
Record values of current I, every 5 s if possible, until $I \Rightarrow 0$

Discharging: Switch to S_2 and record the current, every 5 s, as the charge flows off the capacitor Call this current $-I$, since it is in the opposite direction to the charging current

 That's why centre-zero meters were used

- Plot graphs of I against t for charging and discharging, see (a) and (b) on graph below

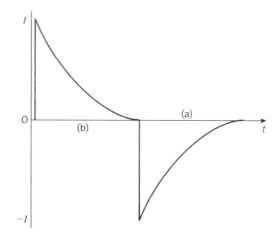

- If a current I amps (coulombs/s) flows for t s, then a charge It coulombs will have been transferred.
  But It is the area under the I/t graph, so charge transferred = Area under I/t graph

  Charge on capacitor = area under I/t graph

The graphs also show how the charging and discharging currents start with a surge and then reduce towards zero

Question

1 A 12V supply is connected across a 200 μF capacitor. What is the charge stored?

Answer

Since $Q = CV$
$$= 200 \times 10^{-6} \times 12 = 2400 \times 10^{-6}$$
Charge stored $= 2.4 \times 10^{-3}$ coulombs

Question

2 What arrangement of resistors has a similar formula to capacitors arranged in parallel?

Answer

Resistors in series, $R = R_1 + R_2$

Question

3 A capacitor of capacitance 200 μF, charge 2.4×10^{-3} C, was disconnected from a battery of emf 12 V and connected in parallel across a 400 μF capacitor

What was the final voltage across the pair of capacitors?

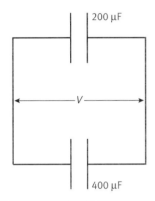

Answer

The charge 2.4×10^{-3} coulombs becomes the total charge, Q, of the system

It will be shared between the 2 capacitors, the larger one storing the larger charge

$$Q = Q_1 + Q_2 = C_1 V + C_2 V$$
$$2.4 \times 10^{-3} = 200 \times 10^{-6} V + 400 \times 10^{-6} V$$
$$= 600 \times 10^{-6} V$$

So ... $V = \dfrac{2.4 \times 10^{-3}}{600 \times 10^{-6}} = \dfrac{2.4}{600 \times 10^{-3}} = \dfrac{2.4}{6 \times 10^{-1}} = \dfrac{24}{6}$

Voltage across pair of capacitors $= 4$ V

Capacitors in parallel

 This is the 'easy one', which is why we'll deal with it first

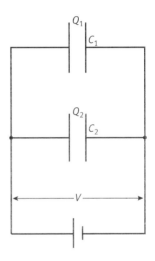

2 capacitors, C_1 and C_2, are connected in **parallel** across a battery, voltage, V

The battery is connected across each of the **parallel capacitors** in the same way, so the

potential across C_1 = potential across C_2 = V

If the charge on $C_1 = Q_1$ and the charge on $C_2 = Q_2$ the total charge on the parallel capacitors is:

$$Q = Q_1 + Q_2$$

 In parallel, capacitors act like one big one

$$CV = C_1 V + C_2 V \qquad [Q = CV]$$

Capacitance in parallel, $C = C_1 + C_2$

Capacitors in series

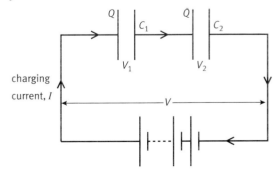

2 capacitors, C_1 and C_2, are connected in **series** across a battery, voltage, V

Since the charging current is the same in the series circuit, for the same length of time, the **charge** on the **series capacitors** is the **same**

Charge on C_1 = Charge on C_2 = Q

The battery voltage is shared between C_1 and C_2. If pd across C_1 = V_1, and the pd across C_2 = V_2, then

$$V = V_1 + V_2$$

$$\frac{Q}{C} = \frac{Q}{C_1} + \frac{Q}{C_2} \qquad \left[V = \frac{Q}{C}\right]$$

Capacitance in series

$$\frac{1}{C} = \frac{1}{C_1} + \frac{1}{C_2} \quad \text{or} \quad C = \frac{C_1 C_2}{C_1 + C_2}$$

:) *Is there a parallel here (sorry) with resistors?*

Question

4 What arrangement of resistors has a similar formula to capacitors arranged in series?

Answer

Resistors in parallel,  $\frac{1}{R} = \frac{1}{R_1} + \frac{1}{R_2}$

learn!	capacitors	resistors
equation	$Q = CV$	$V = RI$
units	farad, F. $\mu F = 10^{-6}$ F	ohm, Ω
series	same charge, Q, share voltage $\frac{1}{C} = \frac{1}{C_1} + \frac{1}{C_2}$ $C = \frac{C_1 C_2}{C_1 + C_2}$	same current, I, share voltage $R = R_1 + R_2$
parallel	same voltage, V, share charge $C = C_1 + C_2$	same voltage, V, share current $\frac{1}{R} = \frac{1}{R_1} + \frac{1}{R_2}$ $R = \frac{R_1 R_2}{R_1 + R_2}$

Questions

5 200 µF and 400 µF capacitors are connected in series and a 12 V battery is connected across them.

a Complete the circuit below showing the +ve and −ve charges on the plates of the capacitors

b Calculate the charge on the 400 µF capacitor

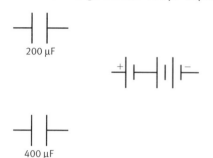

200 µF

400 µF

Answer

a The dotted lines complete the series circuit. The polarity of the charges has also been included on the diagram

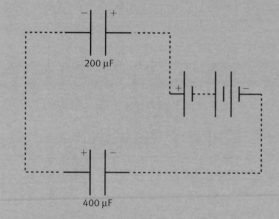

200 µF

400 µF

b Step 1 Find the equivalent capacitance of the 2 in series:

$$\frac{1}{C} = \frac{1}{C_1} + \frac{1}{C_2} \quad \text{or} \quad C = \frac{C_1 C_2}{C_1 + C_2}$$

so $C = \dfrac{200 \times 10^{-6} \times 400 \times 10^{-6}}{(200 + 400) \times 10^{-6}}$

Giving ... $C = \dfrac{80000 \times 10^{-6}}{600 \times 10^{-6}} = \dfrac{800}{6} \times 10^{-6}$ F

Step 2 When connected in series, the same charge Q will collect on each capacitor C, C_1 & C_2
$Q = CV$, so here:

$$Q = \frac{800}{6} \times 10^{-6} \times 12$$

$$= 1600 \times 10^{-6} \text{ Coulombs}$$

Charge on the 400 µF capacitor = 1.6×10^{-3} C

:(*Don't be caught by:*
*C as the symbol for **capacitance***
*and **C** used to represent charge in **coulombs***

:) *Bonuses ... You now also know the charge on the other capacitor (1.6×10^{-3}C) and it's easy to find the pd across the capacitors using:*
$V = \dfrac{Q}{C}$ *each time*

Energy stored in a capacitor

One of the most useful things about a capacitor is that it can store electrical energy, eg, to set off a camera flash bulb

- **Energy stored** is measured in **joules**
  pd across a capacitor is V joules/coulomb
  Charge stored on the capacitor is Q coulombs

- So, for energy in joules, you need to remember
  $W = QV$ ... **but**
  during charging or discharging, V varies between 0 and V volts
  Remember, $Q \propto V$, $Q = CV$

- If Q is plotted against V, the graph will be a straight line

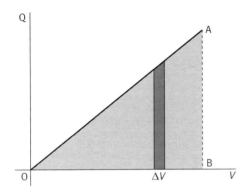

- Energy stored = Charge × Average Voltage

  $$= Q \times \tfrac{1}{2} V$$

Energy stored $= \tfrac{1}{2} QV = \tfrac{1}{2} CV^2 = \dfrac{1}{2} \dfrac{Q^2}{C}$

[since $Q = CV$]

In a charged capacitor: see the above figure

Energy stored = Area under the Q/V graph

Area of triangle   OAB $= \tfrac{1}{2}$ base × height

$$= \tfrac{1}{2} V \times Q$$

Energy stored in capacitor $= \tfrac{1}{2} QV$ joules

 It makes sense that only half of the energy from the source is stored ... energy losses as heat in wires etc

In general:

Energy stored = Sum of strips under graph, Q/V

$$= \Sigma Q \Delta V \ldots \text{you may not need this}$$

 Compare the equation for energy stored in a charged capacitor $= \tfrac{1}{2} QV$ with the energy stored in a stretched spring or wire

$$= \tfrac{1}{2} Fe$$
$$= \text{area under F/e graph}$$

Questions

6

a A capacitor P, of capacitance 100 pF is charged to a pd of 500 V. How much energy is stored in it?

b P is now connected across an uncharged capacitor, S, of capacitance 400 pF. What is the energy stored in P and S?

c What has happened to the 'lost joules'?

Answers

a From above, the energy stored $= \tfrac{1}{2} CV^2$

Energy stored in $P = \tfrac{1}{2} \times 100 \times 10^{-12} \times 500^2$
$= 50 \times 10^{-12} \times 25 \times 10^4$
$= 1250 \times 10^{-8}$
$= 12.5 \times 10^{-6}$ joules

Energy stored in $P = 12.5 \,\mu J$

b

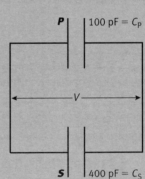

Step 1 Conservation of charge gives:

$$Q = Q_P + Q_S \quad \text{and} \quad Q = CV$$
$$Q = C_P V$$
$$= 100 \times 10^{-12} \times 500$$

So $C_P \times 500 = C_P V + C_S V$

Giving $V = \dfrac{100 \times 500}{100 + 400} = 100 \,V$

Step 2 Combined capacitance of P and S, in parallel,

$$C = C_P + C_S$$
$$= 100 \times 10^{-12} + 400 \times 10^{-12}$$
$$= 500 \times 10^{-12} \,F$$

Step 3
Energy stored in P and S $= \tfrac{1}{2} CV^2$
$$= \tfrac{1}{2} \times 500 \times 10^{-12} \times 100^2$$
$$= 2.5 \times 10^{-6} \text{ joules}$$
$$= 2.5 \,\mu J$$

c They have been converted to heat in the connecting wires as the electrons moved to share the charge

Fields

Any region where a force is acting is known as a **field**. This applies whether the force is produced by:

    gravity
    electric charge
    magnetism
    or other variables.

- **Field lines** can represent fields in magnitude and direction ... yes ... fields are **vectors**

- **Direction** is obviously represented by the direction of the field lines.

- **Magnitude** or **intensity** of the field is represented by the **concentration** of the field lines (the number passing at right angles through unit area at the point gives **field strength**)

Gravitational and **electric** fields are the ones to concentrate on. A table at the end of this section will demonstrate the remarkable similarities in their behaviour.

E22 Gravitational fields

Gravitational force

If 2 masses, m_1 and m_2, are point masses and have their centres a distance r apart, we have Newton to thank for the law of force between them Newton suggested:

$$\text{Force} \propto \frac{\text{product of masses}}{\text{square of distance between them}}$$

Newton's Universal Law of Gravitation

$$F = G\frac{m_1 m_2}{r^2}$$

F = force in newtons if:
m_1 and m_2 = masses in kilograms
r = distance between centres of masses in metres
G = universal gravitational constant
  $= 6.67 \times 10^{-11}\,\text{N}\,\text{m}^2\,\text{kg}^{-2}$

 Notice how tiny G is, so it's not surprising that gravitational force is very weak ... only noticed really when a mass the size of a planet is involved

*Right ... an **Inverse Square Law** again. This should not surprise you, because the field (or region) of gravitational force spreads out in all directions from a mass (eg, the Earth), as does the light from a point light source etc. (see also bottom figure in answer to question 2)*

1

a Name 3 other examples where an Inverse Square Law holds.

b If the distance r doubles between 2 masses what is the effect on the gravitational force, F?

Answers

a 1 Intensity of sound from a point source
   2 Intensity of gamma radiation from a point source
   3 Strength of electric and magnetic fields from point charges and masses

b Newton's Law gives $F = G\frac{m_1 m_2}{r^2}$

If **r** is doubled, and F becomes $F_1 = G\frac{m_1 m_2}{(2r)^2}$

$$= G\frac{m_1 m_2}{4r^2}$$

$$= F/4$$

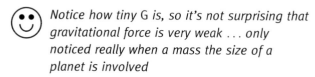 *If the Inverse Square Law holds:*
        Doubling the distance
    quarters the force, field strength, intensity, etc.
            Trebling distance
    divides the force, etc, by 9

Gravitational field strength

The following question will be used to introduce the idea of the strength of a force field.

Questions

2

a Define **gravitational field strength** (g)

b Using Newton's Law of Gravitation, $F = G\frac{m_1 m_2}{r^2}$, show that the gravitational field strength a distance r from a point mass M is given by:

$$g = G\frac{M}{r^2}$$

where G is the gravitational constant.

c Calculate the value of the gravitational field strength of the **Earth**, g_e, at its surface. [mass $= 6.0 \times 10^{24}$ kg, radius $= 6.4 \times 10^6$ m and G $= 6.67 \times 10^{-11}\,\text{N}\,\text{m}^2\,\text{kg}^{-2}$]

Answers

a A mass is in a gravitational field if it feels a gravitational pull or force
The strength of the field

$$g = \text{gravitational force per unit mass}$$

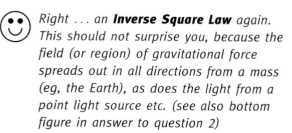

$$g = \frac{\text{gravitational force}}{\text{mass}} = \frac{F}{m}$$

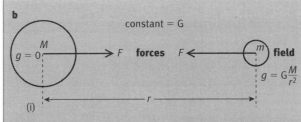

(i)

Let $m_1 = M$ then, for gravitational field acting on any mass $m_2 = m$, a distance r away:

$$F = G\frac{M \times m}{r^2}$$

Gravitational field strength, $g = \dfrac{F}{m} = \dfrac{GMm}{r^2 m}$

Gravitational field strength $g = G\dfrac{M}{r^2}\ \text{N kg}^{-1}$

Alternatively . . . g can be thought of as the gravitational force acting on a unit mass (1 kg) at the point . . .

$$g = G\frac{M \times 1}{r^2} = G\frac{M}{r^2}$$

Here g can take *any* value, it is not *only* the gravitational field at the surface of the Earth

Inside the mass, M, the gravitational field is *not* given by this equation. It falls to zero at the centre of the mass, in a way that depends on how its density changes

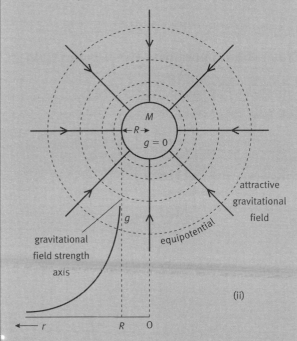

gravitational field strength axis

(ii)

c Step 1 Here the Earth is the mass M, so:

$$g_e = G\frac{M}{r^2} = 6.67 \times 10^{-11} \times \frac{6 \times 10^{24}}{(6.4 \times 10^6)^2}$$

$$= \frac{6.67 \times 6}{6.4 \times 6.4} \times 10$$

Earth's gravitational field strength = 9.8 in magnitude

Step 2 To find the units:

Units of (all) $g = \dfrac{\text{N m}^2\,\text{kg}^{-2} \times \text{kg}}{\text{m}^2} = \text{N for every kg} = \text{N kg}^{-1}$

Earth's gravitational field strength

- g_e . . . usually just called . . . $\boldsymbol{g = 9.81\ \text{N kg}^{-1}}$

Familiar? . . . let's see why

Acceleration caused by gravity

From Newton's 2nd Law (N2L):

Acceleration caused by gravity $= \dfrac{\text{Force}}{\text{Mass}}$

$$= \frac{9.81\ \text{N}}{1\ \text{kg}}$$

So. . .Acceleration, $\quad g = 9.81\ \text{m s}^{-2}$

Remember. . .
Newton = kilogram . metre per second squared
$\quad\quad\quad = \text{kg . m s}^{-2}$
(Force to accelerate 1 kg by 1 m s^{-2})

Questions

3 The figure below represents 2 planets, U and N, each with mass 90×10^{24} kg. Their separation in the solar system is 10^9 miles and they can be treated as point masses.

Calculate the gravitational field strength at the mid-point X between the 2 planets (ignoring the rest of the solar system!)

a caused only by planet U (as if it was on its own)

b caused by both planets, U and N
[1 km = $\frac{5}{8}$ mile]   G = 6.67×10^{-11} N m^2 kg^{-2}

Answers

a

Were you caught? Distance given in miles (from an *American book*), but we need it in **metres**

Step 1 $\quad\quad\quad 1\ \text{km} = \frac{5}{8}\ \text{mile}$

$\quad\quad 10^9\ \text{miles} = 10^9 \times \frac{8}{5} = 1.6 \times 10^9\ \text{km}$

$\quad\quad$ Planet separation $= 1.6 \times 10^{12}\ \text{m}$

Step 2 Gravitational field strength,

$$g = G\frac{M}{r^2} = 6.67 \times 10^{-11}\,\frac{9 \times 10^{25}}{(0.8 \times 10^{12})^2} = \frac{6.67 \times 9}{0.8^2} \times 10^{-10}$$

Field strength, $g = 9.4 \times 10^{-9}\ \text{N kg}^{-1}$

b Field strength caused by both planets, mid-way between them = zero, 0.

Why so easy? . . . Field strengths are vectors. The planets are the same mass, equi-distant from X, their attractions are equal and opposite in direction, so cancel out

Caution *Different masses are often used and the point at which their net field strength is zero is NOT midway*

Gravitational potential

To find out about:

> escape speeds
> weightlessness
> satellite/planetary orbits
> geostationary orbits, etc

it's best to introduce the idea of **gravitational potential**

 (Sorry! So let's try and get our heads around this)

- As in mechanics and current electricity, potential is all about **work done**.

- At *infinity*, ∞... gravitational potential (GP) is called *zero*

 Makes sense because gravitational force and field strength (GF&FS) have reduced to zero at ∞ distances

- GF&FS are **attractive** (masses move closer together)

- So body or mass has to have +*ve* work done *on* it to move it *away* through the attractive GF

  Imagine your hands are stretching a rubber band, you are doing work on it, increasing its potential energy

- $\therefore$ a mass has **−ve** work done **on** it when it moves **in** from ∞

  Now imagine you are letting the stretched rubber band bring your hands together, it is losing its potential energy

 *It can fall to the ground on its own, doing work; **negative** work needs to be done **on** it*

Definition of gravitational potential

Gravitational potential at a point in a gravitational field is defined as the **amount of work needed to bring a unit mass to that point from infinity**

$$V = \frac{W}{m}$$

W = work done in bringing mass m to that point from
   ∞, in Joules
m = mass of body in kg
V = gravitational potential at the point, in $J\,kg^{-1}$

- V is **zero** at infinity
  V is **negative** everywhere else (gravity is attractive)
  V is a **scalar**, like energy

Potential V and field strength, g

- $W = mV$

  so if a mass, m, is moved a small distance, Δr, in a uniform gravitational field, g:

  Work done **on** mass $\Delta W = m\Delta V$

  Work done **by** mass $= -m\Delta V$

and work done **on** mass $=$ force $\times$ distance moved

$$= mg \times \Delta r$$

where g = gravitational field strength

So... $$mg.\Delta r = m\Delta V$$

$$g = \frac{\Delta V}{\Delta r}$$

- In general, for all fields ... $g = \dfrac{dV}{dr}$

 The field strength is the slope or gradient of the V/r graph

Gravitational potential V in a radial field g

Outside a sphere, mass M, radius r:

$$g = \frac{GM}{r^2}$$

and also $$g = \frac{dV}{dr}$$

so... $$\frac{GM}{r^2} = \frac{dV}{dr}$$

Using calculus to sum these small changes, gives

> *Gravitational potential, $V = -\dfrac{GM}{r}$ in $J\,kg^{-1}$*

 Remember that field is a force and potential is work done

Notice that $V \propto \dfrac{1}{r}$. The figure shows the variation of gravitational potential outside the Earth with distance from the centre of the Earth, radius, R

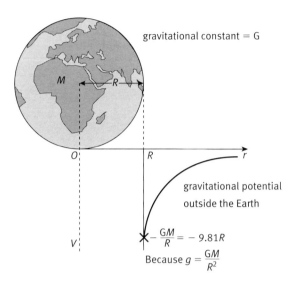

gravitational constant = G

gravitational potential outside the Earth

$-\dfrac{GM}{R} = -9.81R$

Because $g = \dfrac{GM}{R^2}$

Notice $V \Rightarrow 0$ as $r \Rightarrow \infty$ and V is always negative

Earth's gravitational potential at its surface, V_e

If M = Earth's mass, R = Earth's radius:

$$V_e = -\dfrac{GM}{R} = -9.81\,R$$

since

$$g = \dfrac{GM}{R^2}$$

Escape speed

Question

4 What would be the minimum speed needed to fire a bullet right out of the Earth's atmosphere, neglecting air friction?

[Earth's mass = 6×10^{24} kg, radius = 6.4×10^6 m, constant of gravitation = 6.67×10^{-11} N m^2 kg^{-2}]

Answer

Think positive . . . we can do this . . . how?

Gravitational potential is the work done between infinity and the Earth's surface, so the bullet must have this amount of kinetic energy initially if it is to reach infinity (where $V = 0$)

Step 1 Earth's gravitational potential, $V_e = -\dfrac{GM}{R}$

$$V_e = -\dfrac{6.67 \times 10^{-11} \times 6 \times 10^{24}}{6.4 \times 10^6}$$

$$= -6.25 \times 10^7 \text{ J kg}^{-1}$$

Step 2 Initial KE of bullet, mass m, $= \frac{1}{2}mv^2$

To escape, the minimum velocity the bullet needs is given by . . .

$$\frac{1}{2}mv^2 = 6.25 \times 10^7 \times m$$
$$v^2 = 2 \times 6.25 \times 10^7 \text{ m}^2\text{ s}^{-2}$$
$$v = 11.2 \times 10^3 \text{ m s}^{-1}$$

To escape from the Earth, a minimum speed of 11.2 km per sec is needed

 Bonus . . . this is the **escape speed** *from the Earth's surface, ignoring air friction, whatever the mass*
$$= \mathbf{11.2\,km\,s^{-1}}$$

Equipotentials

 At last something that is exactly what it says:

*   A line or surface that connects points of equal potential

*   No work needs to be done to move around an **equipotential**, no energy is exchanged with the gravitational field during such a move

*   The shapes of equipotentials for radial fields were shown on p.83. For uniform fields, the equipotentials are simply parallel lines at right angles to the parallel field see p. 91

*   The Earth's field can be treated as uniform locally near the Earth's surface, although it is obviously radial out into space

Question

5 The figure below shows the gravitational field pattern, dotted, of the Earth and the Moon.
[It is drawn to a scale of rather less than 1:10^{10}]
Notice that the Moon's field has little effect on the Earth's field.

The equipotentials are drawn as solid lines (nearly circles)

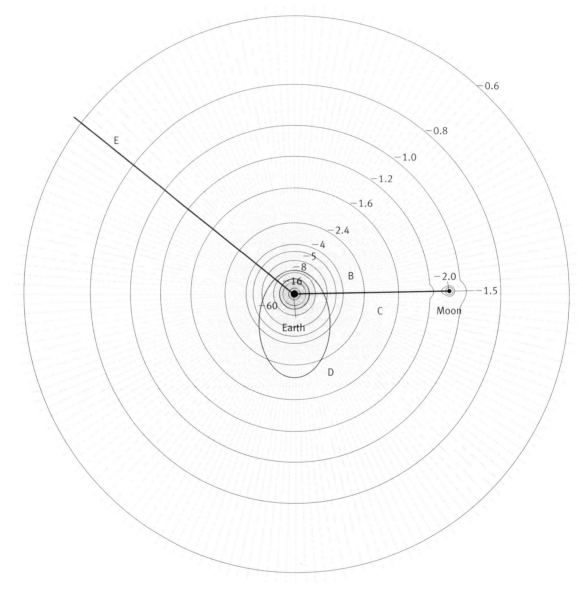

If the Earth's mass $= 6.0 \times 10^{24}$ kg
and the Moon's mass $= 7.4 \times 10^{22}$ kg
there will be a neutral point, X, between them, a distance r_E from the Earth, and r_M from the Moon.
Show that the ratio of $r_E:r_M = 9:1$

Answer

At the neutral point, X:

Earth's field $F_E = F_M$ Moon's field

$$G \frac{M_E}{r_E^2} = G \frac{M_M}{r_M^2}$$

$$\frac{r_E^2}{r_M^2} = \frac{6 \times 10^{24}}{7.4 \times 10^{22}} = \frac{600}{7.4} = \frac{81}{1}$$

So... $r_E:r_M = 9:1$

Changes in gravitational potential energy

- **Uniform field**

Close to the Earth we're on familiar ground... (sorry)...

Change in gravitational PE (rising) = Work done against gravitational force

ΔPE = gravitational force × distance

$$\Delta PE = mg\Delta h$$

where m = mass, kg
g = uniform field ($g_e = 9.81\ \text{N kg}^{-1}$)
Δh = distance moved against field, m

- **Radial field**

Your syllabus may not need this full treatment ... check before you suffer

When a mass, m, moves from a large distance, r_2, to a smaller distance, r_1, in a radial field, where

$$F = \frac{GMm}{r^2}$$

$$\text{Change in gravitational PE} = -\frac{GMm}{r_2} - \left(-\frac{GMm}{r_1}\right)$$

$$\Delta PE = GMm\left(\frac{1}{r_1} - \frac{1}{r_2}\right)$$

ΔPE will be positive because $r_2 > r_1$, so $\frac{1}{r_2} < \frac{1}{r_1}$

Satellite orbits

- To keep a satellite in orbit around the Earth, a centripetal force towards the centre of the Earth is needed $= \frac{mv^2}{r}$
- The strength of the gravitational field provides the force $= \frac{GMm}{r^2}$
- Therefore, $\frac{mv^2}{r} = \frac{GMm}{r^2}$

$$v^2 = \frac{GM}{r}$$

v^2 *does not depend on* m, *only on the radius* r *of the orbit and 'GM' for the planet*

- It's more likely that g_e, the gravitational field strength at the surface of the Earth, will be known

$$g_e = \frac{GM}{R^2} \text{ so } GM = g_e R^2$$

where $g_e = 9.81\ \text{N kg}^{-1}$ and $R = 6.4 \times 10^6$ m

Question

6 At what speed must a satellite travel if it is to orbit the Earth 1.8×10^3 km above its surface? Use the values above for the Earth's gravitational field and radius

Answer

$$\frac{mv^2}{r} = \frac{GMm}{r^2} \text{ so } v^2 = \frac{GM}{r} = \frac{g_e R^2}{r}$$

$$v^2 = \frac{9.81 \times 6.4^2 \times 10^{12}}{(6.4 \times 10^6) + (1.8 \times 10^6)}$$

$$= \frac{401.8 \times 10^{12}}{8.2 \times 10^6} = 49 \times 10^6\ \text{m}^2\,\text{s}^{-2}$$

Orbital speed of satellite = 7 km s^{-1}

Question

7 This question will enable you to work with the time **period of an orbit**
Assuming the Moon takes 28 days to complete a circular orbit of the Earth, calculate the separation of the centres of the Moon and the Earth

Mass of Earth = 6.0×10^{24} kg,
G = $6.7 \times 10^{-11}\ \text{N m}^2\,\text{kg}^{-2}$

Answer

Step 1 If the angular velocity of the satellite Moon is ω

then ... $\frac{mv^2}{r} = mr\omega^2$ [see section B9]

also... $\omega = \frac{2\pi}{T}$

where T = time period in **seconds** ... (watch out)

so ... $v^2 = r^2\omega^2 = \frac{r^2 4\pi^2}{T^2}$ ... (leave as v^2)

Step 2 But ... $v^2 = \frac{GM}{r} = \frac{r^2 4\pi^2}{T^2}$

$$\frac{T^2}{r^3} = \frac{4\pi^2}{GM}$$

Here we need $r^3 = \frac{GMT^2}{4\pi^2} = \frac{6.7 \times 10^{-11} \times 6 \times 10^{24} \times T^2}{4\pi^2}$

$$r^3 = 1.02 \times 10^{13} \times T^2$$

and $T = 28 \times 24 \times 60 \times 60 \approx 2.41 \times 10^6$ seconds

so ... $r^3 = 1.02 \times 10^{13} \times 2.41^2 \times 10^{12}$

$$r = 3.9 \times 10^8\ \text{m}$$

Answer ... a long way from the Earth to the Moon!

Geostationary orbits

The worst thing about these is the spelling!

Some reconnaissance and communications satellites need to hover above the same region of the Earth as it turns on its axis once every 24 hours

This just means that the **period** of the satellite's orbit must be **24** hours and it must orbit around the equator

Geostationary satellites will always seem to be in the same position in the sky above the Earth, unlike the Moon

---

Question

8 Given that, for the Earth:
$GM = 40.2 \times 10^{13} \, \text{N m}^2 \, \text{kg}^{-1}$ and
$R = 6.37 \times 10^3 \, \text{km}$
at what height above the Earth's surface would a geostationary satellite have to orbit?

 Watch your units

Answer

Step 1 A satellite must orbit the Earth once in the same time that the Earth takes to turn once
Period = 24 hours $= 24 \times 60 \times 60 \approx 8.64 \times 10^4 \, \text{s} = T$

Step 2 Referring to the last question (step 2):

$$\frac{T^2}{r^3} = \frac{4\pi^2}{GM} \text{ so } r^3 = \frac{GMT^2}{4\pi^2}$$

$$r^3 = \frac{40.2 \times 10^{13} \times 8.64^2 \times 10^8}{39.5}$$
$$= 75.97 \times 10^{21} \, \text{m}^3$$
$$r = 4.24 \times 10^7 \, \text{m} = 4.24 \times 10^4 \, \text{km}$$

 So, who gave this as the answer? Wrong!

Step 3 r is distance from the centre of the Earth
Height of satellite above the Earth $= r - R$

$$= (4.2 \times 10^4 - 6.37 \times 10^3) \, \text{km}$$
$$= (42 - 6.37) \times 10^3 \, \text{km}$$
$$= 3.56 \times 10^4 \, \text{km} \ldots \textit{watch the 10's}$$

Geostationary satellite orbits at height
$$= 3.56 \times 10^4 \, \text{km}$$

 Things . . . must be getting crowded up there because this *height doesn't depend on the mass of the satellite*

Weightlessness

- Strictly, this only occurs if there is no force acting on the body – way out in space, infinitely distant from all stars and planets.
Or, alternatively, part way between the Earth and the Moon where their gravitational forces of attraction cancel out
- A 'feeling' of **weightlessness** occurs when the only force acting on the body is gravity
It is the reaction with the Earth's surface that enables us to feel our weight
- This is the situation for a satellite far outside the Earth's atmosphere and for any astronaut in it.

They both have the same force keeping them in orbit . . . the gravitational force . . . no others

Consider the forces:

$$\frac{mv^2}{r} = \frac{GMm}{r^2} \rightarrow v^2 = \frac{GM}{r}$$

 m is not involved fortunately, so the satellite and the astronaut move round together!

No other force acts on the astronaut and the satellite. They both experience the same acceleration towards the centre of the Earth (same centripetal force) . . . so they feel weightless

It is the reaction with the floor, etc, that makes us feel our weight

When a lift falls away from under us we lose this reaction and we temporarily feel weightless, with only gravity acting

Comparing fields

 Make your own poster of this table and stick it to the ceiling over your bed . . . no better way to get familiar with it!

gravitational	quantity	electric
$F = G\dfrac{m_1 m_2}{r^2}$ Newton's law of gravitation	force between points: masses/ charges	$F = k\dfrac{Q_1 Q_2}{r^2}$ $k = \dfrac{1}{4\pi\varepsilon_0}$ in free space/air
$\dfrac{F}{m} = g = \dfrac{GM}{r^2}$	**1** radial fields: field strength	$\dfrac{F}{Q} = E = \dfrac{kQ}{r^2}$
$V = -\dfrac{GM}{r}$	potential	$V = \dfrac{kQ}{r}$
$Gm_1 m_2 \left(\dfrac{1}{r_1} - \dfrac{1}{r_2} \right)$	change in potential energy $= \Delta PE$	$kQ_1 Q_2 \left(\dfrac{1}{r_1} - \dfrac{1}{r_2} \right)$
g, at surface of Earth	**2** uniform field: field strength	$E = \dfrac{F}{Q} = \dfrac{V}{d}$
1 always attractive **2** independent of medium **3** small	force	**1** attractive and repulsive **2** depends on ε of medium **3** LARGE

 *Bonus . . . Compare the equations for gravitational fields and electric fields, they are **very** similar. So we're half way there for electric fields . . . **no problem!***

E23 Electric fields

Our world is essentially **neutral**. Atoms generally have exactly the right number of negative electrons to balance their positive protons. If this were not the case, then there are so many atoms that the tiniest imbalance would mean a world so highly charged that the Millennium fireworks would seem like sparklers. We could not get out of bed without a lightning display

However, life is not that exciting. But there are situations (such as a lightning display and the dust on a monitor or television screen) that are the result of electric charge

- Charges cause forces, and charges have fields

Refer to the table at the end of the last section (E22 Gravitational Fields) or, better, to your poster of it.

Electrostatic charges

- **Negative** ... when atoms have **gained** extra electrons, often by friction
  Polythene rubbed with a duster will be charged **n**egatively

- **Positive** ... when atoms have **lost** some electrons, again by friction
  Acetate rubbed by a duster (acetate ... add?)

  What about the duster above, which rubbed electrons off onto the polythene?
  It should be positive (+ve)

- The plates of a charged capacitor, of course, store charges. These will have gained +ve and −ve charges as a result of the flow of electrons off one (+ve) and onto the other (−ve). [Sections D21 and E24]

- The Van de Graaff generator can store the biggest charge in school labs

Electric force

- Masses are surrounded by a region of gravitational force (or field) ... that is attractive only

- Electric charges produce electric forces, so they are surrounded by an electric field ... attractive or repulsive

attractive force	repulsive force
positive and negative	positive and positive
negative and positive	negative and negative
'unlike' charges	**'like' charges**

 Because of the similarity with the work on gravitational fields, questions will be used here to revise the equations

Question

1 Two particles a distance r apart in free space, carrying charges Q_1 and Q_2, experience an electric force, F, between them. What is the relationship that gives the force F?

Answer

$$F \propto \frac{Q_1 Q_2}{r^2}$$

This is known as Coulomb's Law.
It is another Inverse Square Law.
The constant of proportionality, k, depends on the medium between the charges. To simplify other equations, k is replaced by $\frac{1}{4\pi\varepsilon_0}$, another constant

$$F = \frac{Q_1 Q_2}{4\pi\varepsilon_0 r^2}$$

 {...that's physics for you!}

In a vacuum, free space (or air) $F = \dfrac{Q_1 Q_2}{4\pi\varepsilon_0 r^2}$

F in newtons, if Q is in coulombs and r in metres
ε_0 is the permittivity of free space

$$\varepsilon_0 = \mathbf{8.85 \times 10^{-12}} \text{ C}^2\text{ N}^{-1}\text{ m}^{-2} \text{ or F m}^{-1}$$

 *Don't get caught: F m^{-1} is farads per m
F in equation, etc means electric force*

F is positive (+ve) for repulsion ... 'like' charges

F is negative (−ve) for attraction ... 'unlike' charges

Question

2 Two like charges 8 cm apart in air, repel each other with a force of 3.5×10^{-3} N. If one charge is 1.5×10^{-2} µC, find the other charge.

$$[\varepsilon_0 = 8.85 \times 10^{-12} \text{ F m}^{-1}]$$

Answer

 Watch the powers of 10.

$F = \dfrac{Q_1 Q_2}{4\pi\varepsilon_0 r^2}$ so $Q_1 = \dfrac{4\pi\varepsilon_0 r^2 F}{Q_2}$

$$= \frac{4\pi \times 8.85 \times 10^{-12} \times 64 \times 10^{-4} \times 3.5 \times 10^{-3}}{1.5 \times 10^{-8}}$$

$$= 1.7 \times 10^{-7} \text{ C}$$

The second charge is 1.7×10^{-7} C $= 0.17$ µC

Questions

3 Two similar ping-pong balls, X and Y, each of mass 1.3 g and hanging by insulating threads are similarly charged to Q μC

  a Draw a free-body force diagram for one of the balls

  b Find the tension in the thread

  c Find the electrostatic force between them

  d Calculate the charge on one of the balls. They hang as shown in the figure

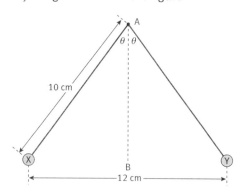

 It's all here folks, take it one bit at a time

Answers

Step 1 ABX and ABY are '3, 4, 5' triangles.

$$\therefore \quad \cos\theta = \tfrac{4}{5} \text{ and } \sin\theta = \tfrac{3}{5}$$

Step 2 **a** Consider ball X, it is in equilibrium from 3 forces:
mg = gravitational force or weight
T = tension in the thread
F = electrostatic force of repulsion from ball Y
A free-body force diagram is drawn below

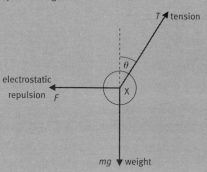

Step 3 **b** Resolving vertically ... $T\cos\theta = mg$

$$T = \frac{1.3 \times 10^{-3} \times 9.81}{\tfrac{4}{5}} = 15.94 \times 10^{-3}$$

$$= 0.016\,\text{N}$$

Step 4 **c** Resolving horizontally ... $T\sin\theta = F$

$$F = 0.016 \times \tfrac{3}{5} = 0.0096\,\text{N}$$

Step 5 **d** Since $F = \dfrac{Q^2}{4\pi\varepsilon_0 r^2}$, $Q^2 = 4\pi\varepsilon_0 r^2 F$

$$Q^2 = 4\pi \times 8.85 \times 10^{-12} \times 0.12^2 \times 0.0096$$

$$= 0.015 \times 10^{-12} = 1.5 \times 10^{-14}\,\text{C}^2$$

$$Q = 1.2 \times 10^{-7}\,\text{C}$$

Charge on one of the balls = 0.12 μC

Electric field strength

An electric field exists wherever there is an electric force acting

- The **strength** of an electric field is defined as the electric **force** acting per **unit +ve charge**

  If F = force in newtons felt by charge q in coulombs in an electric field E, then the units of E are N C^{-1}

$$E = \frac{F}{q}$$

- The **direction** of the **electric field** is given by the path a **positive charge** would take

  An electric field is a **vector** quantity

  The figure below shows the paths a +ve charge would take in various electric fields. −ve charges (eg, electrons) would move against the field

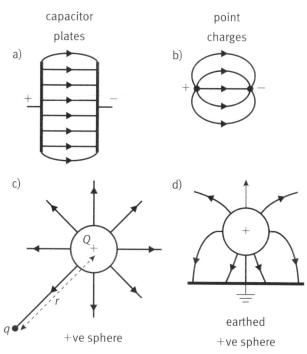

- **Inside** a conductor there is **no** electric field. For the region **outside**, the charge can be taken as concentrated at the **centre** of the conductor

In Figure (c) a charge Q has a **radial** field surrounding it. A distance r away a small charge, q, will feel an electric force, F, where:

$$F = \frac{Qq}{4\pi\varepsilon_0 r^2}$$

so $E = \dfrac{F}{q} = \dfrac{Q}{4\pi\varepsilon_0 r^2} = \dfrac{kQ}{r^2}$

Study and Revise AS and A2 Level Physics

$\therefore$

$$E = \frac{Q}{4\pi\varepsilon_0 r^2}$$

Often, we are dealing with a **uniform** electric field, figure (a) between capacitor plates, X and Y plates of a C.R.O., etc

In figure (a) the **uniform** electric field is represented by parallel field lines running straight across from the +ve plate to the −ve plate except where it bulges at the edges. Again, the arrows indicate the path taken by a unit +ve charge in the field

Electric potential

Question

4 Define the electric potential at a point, P, in an electric field

Answer

The **electric potential** V in a field E is defined as **the work done (or energy transferred) in bringing a unit positive charge from infinity to that point, against the action of the field**

- If an amount of work, W, moves a small charge, q, to P from infinity then:

Electric potential $V = \dfrac{\text{work done}}{\text{charge transferred}}$

$$V = \frac{W}{q} \qquad \text{[joules/coulomb]}$$

Electric potential, V, is measured in volts $= \text{J C}^{-1}$

Notice...

Work done or Energy transferred $= qV$

- Electric **potential = 0 at ∞**... [far from all charges. Similar to gravitational fields]

- Electric potential is a **scalar** quantity

- Positive charges cause a positive potential Negative charges cause a negative potential

Potential, *V* and Field strength, *E*

As with gravitational fields:

Since ... Work done **on** the charge, $W = qV$ If a small charge Δq is moved through a small distance Δr in an electric field, E, the change in potential ΔV is linked to the field as follows:

Work done **on** charge $= \Delta W = +q\Delta V$
Work done **by** charge $= -q\Delta V$

But this is ... force × distance moved $= qE \times \Delta r$

(remember $E = \dfrac{F}{q}$)

So ... $qE\Delta r = -q\Delta V$ (q cancels)

$$E = -\frac{\Delta V}{\Delta r} \qquad \text{using calculus} \ldots$$

For all electric fields, $E = -\dfrac{dV}{dr}$

Minus sign shows that potential is decreasing in the direction of the field

Electric potential in a uniform field

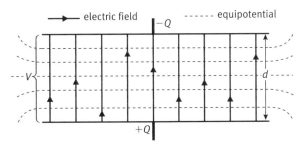

The figure represents the electric field between 2 parallel plates, eg, in a capacitor

A small charge, q, feels a force, F, so the field $E = \dfrac{F}{q} \, \text{N C}^{-1}$.

If there is a potential difference, V, between the plates, a distance d apart:

Since ... $E = -\dfrac{\Delta V}{\Delta r} = -$ potential gradient

$$= \frac{V}{d} \, \text{V m}^{-1}$$

This constant potential gradient means a **uniform** electric field exists

Uniform electric field:

$$E = \frac{F}{q} \, \text{N m}^{-1} \quad \text{or} \quad E = \frac{V}{d} \, \text{V m}^{-1}$$

Electric potential in radial fields

Here ... $E = -\dfrac{dV}{dr}$ and $E = \dfrac{Q}{4\pi\varepsilon_0 r^2}$ using calculus ...

gives

$$V = \frac{Q}{4\pi\varepsilon_0 r}$$

$$\text{Potential } V \text{ in a radial field} = \frac{Q}{4\pi\varepsilon_0 r} \text{ volts}$$

- This would apply to a point charge or, for example, outside a Van de Graaff sphere

- **Inside a charged conductor** no work needs to be done to move the charges, so all points are at the same potential
  The change in potential or potential gradient is zero
  Therefore, the **electric field inside a conductor is zero**

[For the following questions take:

$$\varepsilon_0 = 8.85 \times 10^{-12} \text{ F m}^{-1} \text{ or } C^2 \text{ N}^{-1} \text{ m}^{-2}]$$

Question

5 Find the potential at a point in air 30 cm from a charge of 6.0×10^{-2} nC

 Watch the powers of *10*. Change to m and C. *Remember* nC $= 10^{-9}$C

Answer

$$V = \frac{Q}{4\pi\varepsilon_0 r} = \frac{6 \times 10^{-11}}{4\pi \times 8.85 \times 10^{-12} \times 0.3}$$

$$= 0.18 \times 10 \text{ V}$$

Potential 30 cm from point charge is 1.8 V

Questions

6 An electric field of strength 6.5×10^5 N C^{-1} accelerates a beam of electrons from rest. Find:

a the force on an electron and

b their acceleration

[electronic charge $= 1.6 \times 10^{-19}$ C and mass of an electron $= 9.11 \times 10^{-31}$ kg]

Answers

a $\quad E = \dfrac{F}{q}$ so $F = Eq = 6.5 \times 10^5 \times 1.6 \times 10^{-19}$

$$F = 10.4 \times 10^{-14} \text{ N}$$

The force on an electron is 1.04×10^{-13} newtons

b $F = ma$

So ... $a = \dfrac{F}{m} = \dfrac{1.04 \times 10^{-13}}{9.11 \times 10^{-31}} = 0.114 \times 10^{18} \text{ m s}^{-2}$

The electrons accelerate at 1.14×10^{17} m s^{-2}

Questions

7 An industrial chimney is fitted with parallel metal plates 0.7 m apart. When a large potential difference is put across them, charged smoke and dust can be trapped. If the pd is 40 kV calculate

a the strength of the electric field between the plates

b the charge on a smoke particle if it feels a force $= 1.8 \times 10^{-7}$ N

Answers

a $E = \dfrac{V}{d} = \dfrac{40000}{0.7} = 5.71 \times 10^4$ N C^{-1}

The uniform field between the parallel plates is

$$5.71 \times 10^4 \text{ N C}^{-1} \text{ or V m}^{-1}$$

Here the unit N C^{-1} *is appropriate, because we go on to find the charge on the smoke particle from the force*

b Also ... $E = \dfrac{F}{q}$ so $q = \dfrac{F}{E} = \dfrac{1.8 \times 10^{-7}}{5.71 \times 10^4}$

$$q = 0.315 \times 10^{-11} \text{ C}$$

The charge on the smoke particle is 3.15 pC
[1pC = 1 picocoulomb $= 10^{-12}$ C]

Questions

8 A Van der Graaff generator has a sphere of radius 20 cm

a Calculate the charge it carries if the potential at its surface in air is 100 kV

b Estimate the number of electrons on the surface of the sphere

[electronic charge, e $= 1.6 \times 10^{-19}$C]

Answers

a The sphere can be considered as having a point charge at its centre

Using ... $V = \dfrac{Q}{4\pi\varepsilon_0 r}$ so $Q = 4\pi\varepsilon_0 rV$

$$Q = 4\pi \times 8.85 \times 10^{-12} \times 0.2 \times 10^5 = 22.2 \times 10^{-7} \text{ C}$$

Charge on sphere is 2.22 μC

b Charge carried by one electron $= 1.6 \times 10^{-19}$ C

Number of electrons $= \dfrac{2.22 \times 10^{-6}}{1.6 \times 10^{-19}} = 1.4 \times 10^{13}$!!!

What's the difference between potential and potential difference?

Potential at a point is the work done in bringing unit +ve charge from infinity to the point

Potential difference between two points is the work done in moving a unit +ve charge from one point to the other

Equipotentials

As in a gravitational field, equipotentials are lines joining points of equal potential

The figure below shows the equipotentials for a radial electric field

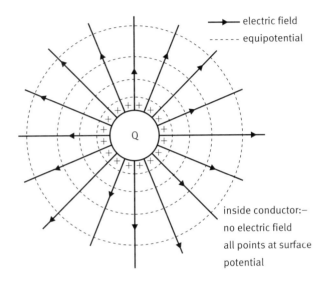

→ electric field
----- equipotential

inside conductor:–
no electric field
all points at surface
potential

Notice that the **equipotential** lines (or surfaces) are always at **right angles** to the electric **field lines**

The equipotential surfaces surrounding a point charge would be concentric spheres, spreading further apart as the distance away increases

E24 Capacitance 2

Beginner's box

- Be confident of all the work learnt in D21 Capacitance 1
- As capacitor decay is exponential, it would be helpful to be familiar with this type of change, described by e^{-x}. (See Sections A1 and G35)
- Know that the uniform electric field between parallel plates, $E = \dfrac{V}{d}$

Parallel plate capacitance

- For a parallel plate capacitor ... $Q \propto V$

  Also, more charge can be stored if the **area** of the plates increases ... $Q \propto A$

  If the plates are **closer together** more charge can be stored (electric field larger) ... $Q \propto \dfrac{1}{d}$

  Combining these factors gives:

  $$Q \propto \frac{VA}{d}$$

  The constant is determined by the **dielectric** (the filling in the sandwich).

  If this is a vacuum (or air, to a close approximation), the constant is the **permittivity** of 'free space' $= \varepsilon_0$.

  $$\boxed{C = \frac{Q}{V} = \varepsilon_0 \frac{A}{d}}$$

For any other medium, eg, waxed paper, polythene and some ceramic materials, its **relative permittivity** $= \varepsilon_r$ must be included

$$\varepsilon_r = \frac{C}{C_0} = \frac{\text{capacitance with dielectric between plates}}{\text{capacitance with vacuum between plates}}$$

$$Q = \varepsilon_0 \varepsilon_r \frac{VA}{d}$$

Finally! ...
$$\boxed{C = \frac{Q}{V} = \varepsilon_0 \varepsilon_r \frac{A}{d}}$$

Permittivity of free space $= \varepsilon_0 = 8.85 \times 10^{-12} \, \text{F m}^{-1}$
Relative permittivity, ε_r, is a ratio, so is just a number with no units.

Question

1 A parallel plate (side 40 cm) capacitor has mica, 2.5 mm thick between its plates. What is the value of its capacitance, if the relative permittivity of mica is 5.5?

Answer

$$C = \varepsilon_0 \varepsilon_r \frac{A}{d}$$

Here ... Area, $A = 0.4 \, \text{m} \times 0.4 \, \text{m}$
$d = 2.5 \times 10^{-3} \, \text{m}$

Given $\varepsilon_0 = 8.85 \times 10^{-12} \, \text{F m}^{-1}$

$$C = 8.85 \times 10^{-12} \times 5.5 \frac{0.4 \times 0.4}{2.5 \times 10^{-3}}$$
$$= 3.12 \times 10^{-9} \, \text{F} = 3{,}120 \times 10^{-12} \, \text{F}$$

Capacitance of parallel plate capacitor $= 3{,}120 \, \text{pF}$

Measurement of capacitance

 EXPERIMENT

A vibrating reed switch very neatly charges and discharges a capacitor rapidly, and results in the current from it being very nearly constant. The circuit is shown in the figure below

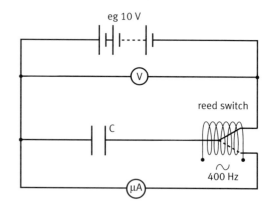

- The springy reed is oscillated by a rectified ac signal, frequency $f \sim 400 \, \text{Hz}$, that repeatedly charges the capacitor from the dc supply and discharges it through the microammeter

- Providing the capacitor is fully charged each time to a charge Q, then Q coulombs flow through the microammeter f times every second:

  Qf coulombs per s = current, I amps
  Current through microammeter, $I = \mathbf{Qf}$
  But $Q = CV$, so ... $I = CVf$

  $$C = \frac{I}{Vf}$$

Using this method, the factors affecting capacitance can be investigated. Check further experimental details in any advanced physics text

Capacitor decay and time constant

Look back at the Experiment in Section D21 (Capacitance 1) where the current, I, was plotted against time, t, during the charging and discharging of a capacitor through a large resistor

The following question will teach you how to analyse such a decay

Questions

2 The figure below shows a typical decay curve for a 30 μF capacitor that was fully charged to 9 V and then discharged through a 20 kΩ resistor

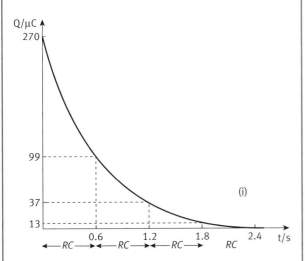

a Find the maximum charge stored on the capacitor

b Calculate the **time constant** for this decay

c Show that the **units** of time constant, RC, are **seconds**

Answers

a $Q = CV = 30 \times 10^{-6} \times 9 = 270\,\mu C$

b Time constant $= RC = 20 \times 10^3 \times 30 \times 10^{-6}$

$\qquad\qquad\qquad = 600 \times 10^{-3}$

$\qquad\qquad\qquad = 0.6\ \text{seconds}$

c Units of time constant, RC, τ

Step 1 $\qquad R\ (\text{ohms}) = \dfrac{V\ (\text{volts})}{I\ (\text{amps})}$

$\qquad\qquad C\ (\text{Farads}) = \dfrac{Q\ (\text{Coulombs})}{V\ (\text{volts})} = \dfrac{It\ (\text{amps} \times \text{s})}{V\ (\text{volts})}$

Step 2 $\qquad RC = \Omega \times F = \dfrac{\text{volts}}{\text{amps}} \times \dfrac{\text{amps} \times \text{s}}{\text{volts}} = \text{s}$

• So units of RC are seconds!

About this **time constant** . . .

As the charge flows off the capacitor, the pd across it will fall. This will mean charge will flow off more slowly

The rate of flow of charge depends on the charge left on the capacitor

[Compare this with the radioactive decay Section G35]

• At any time t: $\quad Q = CV$ and $V = RI$

$\qquad\qquad\qquad$ So $\boldsymbol{Q = RC\,I}$

R and C are constant so $\boldsymbol{Q \propto I}$: the I/t graph will be the same shape as the Q/t graph . . . draw them

RC is known as the **time constant** of the **capacitor**

Meaning of time constant

For a capacitor discharging. . .

$$Q = Q_0 e^{-\frac{t}{RC}} \quad \text{Decay Law}$$

As expected, the decay law shows an **exponential** change. This is expected, because the rate of flow of charge off the plates depends on the charge remaining on them

$$\frac{dQ}{dt} \propto -Q$$

[compare with $\dfrac{dN}{dt} \propto -N$ in radioactivity]

Question

3 In the **decay law**, $Q = Q_0 e^{-\frac{t}{RC}}$, what happens when time, $t = RC$, the time constant?

Answer

$Q = Q_0 e^{-\frac{RC}{RC}} = Q_0 e^{-1} = Q_0 \times \dfrac{1}{e} = Q_0 \dfrac{1}{2.718} = 0.37 Q_0$

So, at time RC, . . . $\dfrac{Q}{Q_0} = 0.37$

charge Q has fallen to 37% of initial value $\simeq \frac{1}{3}$

Show this 37% as a standard position on a Q/t graph
See Fig (i) Question **2**

Questions

4

  a In Question **2** in figure (i), approximately how long does it take for the charge to fall to 90 μC?

  b Calculate, or find from the figure in Question **2**, what charge would remain after another 0.6 s

Answers

a
$$\frac{Q}{Q_0} = \frac{90 \times 10^{-6}}{270 \times 10^{-6}} = \frac{1}{3}$$

So, time taken $\simeq$ time constant $= RC$
$R = 20\,\text{k}\Omega$, $C = 30\,\mu\text{F}$, from 2b) $RC = 0.6\,\text{s}$
Charge falls to 90 μC in about 0.6 seconds

b After another 0.6 s $=$ time constant $= RC$ the charge would have fallen to $\frac{1}{3} \times 90\,\mu\text{C} \simeq 30\,\mu\text{C}$. Check this on the graph

 When a graph is **exponential**, it changes by the same factor in successive equal intervals of time. Here: by 0.37 in every RC seconds (or a time constant interval)

Half-life of capacitor discharge

Question

5 The decay law gives $Q = Q_0 e^{-\frac{t}{RC}}$
At what time will the charge on the capacitor have halved, call this the **half-life**, $t_{1/2}$?

Answer

When $t = t_{1/2}$, $Q = \frac{Q_0}{2}$

Step 1 Substituting in
$$Q = Q_0 e^{-\frac{t_{1/2}}{RC}} \ldots \frac{Q_0}{2} = Q_0 e^{-\frac{t_{1/2}}{RC}}$$

Step 2 Cancelling Q_0 and turning the equation upside down
gives $\ldots e^{\frac{t_{1/2}}{RC}} = 2$

Step 3 Taking natural logs gives: $\frac{t_{1/2}}{RC} = \ln 2$

> **half-life, $t_{1/2} = RC \times \ln 2$**
> **[ln 2 = 0.69]** $\quad = 0.69\,RC$

 Compare with half-life, $t_{1/2} = \frac{\ln 2}{\lambda}$ in radioactivity

Questions

6 The figure below shows the circuit used to charge and discharge a 270 μF capacitor fully. Closing S_1 charges it and switching to S_2 discharges it through the large resistor.

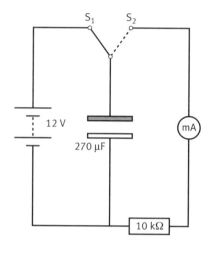

  a What is the time constant for the discharge?

  b Calculate the half-life of the discharge.

  c On the axes below, sketch a graph showing how the current varies with time after the switch is moved to S_2, during the first 3 seconds of discharge.

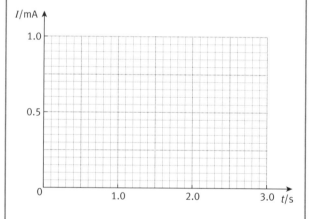

Answers

a Time constant, $\tau = RC$

$\qquad = 10 \times 10^3 \times 270 \times 10^{-6}$

$\qquad = 2.7$ seconds

Or here $\tau = RC$, and $t_{1/2} = 0.69\,RC$ so time

constant $= \dfrac{t_{1/2}}{0.69} = \dfrac{1.9}{0.69} = 2.7\ seconds$

b $t_{1/2} = 0.69RC = 0.69 \times 10 \times 10^3 \times 270 \times 10^{-6}$

$\qquad = 186.3 \times 10^{-2}\,\text{s} = 1.9\,\text{seconds}$

c Notice, current/time, **not** charge/time, during **discharge**

Step 1 Find the initial current

Capacitor charged to 12 V is discharged through $10\text{k}\Omega$ resistor, so using $V = RI$

Initial current, $I_0 = \dfrac{V_0}{R} = \dfrac{12}{10 \times 10^3} = 1.2\,\text{mA}$ at $t = 0$

Step 2 Half-life of the discharge, $t_{1/2} = 1.9\,\text{s}$ (from 6a)

Since $I \propto Q$, the current will have halved in 1.9 s

$I = 0.6\,\text{mA}$ at $t = 1.9\,\text{s}$

Step 3 Time constant for the discharge, $\tau = 2.7\,\text{s}$ (from 6b)

The current will have reduced to $0.37I_0$ in this time (from Question 3).

$\qquad I = 0.37 \times 1.2 \times 10^{-3} = 0.44\,\text{mA}$ at $t = 2.7\,\text{s}$

Step 4 Add the scale to the current axis, remembering

$I_0 = 1.2\,\text{mA}$, $t = 0$;

$I = 0.6\,\text{mA}$, $t = 1.9\,\text{s}$;

$I = 0.44\,\text{mA}$, $t = 2.7\,\text{s}$

Plot these 3 points on the axes and draw a smooth curve to show the exponential decay of current

Check with the dotted curve in graph below

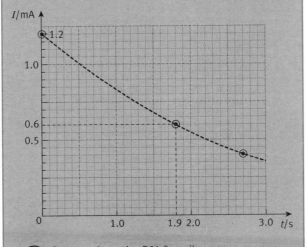

Bonus ... In section D21 Capacitance 1 ...

Charge on capacitor = Area under I/t graph

The area could be estimated by counting squares to give the charge stored ... from the graph

Capacitor curves

Question

8 The figure (i) below shows the shape of the Q/t, V/t and I/t curves for the **charging** process of a capacitor through a resistor.
Complete the chart to show the **discharging** curves.

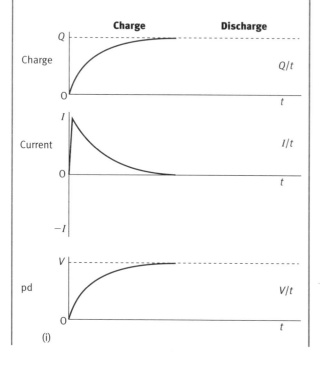

(i)

Answer

Step 1 Remember the charge, Q, flows off exponentially, easily at first, but more slowly as the pd across the capacitor falls

Step 2 $V \propto Q$, ($Q = CV$) so the voltage change matches the charge change in shape

See if you agree with the dotted curves in the figure (ii)

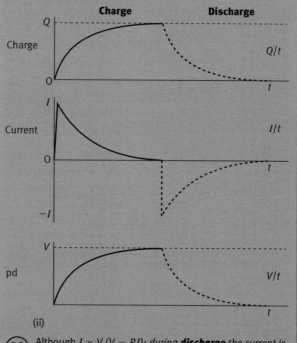

(ii)

☹ Although $I \propto V$ ($V = RI$); during **discharge** the current is flowing **off** the capacitor in the **opposite** direction to the charging current, $-ve$ on the graph.

E25 Magnetic B-fields and forces:

(a.k.a. the 'BIl' and 'Bev' story)

Beginner's box

- Know that magnetic fields are produced by:
  1. permanent magnets
  2. any moving charge or current
- Be familiar with magnetic field patterns (lines of force) for:
  1. permanent magnets (direction N → S)
  2. current flowing in coil
- Know the meaning of a neutral point
- Know that a current-carrying wire in a magnetic field feels a force ... → electric motor

Magnetic fields and forces

Again, any region where magnetic forces are experienced is called a magnetic *field*. The *direction* is the path that a magnetic *North Pole* N would take in the field ... *away* from a North Pole because 'like' poles repel.

- The figure below gives the shapes of some magnetic fields considered in this section. Putting them together helps to compare them.

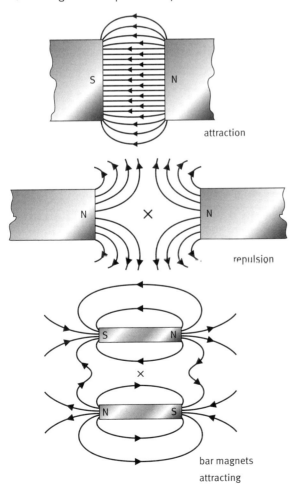

attraction

repulsion

bar magnets
attracting

wire carrying current into page

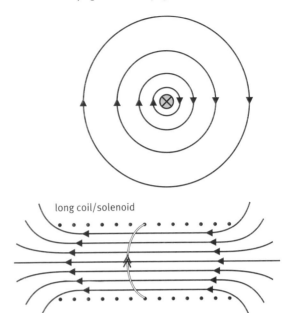

long coil/solenoid

wire carrying
current into page
in a magnetic field

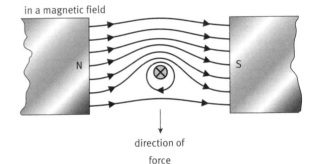

direction of
force

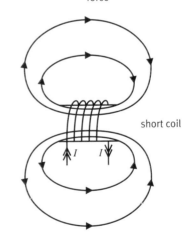

short coil

⊗ indicates current flowing into paper.

Magnetic fields caused by currents

A wire carrying a current has a magnetic field wrapping round it, a bit like the foam lagging round a water pipe

- The direction of the field can be found by the **right hand** screw or **grip** rule (thanks to Maxwell

Imagine you're on a motor-bike ... your right hand revving the engine on the throttle

1 Straight wire carrying a current

If your thumb lies in the direction of the current: your fingers wrap round in the direction of its magnetic field

2 Coil carrying a current

If your fingers wrap round in the direction of the current: your thumb points in the direction of its magnetic field

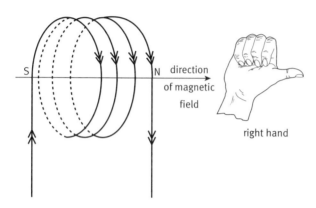

S   N direction of magnetic field

right hand

 Try it, it's easier than it sounds

Magnetic force on a current

 *Now it's the turn of the **left** hand ... prepare to dislocate your fingers*

Any current or charge moving in a magnetic field will feel a force acting on it to move it
(ie, a current-carrying wire will jump in a magnetic field)

This is the result of the magnetic field combining with the current's magnetic field

- The resultant **force direction** is given by **Fleming's left-hand** rule as shown in the figure below

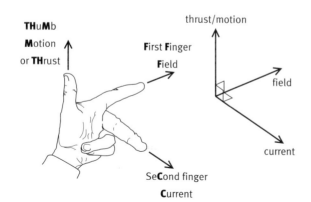

THuMb
Motion or **THrust**

First Finger
Field

thrust/motion

field

current

SeCond finger
Current

 Say after me...

First **F**inger ... **F**ield
se**C**ond finger ... **C**urrent
THumb ... **TH**rust or thu**M**b ... **M**otion

To get your fingers in the correct positions:

1 Using your left hand, hold it out, straight fingers
2 Stick the thumb up in the air
3 Fold 3 fingers round to the palm, leaving the first finger sticking out (at right angles to thumb)
4 Unfold your middle finger, just until it is at right angles to the first finger.

Then align your **f**irst finger with the **f**ield and your se**c**ond finger with the **c**urrent ... without changing the directions of your fingers (that's the skilful bit!)

Your **thumb** will lie in the direction of the **thrust** or resulting **motion**

 Remember you are using conventional current direction

Magnetic field strength

- Magnetic field lines are called **flux**

- The **strength** of a magnetic field of flux is measured in terms of the concentration or **density of the flux** ... **B**

- **Magnetic field strength = Flux density B** is defined in terms of the force the magnetic field applies to a current flowing in it

 That's physicists for you!

- **Flux density B** is a **vector** quantity, direction and magnitude are both important

Force on a straight wire, carrying a current

A current, I, flows in a length, l, of a wire at right angles to a magnetic field of flux density B (its magnetic field strength) ... see the figure below

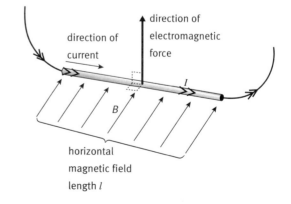

direction of current

direction of electromagnetic force

B

I

horizontal magnetic field
length l

Study and Revise AS and A2 Level Physics

- Use Fleming's left-hand rule to check that the thrust, F, is upwards when the current is flowing left to right

- The magnitude of F increases as current, I, length, l, and field strength, B, increase, so:

$$F = BIl$$

if F in newtons
I in amps
l in metres
then B is in tesla

Magnetic field strength or flux density:

$$B = \frac{F}{Il}$$

where l is the length of conductor at right angles to the field

- If a current of 1 amp flowing in 1 metre of wire at right angles to a uniform magnetic field produces a force of 1 newton on it, then the magnetic field has a strength or flux density of 1 **tesla** (symbol T).

- Comparing units:

  1 tesla = 1 newton per ampere metre
  $= 1\,\text{N}\,\text{A}^{-1}\,\text{m}^{-1}$

- A tesla is another large unit, expect to find microtesla $= \mu\text{T} = 10^{-6}\,\text{T}$, etc

Questions

1 The Earth's magnetic field is taken to flow from south to north

a What must the polarity of the magnetism at the North Pole be?

b In a lab, the horizontal component of the Earth's magnetic field is 1.8×10^{-5} T. A straight piece of wire 2.5 m long, with mass 2.0 g, lies on an insulated bench in a west–east direction. In which direction must a current flow in the wire if it is to jump off the bench?

c Calculate the size of the very large pulse of current needed to make the wire jump.

Answers

a It must be equivalent to a magnetic South Pole, since magnetic field direction is that followed by a unit North Pole

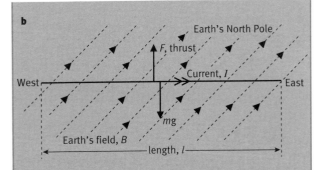

b

Sketch the set-up as in the figure above and use your left hand (Fleming's rule) to line up with:

1 **F**irst **F**inger **F**ield ... into the paper
2 **Th**umb **Th**rust ... which must be upwards
3 So se**C**ond **C**urrent must be left → right in the diagram.

Current must flow from west to east to lift the wire off the bench

c Because ... $F = BIl = 1.8 \times 10^{-5} \times I \times 2.5$

But F = weight of wire $= mg = 2.0 \times 10^{-3} \times 9.81$ N

 Did you forget the 10^{-3}?

So ...
$$BIl = mg$$
$$1.8 \times 10^{-5} \times 2.5 \times I = 2 \times 10^{-3} \times 9.81$$
$$I = \frac{19.62 \times 10^{-3}}{4.5 \times 10^{-5}} = 4.4 \times 10^{2}\,\text{A}$$

A momentary current of 440 amps will make the wire jump.

Don't try this at home ... or in the lab. It would do more than make you jump.

If the conductor is at an angle θ to the field

Check if your syllabus requires this

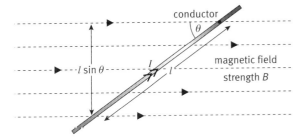

The figure above shows that, when there is an angle θ between the conductor and the field, the effective length of the conductor at right angles to the field is only ... $l\sin\theta$.

So...

$$F = BIl\sin\theta$$

Questions

2 What does this force become when

a $\theta \to 90°$ **b** $\theta \to 0°$?

Answers

a $\theta \to 90°$ then $\sin 90° = 1$ so $F = BIl\sin\theta$ becomes $F = BIl$ ... as expected??

b $\theta \to 0°$ then $\sin 0° \to 0$ so $F \to 0$
There is **no force** when the conductor is **parallel** to the magnetic field or flux.

 EXPERIMENT

Question

3 Describe how you would demonstrate in a school lab that the magnitude of the force on a current-carrying conductor is directly proportional to the current flowing in it, $F \propto I$ and the length of the conductor, $F \propto l$

Answer

A current balance is designed to show this. It consists of a fairly rigid rectangle of wire which can be balanced on two razor blades, as shown in the figure below

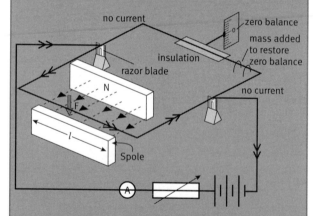

- The current enters via one razor blade, passes round one side of the wire loop, through a magnetic field between the poles of a pair of ceramic magnets and out through the other razor blade
- A variable resistor and ammeter enable the current to be varied and measured
- The direction of the current must give a force down in the magnetic field so that tiny masses (eg, bits of wire) added to the other side of the loop also act downwards to balance the loop. Check that all is correct in the figure

🙁 The tricky, not to say impossible bit, is to balance the wire loop. Sometimes a sensitive top-pan balance is used to 'weigh' the force directly

- For each current, I, balance must be found with a mass, m. Force = mg (g constant), so mass m can be plotted against current, I.
- If the graph is a straight line, then $F \propto I$

To check variation of **F** with **I**

- Use the same arrangement, keep the current, I, constant, but change the length, l, of the wire in the field B.
- Fix two, and then three pairs of ceramic magnets side-by-side to extend the length of the conductor in the field

🙁 This is not that easy, because all the pairs of magnets *must have their* N faces beside each other, and S's opposite. Some firm taping may be necessary

- Find mg for each length, l, which balances the loop (or weigh the force) and check to see if **F** $\propto$ **l**.

🙁 *Before you suffer ... check if your syllabus requires the torque on a coil*

Forces or torque on a coil, carrying a current

A rectangular coil, similar to that in a simple **DC motor**, is shown in the figure below

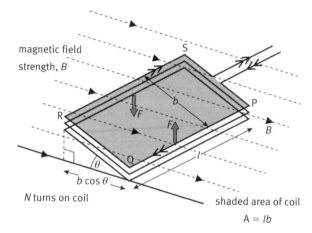

N turns on coil

shaded area of coil
$A = lb$

- θ is the angle between the plane of the coil and the field — it varies as the coil turns.

- With the current flowing as shown, there is a force, F, on one side, PQ, pulling upwards
The current is in the opposite sense on the other side, so the force, also F, will push down on RS. A pair of forces, F, a couple, will turn the coil

- Moment of couple
  = One force $\times \perp r$ distance between them
  = $F \times b\cos\theta$
Moment of couple is called Torque or T
and ... $F = BIl$ for single wire
so ... $F = BIlN$ for N turns of wire

- Combining these we have:
Torque $T = BIlN \times b\cos\theta$
$= BIAN\cos\theta$
where lb = area A of the coil

- $T = BIAN\cos\theta$ holds for any shape plane coil of area A

Questions

4 In what position of the coil will the torque T be

a maximum?

b minimum?

Give the values of T in the 2 positions

Answers

a $T = BIAN \cos \theta$, will be maximum when $\cos \theta = 1$, ie, when $\theta = 0°$

When the coil is parallel to the field, the torque is maximum and $T_{max} = BIAN$

b $T = BIAN \cos \theta$, is minimum when $\cos \theta = 0$, ie, when $\theta = 90°$

When the coil is at right angles to the field, the torque is minimum and $T_{min} = 0$

 Watch out for T = torque and T = tesla . . . they could both be in the same question

Force on a charge in a magnetic field

The figure below represents a length, *l*, of conductor in a uniform magnetic field B. n charges, each with a value of q, move at a drift velocity, v, to carry a current *I*.

 Imagine current I is carried by +ve charges

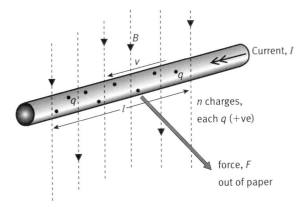

Current, *I*

B

v

q

q

l

n charges, each *q* (+ve)

force, *F* out of paper

If t is the time it takes for a charge to travel the distance *l* . . . Average drift velocity $v = \dfrac{l}{t}$

Total charge moved in *t* seconds = nq

But . . . current $I = \dfrac{\text{charge}}{\text{time}} = \dfrac{nq}{t}$ & $t = \dfrac{l}{v}$

So . . . $I = \dfrac{nqv}{l}$

When a magnetic field B acts at right angles to the flow of charges:

$$\text{Force} = BIl = B\left(\dfrac{nqv}{l}\right)l$$

$$= BnqV$$

- For a single charge, *q*, moving at right angles to a magnetic field B, the force or thrust it feels, *F*, becomes:

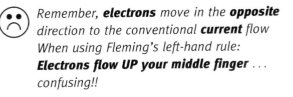

$$F = Bqv$$

if *F* in newtons
q in coulombs
v in metres per second
then *B* is in tesla

- For an electron

$$F = Bev$$

where e = 1.6×10^{-19} C
the charge on an electron

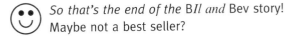 *So that's the end of the BIl and Bev story! Maybe not a best seller?*

*Remember, **electrons** move in the **opposite** direction to the conventional **current** flow When using Fleming's left-hand rule: **Electrons flow UP your middle finger** . . . confusing!!*

Question

5 Calculate the force experienced by electrons moving at 6.5 m s^{-1} at right angles to a uniform magnetic field of flux density 4.5×10^{-3} T.

[Take charge on an electron, e = 1.6×10^{-19} C]

Answer

Force $F = Bev = 4.5 \times 10^{-3} \times 1.6 \times 10^{-19} \times 6.5$
$= 46.8 \times 10^{-22} = 4.7 \times 10^{-21}$ N

 Perhaps as small a force as you're likely to come across

Calculating magnetic flux density B

Again, the magnetic field strength B obeys an Inverse Square Law with regard to distance from a current in a short length of wire.

$$\delta B \propto \dfrac{I \delta l \sin \theta}{4 \pi r^2} \quad \text{Biot–Savart Law}$$

 Don't worry, it's above 'A' level

The constant of proportionality depends on the medium and is called the . . .

permeability of free space, $\mu_0 = 4\pi \times 10^{-7}\,\text{T}\,\text{m}\,\text{A}^{-1}$.

This is a defined value and holds for air as well as a vacuum

Experiment and calculus on the Biot-Savart Law give:

1 Field near a long straight wire

$$B = \frac{\mu_0 I}{2\pi r}$$

where r is the perpendicular distance from the wire carrying a current I

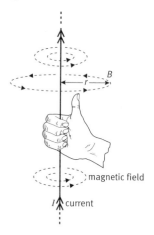

:| $2\pi r$ because of the cylindrical symmetry

2 Field inside a long coil/solenoid

$$B = \mu_0 n I$$

where n is the number of turns/metre for the solenoid carrying a current I

:| *Magnetic field is uniform along the axis near its centre, if it's a **long** coil*

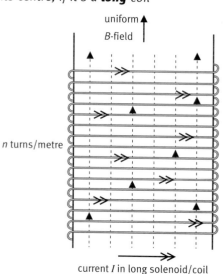

uniform
B-field

n turns/metre

current I in long solenoid/coil

Question

6 Calculate the magnetic flux density at the centre of a long solenoid of 2500 turns and length 40 cm, when a current of 0.3 A flows in it. [$\mu_0 = 4\pi \times 10^{-7}\,\text{T}\,\text{m}\,\text{A}^{-1}$]

Answer

$B = \mu_0 n I$ where n = no. of turns/m

$$= \frac{2500}{0.4} = 6250\,\text{m}^{-1}$$

$B = 4\pi \times 10^{-7} \times 6250 \times 0.3 = 23{,}560 \times 10^{-7}\,\text{T}$

Magnetic flux density in *solenoid* = 2.36 mT

Question

7 What current must flow in an infinitely long straight wire to match this flux density, Question 6, 10 cm from the wire?

Answer

$$B = \frac{\mu_0 I}{2\pi r} \ldots I = \frac{2\pi r B}{\mu_0} = \frac{2\pi \times 0.1 \times 2.36 \times 10^{-3}}{4\pi \times 10^{-7}}$$

$$= 0.118 \times 10^4\,\text{A}$$

A current of 1180 amps would need to flow in the wire!

☠ ***Don't try this at home*** . . . or in the lab

Measuring magnetic field strength/flux density, *B*

Hall probe . . . when a conductor carries a current in a magnetic field a pd is built up across the probe . . . called the **Hall voltage, V_H**

:| *The charges carrying the current feel a force across the flow, $F = Bqv$, which builds up the pd*

- V_H can be used to measure the flux density, B

- V_H enables the sign of the charge carriers in the conductor or semi-conductor to be found

- $V_H \sim$ mV for a semi-conductor, so this is what is used in a **Hall probe**

✳ EXPERIMENT

1 Position the probe at right angles to the unknown magnetic field, pass a small current $I \sim 1\,\text{A}$ through it and measure the Hall voltage, V_H, developed across it, with a high-impedance voltmeter

2 Magnetic field strength/flux density B is found from ... $B = k\dfrac{V_H}{I}$

Force between two wires carrying current

Two long strips of aluminium cooking foil can be hung up and used to demonstrate these forces if about 5 A is passed through them, as in the figure below

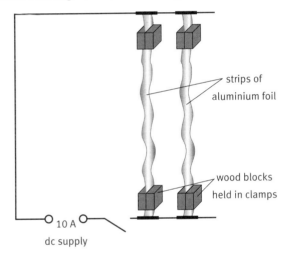

strips of aluminium foil

wood blocks held in clamps

10 A

dc supply

1 Magnetic field/flux method

Currents in **same** direction

- The strips of foil or wires are **attracted** to each other.

  Use the **right-hand grip** rule in Fig. i below to show that the magnetic fields between the wires are in **opposite** directions. They will tend to cancel each other out, making a **neutral point** ✕

  This weak region between the wires will mean the wires are pushed together by the stronger fields outside

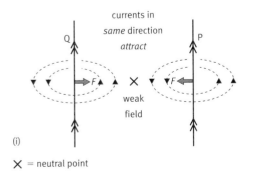

currents in
same direction
attract

weak
field

(i)

✕ = neutral point

Currents in **opposite** directions

- The strips of foil or wires **repel** each other

  This time, the right-hand grip rule in Fig. ii gives the fields in the **same** direction between the wires

  This strong magnetic field pushes the wires apart

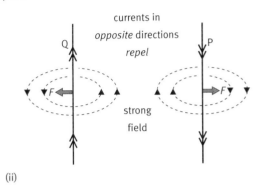

currents in
opposite directions
repel

strong
field

(ii)

2 Fleming's left-hand rule method

Alternatively ... use **Fleming's left-hand rule** to work out the direction of the force/thrust on the conductor in a magnetic field.
In Figs i and ii:

Currents in **same** direction

- Conductor P will be in the field of the current of conductor Q. The R-H grip rule gives this field going back into the paper **at P**

  Fleming's L-H rule on P shows a force/thrust **towards** Q

  Repeating these 2 steps for Q shows that it will move **towards** P

- Currents in the **same** direction **attract** each other

Currents in **opposite** directions

- Start with Q this time ... it is in the field of the current of conductor P. The R-H grip rule gives this field going back into the paper **at Q**

  Fleming's L-H rule on Q shows a force/thrust **away** from P

  Repeating these 2 steps for P shows that it will move **away** from Q

- Currents in **opposite** directions **repel** each other

😐 *Whenever you are drawing magnetic field or flux lines be careful:*

1 Make sure they ***never*** cross each other

2 Draw enough lines, *2–6*, to show the flux pattern fully

3 Field strong — lines close together

Field weak — lines more spread out

4 Around a single wire, as in Figs i and ii, they are concentric circles . . . so make them look like it!

5 If they go behind a wire or conductor, leave a little gap to make this clear, anywhere else they need to be complete loops

6 Examiners are addicted to magnetic field/flux drawing, so it's worth getting it right

Question

8 A solenoid carries a current in the direction shown in the figure below. Add to the diagram the magnetic field that this current produces

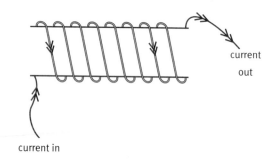

current out

current in

Answer

See dotted lines of flux in the figure

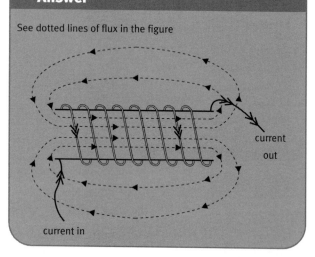

current out

current in

Questions

9 The figure (i) opposite shows two, very long vertical wires that pass through holes in a horizontal sheet of cardboard at P and Q. To start with, there is only a current flowing upwards in wire P

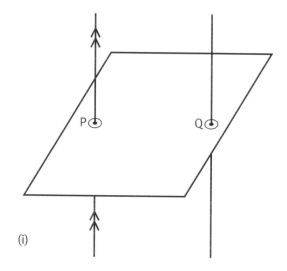

(i)

a Add 5 flux lines to the plan view (ii) to show the magnetic field pattern near P. Include shape, direction and concentration of the lines to represent fully the field strength

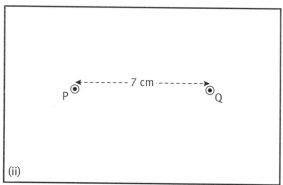

(ii)

P, current up, out of paper

Q, current down, into paper (parts c and d only)

b The current in P is 4.0 A, calculate the magnetic flux density at Q, a distance 7 cm away

[Take $\mu_0 = 4 \times 10^{-7}$ H m^{-1}]

😟 *That makes 3 units for μ_0 . . . T m A^{-1}*
N A^{-2}
and now. . . henrys per metre, H m^{-1}. You can just use $4\pi \times 10^{-7}$ and not worry about units . . . just this once

c A current of 6.0 A is passed in the opposite direction (downwards) through wire Q. Draw an arrow on the diagram to show the resultant direction of the force on Q, using Fleming's rule or by considering the magnetic fields acting on it

d Calculate the force felt on a 2.0 m length of Q.

Answers

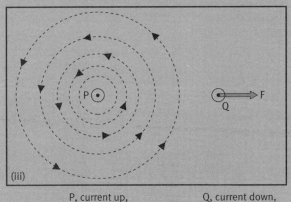

(iii)

P, current up,	Q, current down,
out of paper	into paper
	(parts c and d only)

a The dotted lines on figure (iii)

b $B = \dfrac{\mu_0 I}{2\pi r}$ a distance r from a long straight wire,

carrying a current I.

So ... magnetic flux density $B = \dfrac{4\pi \times 10^{-7} \times 4}{2\pi \times 7 \times 10^{-2}}$

$$= 1.14 \times 10^{-5}\,\text{T}$$

c See shaded arrow on figure (iii)

d $F = BIl = 1.14 \times 10^{-5} \times 6 \times 2 = 1.37 \times 10^{-4}\,\text{N}$

 Sometimes the question's a lot longer than the answers!

 The following work is strictly for potential profs ... check whether your syllabus requires it before attempting it

The ampere

The force between two long wires carrying equal currents allows the ampere to be defined and the value for $\mu_0 = 4\pi \times 10^{-7}\,\text{N A}^{-2}$ to emerge

 You probably won't need this at 'A' level ... but there's no definition quite like it!

The ampere is the current flowing in two infinitely long straight wires 1 metre apart in a vacuum that produces a force of 2×10^{-7} newtons on each metre length of wire

Beat that ... that's physicists for you!

 Question 10 puts the whole section together. It's not impossible if you take it bit by bit ... honest!

Questions

10 Electrons, travelling at right angles to a region of uniform magnetic field of flux density $1.5 \times 10^{-2}\,\text{T}$, have a speed of $2.7 \times 10^8\,\text{m s}^{-1}$ when moving in a circle of diameter 20 cm

a Sketch a diagram to show the direction of the magnetic field that will make the electrons circle clockwise

b Find the mass of an electron if its charge is given by $e = 1.6 \times 10^{-19}\,\text{C}$

Answers

a Use Fleming's left-hand rule on the electrons circling clockwise to find the field direction that will give a thrust towards the centre of the circle

 *Remember ... electrons run **up** your middle finger ... or up into your palm*

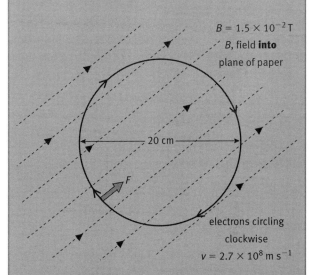

$B = 1.5 \times 10^{-2}\,\text{T}$

B, field **into** plane of paper

20 cm

F

electrons circling clockwise

$v = 2.7 \times 10^8\,\text{m s}^{-1}$

The magnetic field B needs to be **into** the plane of the paper to give thrust F on the electrons towards the centre of the circle

b Step 1 To move in a circle, an electron must have a force towards the centre $= \dfrac{m_e v^2}{r}$ (section B9)

where m_e = mass of the electron we need to find,
r = radius of the circle = 10 cm = 0.1 m
and v = electron speed = $2.7 \times 10^8\,\text{m s}^{-1}$

Step 2 An electron, charge e, moving at right angles to a uniform field feels a force $F = Bev$ (Remember BIl and Bev) This force will provide the centripetal force needed to move the electron in a circle

where B = magnetic field strength = $1.5 \times 10^{-2}\,\text{T}$

Step 3 Therefore, ... $F = \dfrac{m_e v^2}{r} = Bev$

Giving ... $m_e = \dfrac{Ber}{v} = \dfrac{1.5 \times 10^{-2} \times 1.6 \times 10^{-19} \times 0.1}{2.7 \times 10^8}$

$$= 0.89 \times 10^{-30}\,\text{kg} = 8.9 \times 10^{-31}\,\text{kg}$$

Mass of electron is usually given as $9.1 \times 10^{-31}\,\text{kg}$

E26 Electromagnetic induction

Beginner's box

- Know that changing magnetic fields produce, or induce, an emf
- Be familiar with the way a simple dynamo or ac generator works
- Know something about how a transformer works
- Be confident of B-fields as studied in the previous section, E25

About this electromagnetic induction . . .

Without electromagnetic induction it is not exaggerating to say that we would not have the electricity supply that we all rely on at home, in commerce and in business

It may be useful to think of electromagnetic induction as the mirror image or reflection of the force felt by a current in a magnetic field

Before, a current in a magnetic field produced a force ⇒ movement.

- CURRENT + FIELD ⇒ MOVEMENT
- **Fleming's left-hand** rule gave the **direction**

Now, a conductor is forced (moved) through a magnetic field and this **produces an emf and consequently a current**

Or, a magnetic field is forced (moved) through a conductor and this produces an emf and consequently a current

Or, any change in magnetic field, or flux, will **induce an emf**

- MOVEMENT + FIELD ⇒ EMF or CURRENT
- Fleming's **right-hand rule** will give the **direction**

By 1831, Michael Faraday had built the foundations for the production of electricity from a combination of coils and changes in magnetic fields. The following experiments will show you some of the results of his 'electrical revolution'

[Perhaps it followed the Industrial Revolution!?]

How can an emf be induced?

 EXPERIMENT

Figs (i), (ii) and (iii) include the apparatus and lay-out for demonstrating the 3 main ways of inducing emf's and, as a consequence, currents

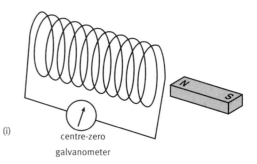

(i) centre-zero galvanometer

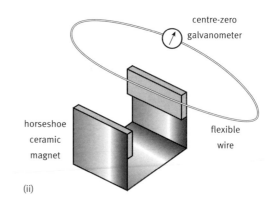

centre-zero galvanometer

horseshoe ceramic magnet

flexible wire

(ii)

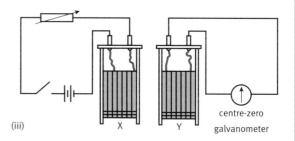

(iii)   X   Y

centre-zero galvanometer

(i)

a Move a bar magnet into, and then out of, a coil connected to a centre-zero galvanometer. See the needle flick first one way, then the other, on the meter

b Now place one end of the coil on some foam [why?!] and drop the magnet into the coil The needle registers a bigger current

c Notice there is only current deflection when the magnet is moving

(ii) Cut down through the magnetic field between the poles of a pair of ceramic magnets with a wire connected to a centre-zero galvanometer See the needle flick one way on the meter

Question

1 Suggest 2 ways of making the needle flick in the opposite direction

Answer

a Pull the wire up through the magnetic field
b Turn the magnets round to reverse the direction of the magnetic flux

(iii) 2 coils (eg, 120 turns) are used. Coil X is connected to a variable current supply to provide a variable magnetic flux. Coil Y is connected to a centre-zero galvanometer

Question

2 Describe 3 ways in which current can be detected by the meter in coil Y

Answer

a Change the current in coil X using the variable resistor
b Switch the current on and off in X
c With current flowing in X, move the 2 coils relative to each other

So the current and emf induced are larger the bigger and faster the change in magnetic flux (the magnetic field lines)

Magnetic flux, ϕ

While studying **magnetic fields** it was convenient to refer to the concentration or density of the magnetic field lines or flux as the **flux density** (B in tesla)

To analyse **changing magnetic flux** it is necessary to know the total number of field lines in the region, eg, down the centre of a coil, of area A ...

Magnetic flux $\quad \phi = BA$
unit of ϕ = weber

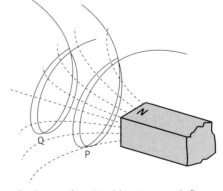

If coil moves from P to Q it cuts magnetic flux,   (i)
so an emf is produced

The figure (i) shows a small coil being moved away from a magnet, from **P** $\Rightarrow$ **Q**

At **P** it has many lines of flux threading through it
At **Q** the field is weaker, so fewer go through it

In moving from **P** to **Q** the coil must have **cut magnetic flux**

An emf will be produced across the coil

If the magnetic flux density is 1 T across an area of 1 m^2 then the flux through it is 1 Wb, or weber

Also, of course ... $B = \dfrac{\phi}{A}$ ... which is why B is called ... flux density ... except that it's an area density, not the usual volume density.

So ... 1 tesla = 1 weber per m^2

But if the coil or solenoid has N turns this flux ϕ passes through or links with each turn to give a ...

Flux linkage $N\phi = BAN$

Question

3 120 turns of fine wire are wound evenly on an insulating tube, length 18 cm, cross-sectional area 8 cm^2. A current of 2.5 A is switched on. What will be the change in flux linkage? [Treat the coil as a long solenoid. $\mu_0 = 4\pi \times 10^{-7} \, \text{T m A}^{-1}$]

Answer

Change in flux linkage is from 0 to $N\phi = BAN$

Step 1 To find B ... for a solenoid, $B = \mu_0 nI$ where n = no. of turns per metre

$$B = 4\pi \times 10^{-7} \times \frac{120}{18 \times 10^{-2}} \times 2.5 = 209 \times 10^{-5} \, \text{T}$$

Step 2 [Watch your units, especially:
Area in m^2 = Area in cm^2 $\times 10^{-4}$]
With current flowing:
Flux linkage = BAN
$= 2.09 \times 10^{-3} \times 8 \times 10^{-4} \times 120$
$= 2000 \times 10^{-3} \times 10^{-4} = 2.0 \times 10^{-4} \, \text{Wb}$

With no current flowing, flux linkage is zero

Change in flux linkage as current is switched on is 2.0×10^{-4} Wb

Laws of electromagnetic (EM) induction

> **1.** Faraday's Law for magnitude of emf
>
> Magnitude of induced emf = rate of **change**
> of flux linkage

Induced emf = $\dfrac{\text{flux cut}}{\text{time taken}} = \dfrac{\text{change in flux linkage}}{\text{time taken}}$

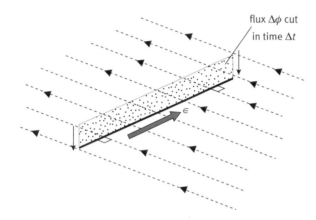

flux $\Delta\phi$ cut in time Δt

In the diagram, a conductor moves steadily through a magnetic field so that it cuts a flux $\Delta\phi$ in a time Δt. This produces an induced emf, $\in$ given by:

$$\in \propto \frac{\Delta\phi}{\Delta t}$$

Units are chosen or defined so that the constant of proportionality is 1:

$$\text{Magnitude of } \in = \frac{\Delta\phi}{\Delta t}$$

If there are N turns of conductor linking with the flux change:

$$\text{Magnitude of } \in = \frac{\text{change in flux linkage}}{\text{time taken}}$$

$$= N\frac{\Delta\phi}{\Delta t}$$

Question

4 [Tricky]

An aircraft with a wing span of 58 m is cruising due west in level flight at 840 km hr^{-1}, over the British Isles where the vertical component of the Earth's magnetic field is 3.8×10^{-5} T. Calculate the induced voltage between the wing-tips

Answer

Step 1 $\in = N\dfrac{\Delta\phi}{\Delta t}$, $N = 1$. Here $\in = \dfrac{\Delta\phi}{\Delta t}$

Step 2 Here ... $\phi = BA$ ... so $\dfrac{\Delta\phi}{\Delta t} = B\dfrac{\Delta A}{\Delta t}$ ①

(since B is a uniform field)

ΔA is the area of flux cut by the wings in time Δt

Travelling at speed v m s^{-1}, wing span l m,

$\dfrac{\Delta A}{\Delta t}$ becomes ... $\dfrac{\Delta A}{\Delta t} = lv$ ... ② sketch it out. ($\Delta t = ls$)

Step 3 Combining these equations ① and ② gives:

$$\in = Blv$$

● This equation holds for any straight conductor moving steadily, at right angles, through a uniform magnetic field

Induced emf across wing-tips $\in = Blv$

$$\in = 3.8 \times 10^{-5} \times 58 \times \frac{840 \times 10^3}{60 \times 60}$$

$$= 514 \times 10^{-3} \text{ V}$$

Induced emf across wing-tips is just over 0.5 volt

> **2.** Lenz's Law for direction of emf
>
> The direction of the induced emf and current always produces effects to oppose the change that causes it

❄ EXPERIMENT

Consider again Expt (i) above and Fig. i where a bar magnet was moved in and out of a coil connected to a centre-zero galvanometer

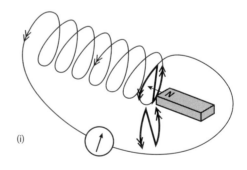

(i)

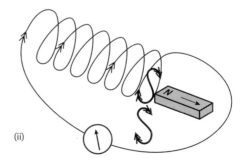

(ii)

Confirm that:

a When a N-Pole is moved into the coil, an emf and current are induced
The current is anticlockwise creating a North Pole at that end of the coil
This induced North Pole repels the motion of the magnet coming towards it, see Fig. i
[It tries to keep the approaching N-Pole of the magnet out, by repulsion]

b When the N-Pole is moved out, a South Pole is induced at that end of the coil. This South Pole attracts the magnet, which is moving away from the coil, see Fig. ii
[It tries to keep the escaping N-Pole in, by attraction]

 *After all, if moving a N-Pole **in** induced a South Pole, it would be attracted faster and faster increasing the induced emf ... great ... but life's not like that!*

- Lenz's Law is needed for EM induction to satisfy the Law of Conservation of Energy

- A negative sign is used to indicate Lenz's law of opposition

A combination of Faraday's and Lenz's Laws can be expressed by:

$$\text{induced emf, } \in = -N\frac{\Delta\phi}{\Delta t}$$

where $\Delta\phi$ = flux change/Wb in time Δt/s and N = no of turns

Eddy currents

 Don't miss this, it's a favourite

 EXPERIMENT

a Borrow a solid copper cylinder and fix a loop of thread to it

b Use a pile of coins of similar diameter to make up a cylinder of the same dimensions. Fix them together with thread, leaving a loop to suspend their cylinder by

c Arrange a *large* horseshoe magnet on the bench with its jaws facing upwards.

d Twist up the suspension thread of the solid cylinder, lower it into the gap between the poles of the magnet ... and let go

e Repeat **d** with the coins cylinder

f Result ... the solid cylinder stops, almost immediately, in the magnetic field ... the coins cylinder goes on twisting and turning as they both would just out in air

The strange result with the cylinders above is described by Lenz's Law!

When the copper cylinder tried to spin in the magnetic field it was cutting magnetic flux. **Lenz's Law** says that the emf induced will **oppose** the change ... so here the currents in the cylinder did just that ... and stopped the spinning

This is known as magnetic braking. The opposing induced currents are called **eddy currents**

The coins cylinder went on turning because the gaps/breaks between the coins introduced electric insulation into the cylinder, so that the swirling eddy currents could not be induced although an emf was induced

- Eddy current braking can be useful, but eddy currents cause heating in cores and energy losses unless they are prevented

- By **laminating** a core they can be reduced. To do this, for instance, the iron core of a transformer is made up of thin layers of iron, each one dipped in insulating varnish and then sealed together (a bit like the cylinder of coins).
Magnetic flux is unaffected by the varnish, only the eddy currents can't flow

Fleming's right-hand rule

 Finger dislocation time again, right hand this time! To help you remember which hand ... try this:

Here, we're ... generating electricity, call this ... gene-***right**-ing electricity*

(Sorry ... they don't get any worse than that!)

This means the magnetic force/motor rule is the other one, the left-hand one.

- The **induced current direction** is given by **Fleming's right-hand rule**

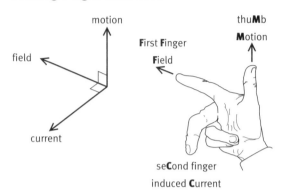

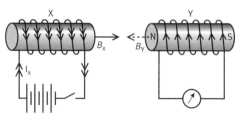

The figure shows the fingers of the right hand, set up as a mirror image of the left-hand rule

If a conductor **moves** in the direction of the **thumb** through a magnetic flux or **field** in the direction of the **first finger**, then a **current** will be induced in the direction of the **second** finger

 Say after me...
First Finger ... Field
thuMb ... Motion
seCond finger ... Current

Refer back to the beginning of Section **E25**, Magnetic B-fields, p. 100, to help you get your fingers in the right positions

Question

5   Look again at Question **4**, p. 110
    Over the British Isles, the Earth's magnetic field is down, towards the North Pole. Use Fleming's right-hand rule to find the direction of the induced emf across the wings of the plane

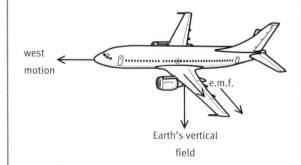

Answer

The sketch shows the plane moving west through the Earth's downward magnetic field. Fleming's R-H rule gives the direction of the induced emf towards us, out of the paper

 Fleming's R-H rule can be used here to find the induced emf direction, because emf goes from +ve to −ve like current

Questions

6   The figure below shows two similar coils on the same axis. Coil X has a dc supply, coil Y is connected to a centre-zero galvanometer

When the switch is closed a magnetic field, B_X, is formed along the axis of X as shown. This induces a current temporarily in Y, which is shown on the meter. This current in Y will have its own magnetic field, B_Y, along its axis

a   Draw an arrow on the diagram in the direction of this field, label it B_Y

b   Use Lenz's Law to explain its direction

c   Why is there only a pulse of current in Y?

Answers

a   See dotted line labelled B_Y, in the figure

 The following answer is expanded for teaching purposes:

Step 2 would be an adequate exam answer

b   Step 1   Arrows have been added to the figure to show the current direction in coil X. The right-hand grip rule on coil X confirms that its field B_X is out of the end towards Y, this must be its magnetic North Pole

    Step 2   Lenz's Law says that the direction of an induced emf always opposes any change of flux. Because the current I_X switching **on** (increasing) produced an increasing field B_X, the emf, and so field, induced in Y, will try to reduce B_X or oppose it. The magnetic field B_Y will, therefore, be in the opposite direction to B_X as shown

    Step 3   This will mean a magnetic North Pole has been induced in Y, with its field out towards X. The direction of the induced current in Y can also be found, by the right-hand grip rule. It has been shown on the figure to complete the teaching

c   emf and current are only induced while there is changing flux. Once the current is established in coil X, there will be no further change in B_X, so no induced emf or current ... unless I_X is switched off or changed in some way

 Tricky terms:
1   field & flux ... either of these can generally be used to refer to regions of magnetic force
2   induced emf & current ... changing magnetic flux results in an induced emf in a conductor (electrons are pushed sideways by the changing field)
If there is a circuit connected to the conductor, this emf will make an induced current flow while the flux is changing

Transformers

Although emf's and currents have been induced in this section, most of them have been brief pulses ... only while a current has been switched on or off etc. (Question **6** was a very simple transformer)

The beauty of a transformer is that it allows an alternating voltage to be changed or transformed in size ... with no moving parts to wear out

- A changing flux is needed for an induced emf. An alternating current (ac) has a current that is continually changing

  If a coil (primary) carried ac, then it would have a continually changing flux in its core

  If this core is linked to a secondary coil, this changing flux would induce an emf in the secondary. This would also be alternating

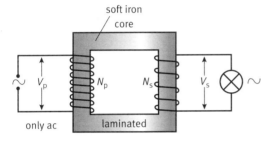

The figure diagrammatically represents 2 coils linked in this way by a soft iron core

Transformer voltage ratio

 EXPERIMENT

Link 2 coils with different numbers of turns, by using a laminated soft iron core, held tightly together with an iron clip

(eg, primary N_p = 120 turns
   secondary N_s = 240 turns)

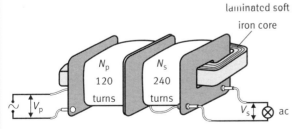

1 Connect an alternating 6 V supply across the primary. Use a multimeter to measure this alternating primary voltage V_p

2 Connect a lamp across the secondary and use a multimeter to measure the alternating secondary voltage V_s

3 N_p = 120 turns, N_s = 240 turns
   V_p = 6 V ... hopefully, $V_s \sim$ 12 V

If possible, repeat these measurements using different numbers of turns, etc, and show that:

$$\frac{V_p}{V_s} = \frac{N_p}{N_s}$$ where V_p = primary emf

V_s and V_p are alternating

V_s = secondary voltage

N_p = no. of primary turns

N_s = no. of secondary turns

- It looks as though we're getting something for nothing here. The input voltage was 6 V and the output voltage near 12 V

Again, life's not like that

The output power won't even be equal to the input power, as no transformer will be 100% efficient

Output power $\lesssim$ Input power

The voltage may have increased, but the current will have decreased

Questions

7 A 1 kW electric iron, which was purchased in the UK to operate on 240 V ac, is to be used in the USA on only 110 V ac

a What would the turns ratio of a transformer need to be, for the iron to be used in the USA?

b Estimate the size of the currents that would flow in the coils. What assumption has been made?

Answers

a The iron needs to be across the secondary coil, N_s turns, at 240 V (V_s) and the primary with N_p turns has the 110 V (V_p) supply across it.

Because ... $\dfrac{V_p}{V_s} = \dfrac{N_p}{N_s} = \dfrac{110}{240} = 0.458$

the secondary must have over twice the number of turns that the primary has ... **a step-up transformer**

b The answer to **a** has assumed a 100% efficient transformer The power of the iron needs to be 1000 W at 240 V.

Secondary current $I_s = \dfrac{P_s}{V_s}$ ... $P = VI$

$$= \frac{1000}{240} = 4.17 \, A$$

Primary current $I_p = \dfrac{P_p}{V_p} = \dfrac{1000}{110} = 9.1 \, A$

Efficiency of a transformer

$$\text{efficiency} = \frac{\text{power output}}{\text{power input}}$$

$$= \frac{\text{power output}}{\text{power input}} \times 100 \text{ as \% age}$$

This will never be 100% because of the following losses:

Transformer losses

- The core must be of soft iron since the flux in it is continually changing. The flux will increase with the current in the primary, reduce as its reduces, and reverse in direction as the current reverses, etc

  If it is a mains supply ac, this reversal and cycle will happen 50 times a second, (frequency of mains ac = 50 Hz)

  All this magnetic activity in the soft iron will cause considerable heating losses. These are known as hysteresis losses. They are reduced by using special alloys, eg, permalloy, for the core

- The core is laminated to reduce eddy current heating

- Thick wires are used for the coils to reduce resistive heating losses

- The most efficient transformers are the largest transformers ... biggest is best

  A large transformer, eg, at an electricity sub-station, will need to be oil cooled

E27 ac Theory

This is a topic based on the behaviour and mathematics of **alternating currents and emf's**

- **What's the use of** alternating currents and emf's?

  An alternating pd is necessary to provide an alternating flux in a transformer.

  Alternating flux is necessary to induce a larger or smaller pd in the secondary coil

  Step-up and step-down transformers are vital for easy, efficient electricity grid transmissions

  The grid carries up to 400 kV
  Heavy industry uses 33 kV
  Our mains supply is 240 V

- When the polarity ($\pm$ or $\mp$) of an emf changes with time it can be called an **alternating emf**. The simplest emf/voltage oscillations vary **sinusoidally**

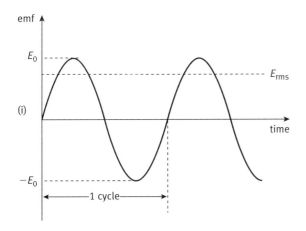

(i)

and are described using

$$E = E_0 \sin \omega t \quad \text{or} \quad V = V_0 \sin \omega t$$

E = emf at time t
E_0 = maximum (peak) emf
ω = angular frequency of supply (rad s^{-1})

- An alternating emf causes electrons to oscillate about a fixed position usually many times a second, instead of a continual drift in one direction. The drift speed of these electrons is zero
  This is called an **alternating current**

  The simplest alternating current oscillations are sinusoidal

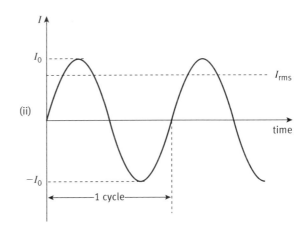

(ii)

and can be described using

$$I = I_0 \sin \omega t$$

I = current at time t
I_0 = maximum (peak) current

- Refer back to circular motion (section B9) and remind yourself
  $$\omega t = 2\pi f t = \theta$$
  Where f is the frequency of the supply

  :) In the UK the mains frequency is *50* Hz

  So $2\pi f$ can be substituted in the equations above for ωt

  $$\text{e.g } I_0 \sin \omega t = I_0 \sin 2\pi f t$$

  :| *Not all alternating currents/emfs are sinusoidal. Figure iii below*

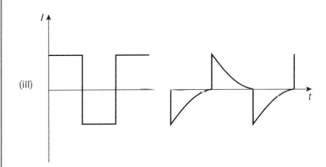

(iii)

rms values

The mains voltage is given as 240 V, yet you know it is not a steady value. It is useful to have an **effective** ac value to compare with dc. This effective value is called the rms (root mean square) value

If a dc supply produces a certain heating effect in a resistor and . . .

an ac supply produces the same heating effect then. . .

current of direct supply = **rms current** of alternating supply

voltage of direct supply = **rms voltage** of alternating supply

$$I_{rms} = \frac{I_0}{\sqrt{2}} \qquad V_{rms} = \frac{V_0}{\sqrt{2}}$$

where I_0 = peak alternating current
V_0 = peak alternating voltage

 Use resistance R as you normally would in questions. There is no such thing as R_{rms}

Question

1 What is the peak voltage of the 240 V mains supply in the UK?

Answer

240 V is the rms value,

$$V_{rms} = \frac{V_0}{\sqrt{2}} \qquad \therefore \quad V_0 = \sqrt{2} \times V_{rms} \simeq 339\,V$$

Power in an ac circuit

It can be shown that the power in an ac circuit is given by. . .

$$P = I_{rms} V_{rms}$$

$$= \frac{I_0}{\sqrt{2}} \times \frac{V_0}{\sqrt{2}}$$

$$= \tfrac{1}{2} I_0 V_0$$

So the **average power** dissipated through a resistor in an ac circuit is half the maximum possible power

$$P = \tfrac{1}{2} I_0 V_0$$

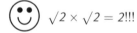 $\sqrt{2} \times \sqrt{2} = 2$!!!

Questions

2 A resistor, 100 Ω, is connected to an alternating, 240 V supply. Calculate

a The average power dissipation in the resistor

b The maximum instantaneous power dissipation in the resistor

Answers

a Average power, $P = I_{rms} V_{rms}$

where, using '$V = IR$' $I_{rms} = \dfrac{V_{rms}}{R}$

$$\therefore \quad P = \frac{V_{rms}^2}{R} = \frac{240^2}{100} = 576\,W$$

b Maximum instantaneous power $= I_0 V_0$
$= \sqrt{2} \times I_{rms} \times \sqrt{2} \times V_{rms}$
$= 2 \times 576 = 1152\,W$

Questions

3 An ac supply is connected to a lightbulb. It radiates with an intensity, X. A 9 V battery is now connected to the bulb and it glows with the same intensity

Assume any heat losses by the bulb are negligible!

a Calculate the rms value of the supply

b Calculate the peak voltage of the supply

Answers

a Using the definition of rms,
$V_{rms} = 9\,V$

b $V_{rms} = \dfrac{V_0}{\sqrt{2}} \qquad \therefore \quad V_0 = \sqrt{2} \times 9 = 12.7\,V$

Questions

4 An alternating supply delivers a sinusoidal voltage

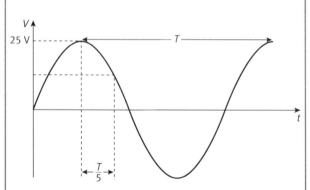

a What is the value of the voltage $\frac{1}{5}$ of a cycle after the peak voltage of 25 V has been reached?

b If the resistance of the circuit is 6 Ω, what will be the current at the voltage calculated above?

Answers

 Remember $\theta = \omega t = 2\pi ft$

a $V = V_0 \sin\theta$

At the peak when $V = V_0$, $\sin\theta = 1$ $\therefore$ $\theta = 90°$

A cycle $= 360°$ so $\frac{1}{5}$ of a cycle $= \frac{360}{5} = 72°$

So $\frac{1}{5}$ of a cycle after the peak is $90 + 72 = 162°$

$\therefore$ $V = V_0 \sin\theta = 25 \sin 162° = 7.7\,V$

 Make sure your calculator is on DEG not RAD

b $I = \dfrac{V}{R} = \dfrac{7.7}{6} = 1.3\,A$

Notice here, rms values have not been asked for, *simply another instantaneous value!*

Question

5 Here is a graph showing the sinusoidal variation of a mains supply, 240 V, 50 Hz

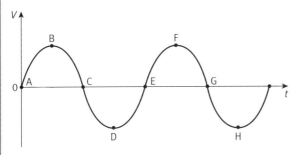

a Eight positions are labelled on the graph. Which represent power dissipation at a maximum and at a minimum?

b What is the time period of one oscillation?

Answers

a Maximum power = B, D, F, H

   Minimum power = A, C, E, G

b $f = 50\,Hz = \dfrac{1}{T}$ $\therefore$ $T = \dfrac{1}{50} = 0.02\,s$

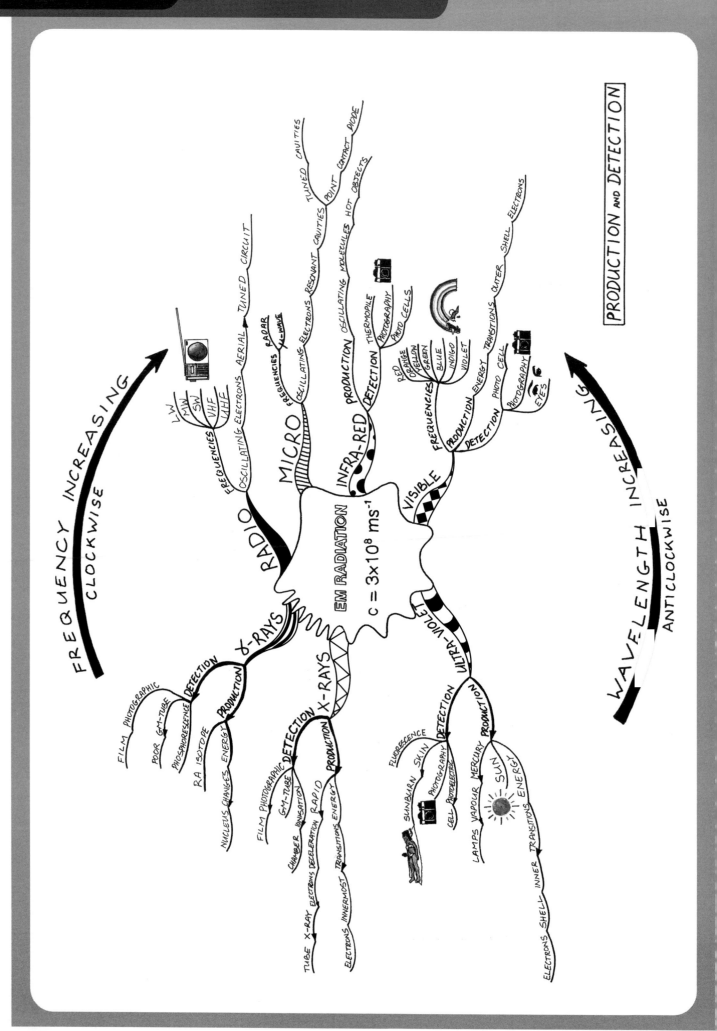

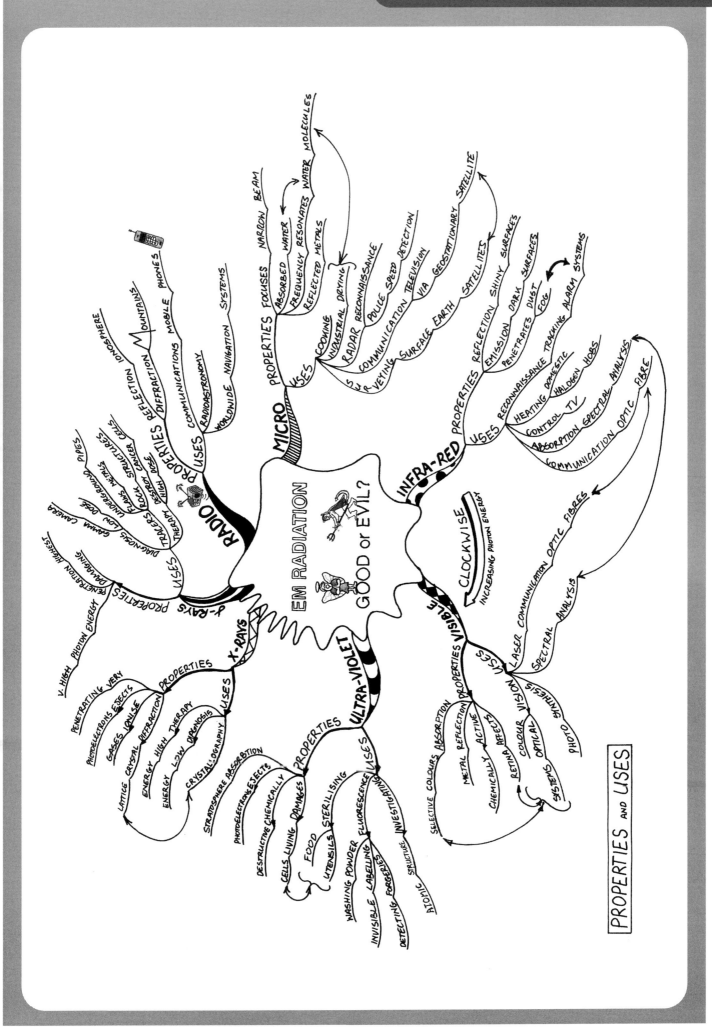

F28 Getting to know waves

Beginner's box

- From your GCSE work you should:
- Know the meaning and units of the following terms: wavelength, frequency, amplitude
- Know that: wave **speed = frequency × wavelength**.

  Remind yourself of the wave patterns produced in a ripple tank showing reflection, refraction, diffusion and interference

Question

1 The frequency of Capital Radio is 95.8 MHz. If the speed of electromagnetic (radio) waves is 3.0×10^8 m s^{-1} what is the wavelength of Capital Radio?

Answer

Using $v = f\lambda \rightarrow \lambda = \dfrac{v}{f} = \dfrac{3.0 \times 10^8}{95.8 \times 10^6} = 0.0313 \times 10^2$

Capital Radio wavelength = 3.13 m

Waves carry or store energy

Progressive/travelling waves carry energy
Standing/stationary waves store energy

Wave types

1 <u>Transverse waves</u>

   Examples:

   waves on the sea and ripples on a pond
   Mexican wave
   radio waves ⎫
   light waves ⎬ all electromagnetic waves
   microwaves ⎭
   guitar strings

Question

2 Can you name 2 others?

   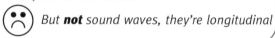 But **not** sound waves, they're longitudinal

- All vibrations are at **right angles** to direction of energy transfer
- Can set up standing waves, as on a guitar string
- Can be polarised

2 <u>Longitudinal waves</u>

   Examples: sound waves
   compression waves, such as those produced by earthquakes

- All vibrations are **along the direction** of transfer of energy
- Can set up standing waves as in a saxophone
- Cannot be polarised

Graphical representation

Both types of wave, transverse and longitudinal, can be shown as:

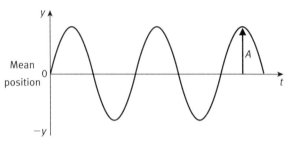

Where y = displacement from mean position

(A2 students will recognise the equation of this curve as $y = A\sin\omega t$, see **F30** Oscillations).

Question

3 How many wavelengths are shown above?

Answer

2.5

Interference

Interference all around

Look around you to see examples of light interference: they are often beautiful

   colours in CD's
   soap bubbles
   oil patches on roads

Question

4 Can you name 2 others?

Questions

5
   a Why are rainbows, prisms and diamonds not included?

   b What causes their spectral colours?

Answers

a Interference is not the cause of their colours
b Refraction at different speeds, of different frequencies or colours, through glass or water

Tuning fork twist

TRY THIS ... don't miss it

Borrow a tuning fork
Sound it/bang it on cork or similar material
Hold it vertically close to one ear
Twist it quite slowly through one complete turn turn/360°,
listening carefully
Try this a few times

Question

6 What do you notice about the level/intensity of sound?

Answer

It rises and falls with 4 quiet patches in one turn

Think about this while revising the following:

1 **Destructive interference** in quiet regions/patches:

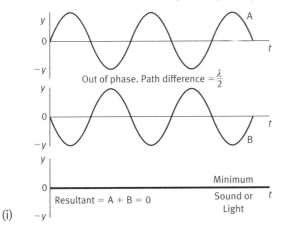

(i)

- A and B must be of the same wavelength, frequency and amplitude for complete destruction

2 **Constructive interference** in loud regions/patches:

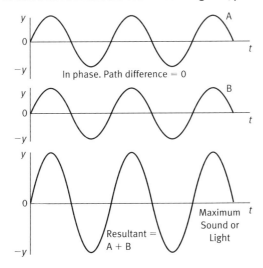

(ii)

If you want to know about those tuning forks

C represents a compression being produced
R represents a decompression/rarefaction being produced
Points along the diagonals, dotted, receive compressions and rarefactions at the same time so that the two sound waves destroy each other. An example of destructive interference that you hear (or not!)
Fig. i on the left represents it graphically

Path difference

1 Destructive interference (see Fig. i)

Path difference $= \dfrac{\lambda}{2} = \dfrac{\text{wavelength}}{2}$

A and B are out of phase with each other
To change wave B to be in phase with wave A it would have to be moved half a wavelength to the left or right

It would also be in phase if it was moved $\dfrac{3\lambda}{2}, \dfrac{5\lambda}{2}$ etc, so:

- Destructive interference when:

Path difference $= \dfrac{\lambda}{2}, \dfrac{3\lambda}{2}, \dfrac{5\lambda}{2}$ etc

2 Constructive interference (see Fig. ii)

Path difference $= 0$

A and B are in phase (in time) with each other. To change wave B so that it would still be in phase with wave A, it could be moved one whole wavelength to the left or right or $2\lambda, 3\lambda$, etc, so:

- Constructive interference when:

Path difference $= 0, \lambda, 2\lambda$, etc

To sum up:

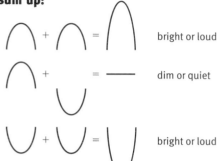

bright or loud

dim or quiet

bright or loud

Superposition of waves

Destructive and constructive interference has been the result of the superimposing of the waves A and B, or superposition

Throughout: the displacements, *y*, at any instant have been vector summed to give the resultant displacement

Any two waves meeting will combine in this way to give the resultant

Questions

7 Two whistles, P and Q, are blown together:
a which note is louder, P or Q?
b which note is higher, P or Q?
c check that R is the result of super-imposing P and Q

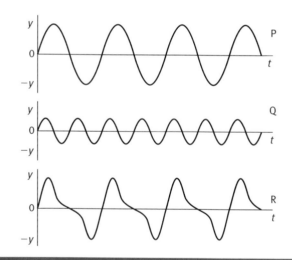

Answers

a P ... bigger amplitude
b Q ... smaller wavelength, bigger frequency
c Rule many lines vertically down through the P, Q and R graphs at small time intervals. Add the *y*-values for P and Q and see that they vector sum to the *y*-value of R, at each time chosen

 Vector sum means ... take into account whether the y-value is +ve or −ve ... and then add

Know it all box

by now you should know:	sure	shaky	unsure
the difference between longitudinal and transverse waves			
the meaning of constructive and destructive interference			
the graphical representation of waves			
superposition of waves			
result of in phase and out of phase waves			
the effect of path difference			

If you're unsure, go back to your notes and textbooks, then try again later

If you're shaky on some, come back to these in a day or two

If you're sure — then we're doing all right!

Study and Revise AS and A2 Level Physics

F29 Diffraction and polarisation

Beginner's box

- Make sure you are confident of the previous chapter F27 Getting to know waves
- Know the meaning of the word

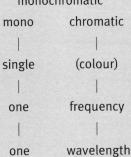

monochromatic

mono   chromatic

single   (colour)

one   frequency

one   wavelength

 Colour is bracketed above because it would not be accepted as an exam answer

So monochromatic light is light of only one wavelength

- Light wavelengths are often measured in **nm**

nm
/ | \
nano | metre

10^{-9} metre

nano/nine easy to remember

Laser red light has a wavelength $\approx 600\,\text{nm}$

- A wavefront is a surface on which all points along are in phase or in step with each other

- A photon can be thought of as a burst or pulse of waves

Single slit diffraction

water in harbour
ripple tank } All of these show spreading of a wavefront when it is restricted by an obstacle or slit
laser light
microwaves

 Take usual precautions when teacher uses laser

1 A **laser** may show the effect most clearly

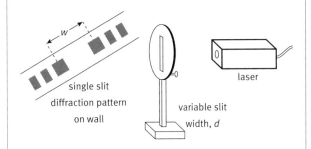

single slit diffraction pattern on wall

variable slit width, d

laser

The width of the central diffraction maximum is marked on the diagrams as w

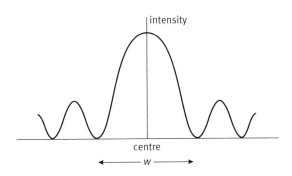

intensity

centre

$\longleftarrow w \longrightarrow$

Using a slit of variable width, d, shows that:

    as d increases, w decreases
    as d decreases, w increases

2 Set up a **ripple tank** with a single slit in front of the straight/plane ripples produced by a vibrating motor and straight bar, and just touching the water

Change the frequency of the motor using a variable resistor in series with it to change the wavelength, λ, of the ripples to show that:

    as λ increases, w increases
    as λ decreases, w decreases

For maximum diffraction spread, you need:
narrrow slit
large wavelength

Questions

1

a Which would be diffracted most? Red light or blue light?

b Which would be diffracted most? Visible light or microwaves?

Answers

a Red light is diffracted most
b Microwaves are diffracted more than visible

 About those <u>dark</u> bands in the single slit laser diffraction pattern:
(only if you're interested)
OK, it's common sense that waves spread out on the far side of an obstacle
But why <u>dark</u> bands?

Remember light wavelengths are <u>very</u> small ($\sim 600\,\text{nm}$)
The slit you are using is $\sim 0.1\,\text{mm}$ wide

- To find the number of wavelengths across the slit width, N:

$$N \sim \frac{0.1\,\text{mm}}{600\,\text{nm}}$$

$$= \frac{10^{-1} \times 10^{-3}}{600 \times 10^{-9}} = \frac{10^{-4}}{6 \times 10^{-7}}$$

$$\sim \frac{10^3}{6} > 150$$

So the slit is *very* wide cf. the wavelength ($> 150\lambda$)

- The waves passing straight through will be in phase to give the central maximum

- As the angle out from the centre increases light through different parts of the slit will travel different path lengths to reach the screen

    When such path differences $= \dfrac{\lambda}{2}$ we know that destructive interference occurs → darkness in the pattern

Conditions for interference

For a steady, clear interference pattern to be observed the 2 interfering beams/waves must have

1 same wavelength

2 same amplitude
if the destruction is to be complete and give real darkness

3 coherence

Coherent sources are those with synchronised phase changes between them

Teachers and textbooks will all tell you that for clear patterns of interference to occur then the interfering beams must be 'coherent'

Literally, this means they must understand each other, or stick together

In practice this means they must change in time with each other

- *The rise and fall of one wave exactly match the rise and fall of the other*

Laser light is highly coherent as the atoms are stimulated to produce photons in phase, which results in coherent bursts of waves lasting about a second (cf. 10 ns for ordinary light sources)

But even 2 lasers will not be coherent with each other

- *One original light source must be split into the two beams that are to interfere, if a steady pattern is to result*

This can be done by using 2 slits or reflections from the 2 surfaces of a soap bubble or oil film on the road, etc

- *The path difference between 2 interfering wavelets must not be greater than about 30 cm or they will no longer be coherent and will not give a clear interference pattern*

Questions

2 2 whistles, frequency 2 kHz, are blown 2 m apart, at the same time
As you walk across a line 10 m away you hear the note rise and fall

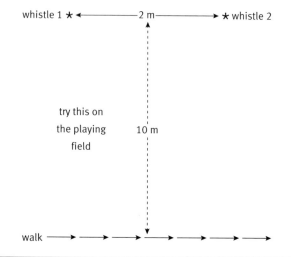

a Why can you hear this interference pattern from separate whistles, but not from separate light sources?

b Draw in a path you would have to follow to hear steady, unfluctuating sound

Answers

a Because the whistles can produce continuous pulses of sound waves that last much longer than light pulses

b - - - - - - - - - a symmetrical path between two sets of waves

Two-slit interference

- This example of the 2 whistles was similar to 2-slit interference. The combined or superimposed signal consisted of a note rising and falling in intensity, heard as you walked across $\longrightarrow$ $\longrightarrow$

- When a vibrating bar causes 2 dippers to make waves in a ripple tank:

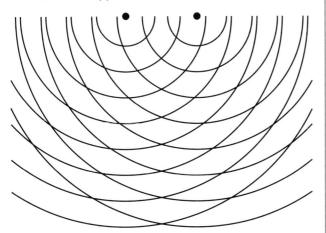

The curved lines represent crests, with gaps for troughs in between

Constructive interference

- Along the central symmetrical line the crests coincide with crests (and troughs with troughs). The waves from the 2 sources are in phase, constructive interference occurs and the resultant ripple is strong
  The path length from each dipper/source is the same ...... no path difference

- Sketch in 2 further directions, one on each side of the central line where crests coincide
  Along each of these the ripple/wave from one dipper has travelled just one wavelength further than from the other dipper

Wavelength, λ, is the path difference for constructive interference (or 2λ, 3λ etc)

Again, strong ripples in these directions

(See **F28** Constructive interference)

Destructive interference

- Between these strong ripple directions regions of quiet water can be seen
  Here destructive interference is occurring
  Yes, crests from one dipper are coinciding or meeting with troughs from the other and destroying each other

Question

3 What is the path difference between ripples or waves from the 2 dippers for destructive interference?

Answer

$\dfrac{\lambda}{2}, \dfrac{3\lambda}{2}, \dfrac{5\lambda}{2}$ = **Path difference for destructive interference**

 EXPERIMENT

 *Do make sure you see this interference pattern clearly for yourself*

If you stand the ripple tank on the bench, with the 12 V bulb shining up under it, you will see clear patterns on the ceiling

Use only 1 cm of water and have the dippers just touching the water

Have the motor vibrating as slowly as possible (use a rheostat/variable resistor in series)

Once you have seen those fingers of ripples and quiet patches of water fanning out and really grasped the reasons given above, you can apply it to your work with:

    microwaves
    laser light

and other interference situations.

Spacing of interference fringes

While working with the ripple tank, check out the following:

    As you reduce the wavelength, λ, of the ripples, the interference pattern closes up, like closing the fingers of a hand

    Small wavelengths, λ, smaller fringe spacing, x

$$x \propto \lambda$$

    The further away from the dippers, D, the larger the fringe spacing x

Bigger screen distances, D, larger fringe spacing, x

$$x \propto D$$

Move the dippers further apart on the bar, s, again the interference pattern closes up.
Larger source spacings, s, smaller fringe spacing, x

$$x \propto \frac{1}{s}$$

Equation for fringe spacing, x

$$x = \frac{\lambda D}{s}$$

Remember that this formula is true only when $D \gg \lambda$ and $D \gg s$

So, for the very small wavelengths of light, tiny slit separations are needed if any fringes are to be visible to the naked eye ($s < 1\,\text{mm}$)

Measurement of wavelength, λ

2-slit interference can be used to measure the wavelength of the source because

$$\lambda = \frac{xs}{D}$$ [excess over big D!]

Question

4 For laser red light, $\lambda \approx 600\,\text{nm}$
If the slit-to-screen distance $D = 3.4\,\text{m}$, and the 2-slit-separation $s = 1\,\text{mm}$, what would be the fringe separation, x?

Answer

Using $x = \dfrac{\lambda D}{s} = \dfrac{600 \times 10^{-9} \times 3.4}{10^{-3}} = 600 \times 10^{-4} \times 3.4$

$x = 20.4 \times 10^{-4}\,\text{m} = 2.04\,\text{mm}$

 EXPERIMENT WITH A LASER

To find λ: x, s and D must all be measured

Using a laser, 2 slits and screen: (see expt. 1, p. 123)
For greater accuracy measure the distance across 10 bright fringes and divide by 10 to find x
s will often be given for a pair of slits, or use a travelling microscope
D is very large so can be measured with a tape or metre rule

Conditions for clear interference fringes

- Coherent sources (from one original source)

- Region where the waves overlap

- Small path length differences $\sim$ a few wavelengths

- Beams of same wavelength

- Similar intensities of the interfering beams so that their similar amplitudes will cancel to near zero at destructive interference

Question

5 A micrometer eyepiece is used to examine the interference fringes produced by 2 slits, 0.7 mm apart, lit by a sodium light

The eyepiece is 90 cm from the slits and 15 bright fringes are counted in 11.36 mm.

What is the wavelength of the sodium (Na) light?

Answer

Step 1

$$\lambda = \frac{xs}{D} \text{ and } x = \frac{11.36 \times 10^{-3}}{15}$$

Step 2

$$\lambda = \frac{11.36 \times 10^{-3} \times 0.7 \times 10^{-3}}{15 \times 0.9}$$

$$= 5.89 \times 10^{-1} \times 10^{-6} = 589 \times 10^{-9}\,\text{m}$$

Wavelength of sodium light $= 589\,\text{nm}$

Questions

6

dark   bright

(a) (b) (c) (d) (e)

The diagram above shows the 2-slit interference pattern made by monochromatic light falling on slits 0.6 mm apart. The screen showing the pattern was 2.0 m from the slits

a Use the diagram (magnified 3 times) to find the actual fringe spacing

b What was the wavelength of the light?

c If (c) is the centre of the interference pattern, which of the fringes (a)–(e) are where the light from one slit has travelled one wavelength further than the other?

Answers

a In the figure:

8 fringes in 5.5 cm, so 1 fringe in $\dfrac{5.5}{8}$ cm $= 0.69$ cm

$\times 3$ magnification means $x = \dfrac{0.69}{3}$ cm $= 0.23$ cm

Actual fringe spacing $= 2.3$ mm

b $\lambda = \dfrac{xs}{D} = \dfrac{2.3 \times 10^{-3} \times 0.6 \times 10^{-3}}{2} = 6.9 \times 10^{-6}$ m $= 690$ nm

c (b) and (d)

Standing waves ... interference by reflection

Playtime

With a friend, stretch a long 'slinky' spring along the floor

Send transverse waves (wave types p. 120) down the spring from one end, while the other end is held steady, to act as a reflector

Increase the frequency of the vibrations until the whole spring becomes *alive* with the large amplitude waves standing on it, as shown below:

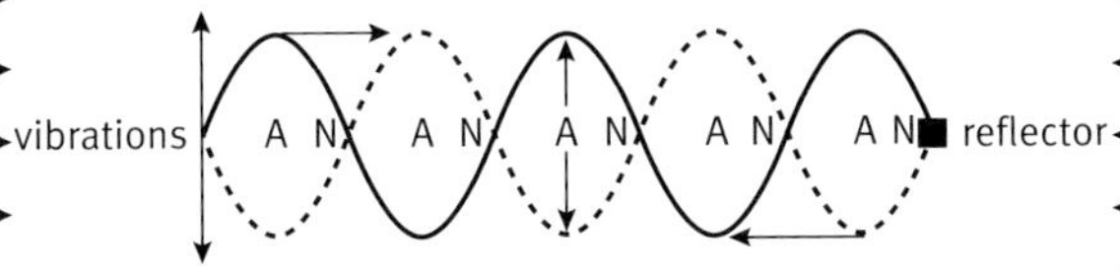

The solid wave in the figure, travelling →, is interfering/combining with the dotted wave reflected back ← in the opposite direction

Questions

7 In the figure above

a What do **N** and **A** stand for?

b How many wavelengths are shown?

c What is the distance, in λ's, between **N**'s and between an **A** and an adjacent **N**?

Answers

a N = Node (no displacement) and antinode = A

b $2\frac{1}{2}$

c $\dfrac{\lambda}{2}$ between N's and $\dfrac{\lambda}{4}$ between A and N

• **These are the conditions for standing waves to occur**

The 2 waves must be of equal wavelength and amplitude, and travelling in opposite directions on the system

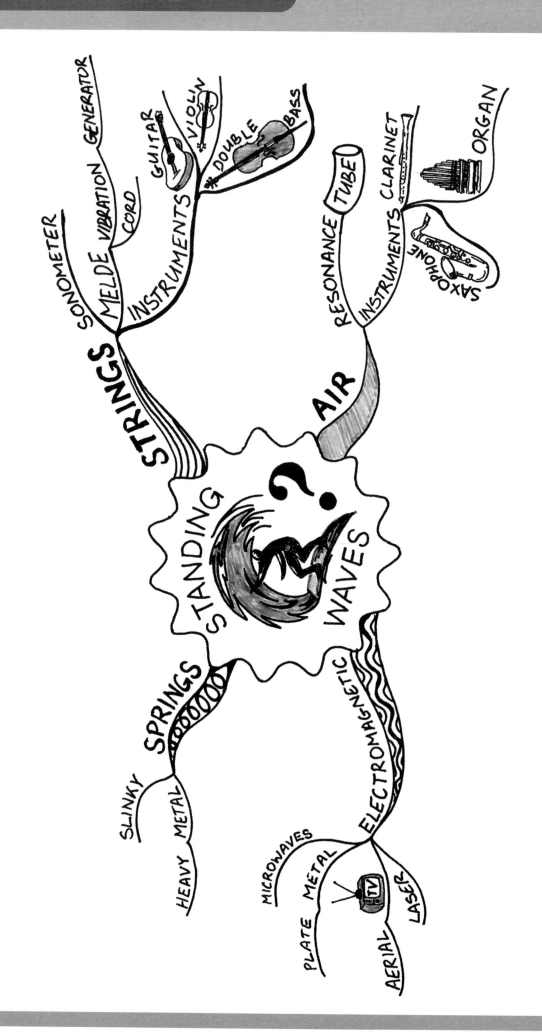

Resonance

The slinky, on p. 127, could be said to be **resonating**

It is obviously storing a lot of energy, often a useful property of resonance. It occurs when:

frequency of vibrator = natural frequency of the system

The vibrator is in time/phase with the oscillating system

It reinforces the system's natural oscillations

This causes a build-up of amplitude and much energy is stored

Examples of resonance

a In **microwave cookers** the frequency of microwaves is chosen to match the frequency of the water molecules in food, causing them to resonate and gain KE. The temperature of any food containing water is raised very quickly and efficiently.

b In **ac circuits** a pair of am inductors and a capacitor can be selected to resonate to a certain frequency and so tune to a particular station, eg, 95.8 MHz

Question

8 Sketch a graph showing the change in amplitude of such a signal, b) above, as the tuning signal frequency is increased through it

Answer

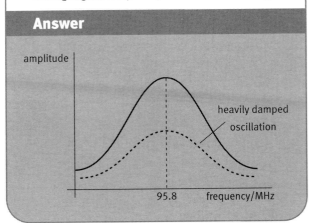

Questions

9 6 pendulums are hung from a single string. Pendulum **P** is the heavier driving bob and is displaced (out of the paper) by a few cm and allowed to swing at right angles to the plane of the paper

Ask to see Barton's pendulum oscillating in the lab.

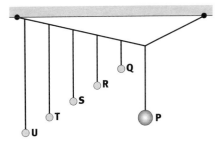

a Which pendulum eventually swings with the greatest amplitude? Explain your answer

b Describe and explain the motion of the other bobs

Answers

a Pendulum **S** has the largest amplitude. It is nearly the same length as the driver, **P**, and so its natural frequency is the same as the forcing frequency and it resonates with **P**. The oscillations of **S** lag behind those of **P** by $\frac{\pi}{2}$ rad

b **T** and **U** both vibrate, but with a smaller amplitude than **P** as they are longer, and out of phase with **P**
R and **Q** also vibrate at a smaller amplitude than **P** because they are shorter. They oscillate almost in phase with **P**

Playtime

Have a go on the swings on the way home. Push a friend with the right frequency to cause resonance . . . *no accidents please!*

Question

10 When can resonance be a nuisance and how can it be avoided?
Think of sound systems, cars, bridges, spinning drum vibrating in a washing machine, etc

Polarisation

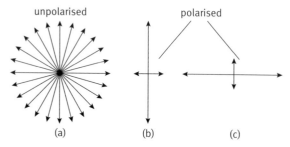

unpolarised   polarised

(a)   (b)   (c)

Transverse waves travelling out of (or into) the paper

Most light we receive is unpolarised

(a) This represents light approaching us head-on and contains all directions of vibration (of the E-field) like the spokes of a bicycle wheel, or the London Eye (the Millennium wheel)

(b) and (c) represent polarised or directional light or radiation where most of the directions in **(a)** have been absorbed or removed in some other way

Sound cannot be polarised

Question

11 Why can't sound be polarised?

Answer

Sound consists only of vibrations along its direction of energy transfer, called longitudinal waves

Only transverse waves, with many directions of vibration (see **(a)** above), can have some absorbed, to leave mainly one direction, as in **(b)** and **(c)**

In an exam, Question **11** might read:

a Can longitudinal waves be polarised? or

b How can you differentiate between longitudinal and transverse waves?

So why do we use polaroid sunglasses?

Polaroid is a material that contains aligned minute crystals that absorb all but one direction of vibration of light, ie, they polarise it

When reflection occurs from the surface of the sea, snow, or wet roads only the light vibrations parallel to the surface are reflected (like a stone skimming off water?)

This reflected light is mainly horizontally polarised, most of the surfaces are horizontal. The polaroid in the sunglasses is arranged to absorb these horizontal vibrations that cause the glare and allow the rest of the light through

- **Result:** Using polaroid sunglasses we can see in bright sunlight, without the nuisance of glare

To check if light or another waveform (eg, microwaves) is polarised, the clue is to rotate the analyser through 180° in the path of the beam. If the **intensity** received **changes,** this confirms **polarisation**

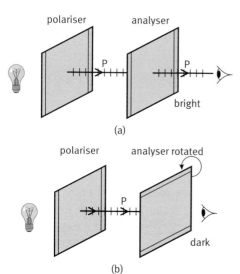

polariser   analyser

P   P

bright

(a)

polariser   analyser rotated

P

dark

(b)

P = polarised light

‖ = direction of vibration not absorbed

Photoelasticity

 EXPERIMENT

Don't miss this (even if you have to buy a new ruler afterwards)

With the polaroids 'crossed' and lit as in (b) above:

Hold a polythene or perspex ruler, or set-square between crossed polaroids and bend or stress the ruler, etc

Patterns, something like soap bubble colours, will appear most concentrated where the stress is greatest

They form a contour map of the stress in the object and can help in analysing this stress

Such a model of, for example, a cranehook, can be redesigned to reduce the stress or to show where extra strength is needed

This strange, beautiful and useful phenomenon is known as **photoelastic stress analysis**

[It happens because the material, when under stress, responds in different ways to differently polarised light of different colours ... it uses interference]

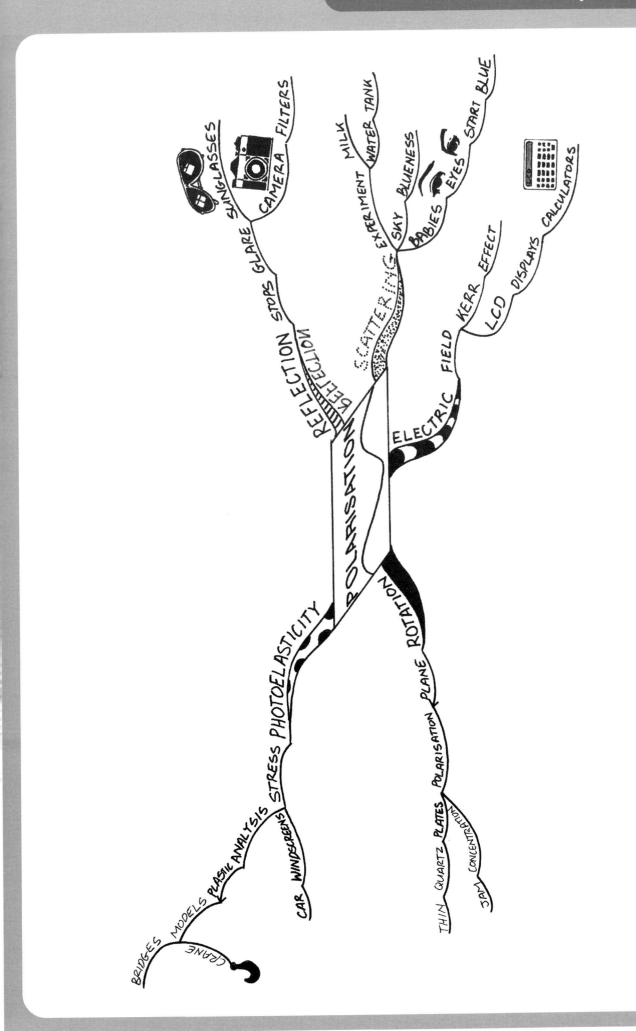

F30 Oscillations

Beginner's box

* Meaning of angular measure in radians, rad
  A turn through an angle of

  360° is called 2π rad

  180° is called 1π rad

Question

1 What is $\dfrac{\pi}{2}$ rad equivalent to in degrees?

Answer

90°

* $\cos 0° = 1$ $\sin 0° = 0$
* $\cos 90° = 0$ $\sin 90° = 1$
* **Hooke's Law** for an **elastic** spring, rope, wire, etc

$$F = kx$$

where F is the restoring force
k is the elastic or force constant
x is the extension or displacement from the mean position

Simple harmonic motion (SHM)

simple harmonic oscillations	other oscillations
swing, with gravity only	swing being pushed
trolley between 2 springs	springy pendulum and magnets
liquid swinging in U-tube	pogo stick
alternating current	rectified ac
bouncing spring	bouncing ball
marble in watch glass	skateboard on curved ramp
bungee jumping	yoyo

SHM is the result of a restoring force, F, that is proportional to the displacement.

$$F = -kx$$

x = displacement of body from mean or rest position
k = positive constant
(eg, spring constant, units $N\,m^{-1}$)

 The minus sign is there because F is measured towards the rest position, whereas x is measured away from it

Forces acting during bouncing spring

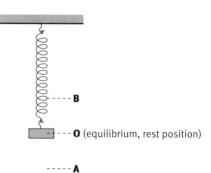

The load is pulled down to position **A** and then released

Questions

2 For the bouncing spring above:
a Describe the forces acting during one complete oscillation, (ie, until it reaches **A** again, ready to rise up again)

b Sketch a graph to show the velocity of the load as it changes with time during this oscillation (show upward motion as positive velocity)

Answers

a **A–O** elastic restoring force (ERF) pulls it back towards **O**
At **O** ERF = 0, zero. But because of inertia, it overshoots
O–B, ERF acts towards **O**, slowing it down to stop
At **B**, load stops, then moves back down, under ERF
At **O**, ERF = 0 as above,
O–A as **O–B**

 Remember, gravity is also acting throughout, slowing down motion upwards and accelerating motion downwards

b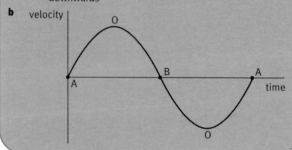

Question

3 Why are the '**other oscillations**' in the table **not** simple harmonic?

Answer

Because the restoring force is proportional to the displacement

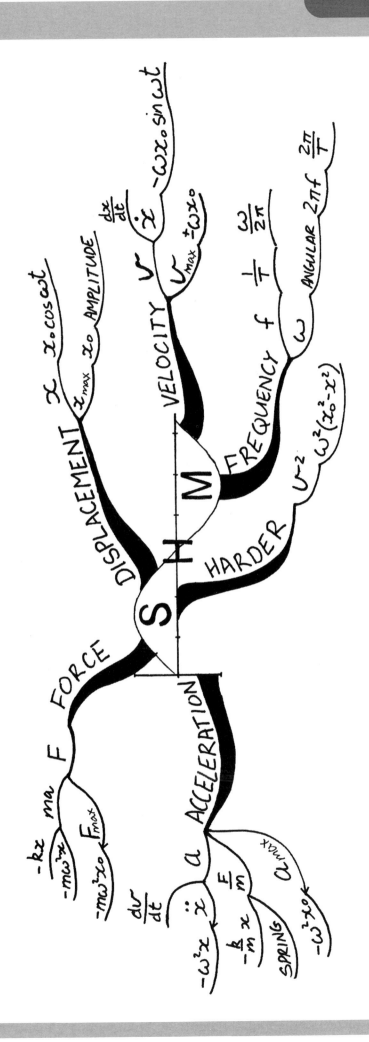

Simple harmonic motion (SHM)

SHM is often defined in terms of the angular frequency, ω, of the motion, so that the equation

$$F = -kx \text{ becomes}$$

$$F = -m\omega^2 x$$

where m = mass of the body

Also Newton's Second Law (N2L) tells us that

$$F = ma$$

$$\therefore \quad ma = -m\omega^2 x$$

So SHM will occur when the acceleration, a, of the body at a displacement, x, is given by:

$$a = -\omega^2 x$$

Simple harmonic motion is defined by:

$$a = -\omega^2 x$$

The acceleration of a body which is directed towards a fixed point, and is proportional to its displacement from it, will result in that body moving with SHM

SHM variation of:

displacement x with time

velocity $v = \dfrac{dx}{dt} = \dot{x}$ with time

acceleration $a = \dfrac{dv}{dt} = \ddot{x}$ with time

Imagine a pendulum starting to swing from its maximum displacement (or amplitude) position

When $t = 0$, $x = x_0$ and x_0 = amplitude

a   Displacement, $x = x_0 \cos \omega t$ [given] **(a)**

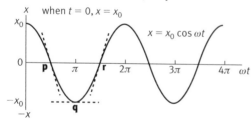

a) displacement curve

b   Velocity, $v = \dfrac{dx}{dt}$

or, the slope of the displacement curve

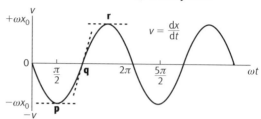

b) velocity curve

Velocity, $v = -\omega x_0 \sin \omega t$ **(b)**

Check the **slope** of the x curve at **p**, **q**, and **r**. See that this is what the v curve shows:

At **p**   maximum negative velocity down

At **q**   zero,

At **r**   maximum positive velocity moving up

c   Acceleration, $v = \dfrac{dx}{dt}$,

or the slope of the velocity curve

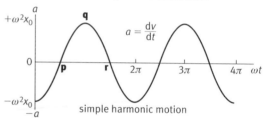

c) acceleration curve

simple harmonic motion

Acceleration, $a = -\omega^2 x_0 \cos \omega t$ **(c)**

Again, check **p**, **q**, and **r** from the v curve **slopes**

p   Zero acceleration

q   maximum positive acceleration

r   zero acceleration

Question

4   Can you see where the equation $a = -\omega^2 x$ came from?

Answer

Combine equations **(a)** and **(c)**
Substitute **(a)** $x = x_0 \cos \omega t$ into
(c) $a = -\omega^2 x_0 \cos \omega t$, then $a = -\omega^2 x$

displacement	velocity	acceleration
$x = x_0 \cos \omega t$	$v = -\omega x_0 \sin \omega t$	$a = -\omega^2 x_0 \cos \omega t$
	$v = \pm \omega \sqrt{x_0^2 - x^2}$	$a = -\omega^2 x$
$x_{max} = x_0$	$v_{max} = \pm \omega x_0$	$a_{max} = -\omega^2 x_0$

Also $\omega = 2\pi f$ and $F = ma$

Period and frequency of SHM

- **Period**, T = time for 1 complete oscillation in seconds, s

- **Frequency**, f = number of oscillations in 1 s in hertz, Hz

and $T = \dfrac{1}{f}$ or $f = \dfrac{1}{T}$

- **Angular frequency**, $\omega = \dfrac{2\pi}{T}$ rad s^{-1} = $2\pi f$

$T = \dfrac{1}{f}$ and $T = \dfrac{2\pi}{\omega}$

(See examples using radians in Section A1)

period	frequency	angular frequency
T	f	ω
seconds, s	hertz, Hz	rad/sec
$\dfrac{1}{f}$	$\dfrac{1}{T}$	$\dfrac{2\pi}{T}$
$\dfrac{2\pi}{\omega}$	$\dfrac{\omega}{2\pi}$	$2\pi f$

 This next part could seriously damage your health. If you're not a mathematician … skip it

Velocity

From graph **b)** v varies sinusoidally. The maximum value for sine is 1 so:

$$v_{max} = \pm\omega x_0 \text{ as shown from (b)}$$

$$= \pm 2\pi f x_0$$

In general $v^2 = \omega^2(x_0^2 - x^2)$ [given]

so $v = \pm\omega\sqrt{x_0^2 - x^2}$

$$= \pm 2\pi f \sqrt{x_0^2 - x^2}$$

 After all that, let's see what these equations can find out for us

Question

5 Some ripples on water travel at 0.15 m s^{-1}, have a wavelength of 30 mm and an amplitude of 10 mm. What is the maximum velocity of a point on the water surface?

Answer

$v = 0.15$ m s^{-1}, $\lambda = 30$ mm, $x_0 = 10$ mm

Step 1 Use $v = f\lambda$ to find the frequency of the ripples

$$f = \frac{v}{\lambda} = \frac{0.15}{30 \times 10^{-3}} = \frac{15 \times 10^{-2}}{30 \times 10^{-3}} = 0.5 \times 10 = 5.0 \text{ Hz}$$

Step 2 Use $v_{max} = \pm 2\pi f x_0$ to find the maximum velocity of the duck

$$v_{max} = \pm 2\pi \times 5 \times 10 \times 10^{-3}$$
$$= \pm\pi \times 10^{-1}$$
$$= \pm 0.31 \text{ m s}^{-1} \text{ or } 30 \text{ cm s}^{-1}$$

Maximum velocity = 31 cm s^{-1}

Questions

6 A Malteser rolls in a smooth bowl with SHM of amplitude 30 mm. Its mass is 10 g and the maximum force acting on it is 0.05 N
Find

a its maximum velocity

b its period of oscillation

 The clue to the SHM questions is often to find ω, and then use it in the other equations (table on p. 134) to find what you need

Answers

$m = 10$ g, $x_0 = 30$ mm, $F_{max} = 0.05$ N

a Here you are given a force and a mass so $F = ma$ will give the maximum acceleration

Step 1 $a_{max} = \dfrac{F_{max}}{m} = \dfrac{0.05}{10 \times 10^{-3}} = \dfrac{5 \times 10^{-2}}{10 \times 10^{-3}} = 0.5 \times 10$

$= 5.0$ m s^{-2}

The acceleration is maximum, when the displacement is maximum, i.e. $x = x_0$ in magnitude

Step 2 For SHM $a = -\omega^2 x$, $a_{max} = -\omega^2 x_0$

Ignoring the $-$ve sign to find the magnitude of ω

$$\omega^2 = \frac{a_{max}}{x_0} = \frac{5}{30 \times 10^{-3}} = \frac{500}{3} = 167$$

$$\omega = 13 \text{ rad s}^{-1}$$

Step 3 Use $v_{max} = \pm\omega x_0$ to find maximum velocity of the Malteser, $v_{max} = \pm 13 \times 30 \times 10^{-3}$
$$= \pm 0.39 \text{ m s}^{-1} = 39 \text{ cm s}^{-1}$$

b For the period of oscillation, $T = \dfrac{2\pi}{\omega}$

$$T = \frac{2\pi}{12.9} = 0.49 \text{ s}$$

Alternatively, $\omega = 2\pi f$, so you can work through, all in terms of $2\pi f$ if you prefer. ω is used mainly to simplify the equations

Bouncing spring a.k.a. Bungee jumping!

When Hooke's Law is obeyed, $F = -kx$ and the motion is simple harmonic

So $F = -m\omega^2 x$ and $-kx = -m\omega^2 x$

The period, T, of a mass-spring system is given as

$$T = 2\pi\sqrt{\frac{m}{k}}$$

where k is the spring constant

 EXPERIMENT

To find the effect of a change in m and k on T

Choose 3 springs as near alike as possible.

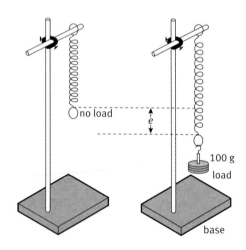

Check Hooke's Law holds:

a Load each spring in turn with increasing 100 g masses and measure the **extension** for each load, e

Take each new load off and check that the spring has returned to its original position and length (not overstretched)

Plot load against extension

If this is a straight line through the origin then Hooke's Law,

$$F = -kx, \text{ holds for that spring}$$

Changing mass, m:

b With **one** spring as above, again increase the load in 100 g steps

This time, pull the load down a *little* and release it

Use a stopwatch to time 10 complete oscillations

(One oscillation is one bounce up and down, time T seconds = the **period**)

For accuracy, repeat this timing

Average the two values of 10T

Find T in s (remember to divide by 10)

Do this for 5 increasing loads (100–500 g)

Plot T^2/s^2 against m/g

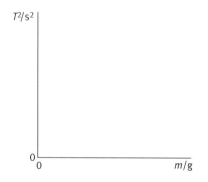

This notation T^2/s^2 or m/g is commonly used to label axes of graphs, etc, and can be confusing

Take for example:
A load in grams of mass, m = 150 g

$$\text{Then, } \frac{m}{g} = 150$$

or, as the notation says, m/g = 150

So, it's simply a way of including the units on the axes, leaving just the numerical values to be plotted on the graph

Another way of showing this could be:

$$m/kg \times 10^{-3} = 150$$

Questions **7–10** are about this experiment

Question

7 If $T = 2\pi\sqrt{\frac{m}{k}}$ what will you expect the graph of T^2 against m to look like?

Answer

A straight line through (0, 0), the origin

Question

8 How else could you have used your results for T and m to confirm $T = 2\pi\sqrt{\frac{m}{k}}$?

Answer

Plot T against $\sqrt{m}$, again a straight line through the origin

Never feed the values into the equation. If you have a set of results always plot a graph

Question

9 Tricky. How could you find k from the T^2 against m graph?

Answer

$$T^2 = 4\pi^2 \frac{m}{k} = \frac{4\pi^2}{k}.m$$

Slope or gradient $= \dfrac{4\pi^2}{k}$ Hence $k = \dfrac{4\pi^2}{\text{gradient}}$

 EXPERIMENT

To investigate effect of changing k: (Tricky!)

c Choose a load, eg, 200 g. You have already found T_1 for 200 g for **one** spring with constant k.

1 Fix 2 springs together side-by-side (in parallel), with a combined constant of $2k$
Use the same load, 200 g
Find the new period, T_2

2 Repeat with 3 springs side-by-side (like a chest expander) with 200 g load to find T_3

3 Plot T^2 against $\dfrac{1}{k}, \dfrac{1}{2k}, \dfrac{1}{3k}$, etc

If $T^2 = 4\pi^2 m.\dfrac{1}{k}$ the graph will be linear

You should realise that 3 points on a graph are insufficient to verify the effect of changing k. Three points give only an indication of a possible trend.

Questions

10 If $T^2 = 4\pi^2 \dfrac{m}{k}$:

a Will you expect a linear graph?
b What will the gradient give?

Answers

a Yes
b $4\pi^2 m$

11 A girl, of mass 55 kg, jumps off a high platform firmly attached to a 15 m elastic rope. After her fall she bounces until she hangs still, when the rope measures 18.3 m

a Find the elastic constant, k, of the rope (its spring stiffness)
b What is the time period, T, of her bounce?
c Describe the energy changes taking place during the bouncing

Answers

$m = 55$ kg, *Extension* $= 18.3 - 15$ m

a $k = \dfrac{load}{extension} = \dfrac{55 \times 9.8}{3.3} = 160$ N m^{-1}

b $T = 2\pi\sqrt{\dfrac{m}{k}} = 2\pi\sqrt{\dfrac{55}{160}} = 3.6$ s

c Energy changes while bouncing:
While **falling down**:
Gravitational PE $\Rightarrow$ Kinetic energy until rope starts to stretch, this slows her fall
Gravitational PE + KE $\Rightarrow$ Elastic PE in rope
While **bouncing up**:
Elastic PE in rope $\Rightarrow$ KE + gravitational PE until girl is at highest point when KE = 0

Simple pendulum, eg, grandfather clock

For small angles of swing, the period T of a pendulum of length, *l*, is given by

$$T = 2\pi\sqrt{\frac{l}{g}}$$

 This does not include the mass of the pendulum, nor the size of the angle of swing

Questions

12 Given simple lab. equipment, how could you show that:

a $T = 2\pi\sqrt{\dfrac{l}{g}}$ does not depend on

   i the angle of swing

   ii the mass of the bob

b Describe an experiment to measure *g*, the acceleration due to gravity, using a simple pendulum

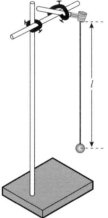

Answers

a Firstly, **angle of swing**: Use a split cork to suspend a pendulum bob from a clamp stand

   1 Measure *l* from the bottom of the cork to the centre of the bob (add the radius of the bob to the string length)

   2 Find the time for 10 swings (10*T*) from a certain angle of release

   3 Repeat and average, find T

   4 Keep *l* and the bob the same. Find 5 more values for T for different release angles

- In this way confirm that for **small angles of swing, the time period is independent of the amplitude**. This is a characteristic of simple harmonic motion. The angle of swing must be less than about 5°

Secondly **mass**: Use a lump of plasticine as the bob, of mass *m*. Keep the same length, *l*, as in **a**

   1 Find the time period, T, as before, for a small angle of swing

   2 Remove some plasticine and find the new *T*

   3 Repeat this 5 more times

- In this way confirm that the **mass of the pendulum does not affect T either**

b To measure *g*, the acceleration due to gravity
(Look up Section **B8**, and revise the 'trap door experiment' for measuring ***g***)

- Measure T as before for different lengths, *l*

l/m	10T_1/s	10T_2/s	Avge 10T/s	T/s	T^2/s²
0.15					

 15 cm is suggested as a minimum length because the frequency becomes too high, and T too small to measure accurately at shorter lengths

- Plot T^2 against *l* because

$$T = 2\pi\sqrt{\frac{l}{g}} \text{ so}$$

$$T^2 = \frac{4\pi^2}{g}.l \text{ similar to}$$

$$\downarrow \qquad \downarrow \downarrow$$
$$y = \quad m. \; x$$

so that slope or gradient $= \dfrac{4\pi^2}{g}$

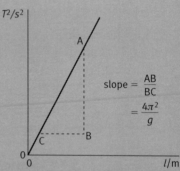

$$\text{slope} = \frac{AB}{BC}$$
$$= \frac{4\pi^2}{g}$$

For accuracy A & C should be as far apart as possible.

- Find $g = \dfrac{4\pi^2}{\text{slope}} \text{ m s}^{-2}$

Questions

13 The period of a simple pendulum is measured as 1.5 s. The mass of the bob is 70 g

a What is the length of the pendulum?

b The bob is pulled aside through 6 cm and released. What is its displacement after 0.5 s?

Answers

$T = 1.5\,\text{s}, m = 70\,\text{g}, x_0 = 6\,\text{cm}, t = 0.5\,\text{s}, g = 9.8\,\text{m s}^{-2}$

a $T = 2\pi\sqrt{\dfrac{l}{g}}$ so, $T^2 = 4\pi^2 \cdot \dfrac{l}{g}$

$$l = \frac{T^2 g}{4\pi^2} = \frac{1.5^2 \times 9.8}{4\pi^2} = 0.56\,\text{m} = 56\,\text{cm}$$

b $x = x_0 \cos \omega t$ from (p. 134)

Step 1 Need to find $\omega = \dfrac{2\pi}{T} = \dfrac{2\pi}{1.5} = 4.19\,\text{rad s}^{-1}$

Step 2 Then $x = 0.06 \cos(4.19 \times 0.5) = 0.06 \cos 2.09$

 Don't get caught ... 2.09 is in radians

Displacement, $x = -0.03\,\text{m}$ (beyond the mean position)

Energy and SHM

x_0 is the maximum displacement

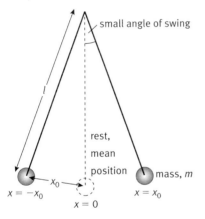

small angle of swing

rest, mean position

mass, m

$x = -x_0$ x_0 $x = x_0$

$x = 0$

$x = -x_0$	$x = 0$	$x = x_0$
$v = 0$	$v = \pm v_{max}$	$v = 0$
$a = a_{max}$	$a = 0$	$a = -a_{max}$
$KE = 0$	$KE = KE_{max}$	$KE = 0$
	$= \frac{1}{2}mv_{max}^2$	
$PE = max$	$PE = min$	$PE = max$

Total energy.........................$KE + PE = $ const.

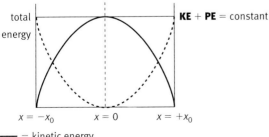

total energy

$KE + PE = $ constant

$x = -x_0$ $x = 0$ $x = +x_0$

—— = kinetic energy

---- = potential energy

Generally **KE** + **PE** = Total energy of the body

= constant

- **KE** $= \frac{1}{2}mv^2$

  $= \frac{1}{2}m\omega^2(x_0^2 - x^2)$ from (p. 135)

So KE is maximum when $x = 0$

$$\textbf{KE}_{max} = \tfrac{1}{2}m\omega^2 x_0^2 \text{ when } x = 0$$

KE is the total energy of the body when $x = 0$

- **PE** = Total energy of body − **KE**

- **PE** $= \frac{1}{2}m\omega^2 x_0^2 - \frac{1}{2}m\omega^2(x_0^2 - x^2)$

  $= \frac{1}{2}m\omega^2 x^2$ at **any** point

So PE is maximum when $x = x_0$

$$\textbf{PE}_{max} = \tfrac{1}{2}m\omega^2 x_0^2 \text{ when } x = x_0$$

PE is the total energy of the body when $x = x_0$

Question

14 What is the maximum KE of the pendulum bob in question **13**?

Answer

$KE = \frac{1}{2}m\omega^2 x_0^2$ $m = 70\,\text{g}$

$= \frac{1}{2}0.07 \times 4.19^2 \times 0.06^2$ $x_0 = 6\,\text{cm}$

$= 0.035 \times 17.556 \times 0.0036$ $\omega = 4.19\,\text{rad s}^{-1}$

$= 0.0022$ joule

$= 2.2\,\text{mJ}$

F31 Materials 1: Young modulus

Beginner's box

- At GCSE you were familiar with Hooke's Law:

  'The extension of a spring is proportional to the force applied.'

- This idea will be stretched (tee hee) here

Hooke's Law

To understand materials fully you must take all of their properties into consideration

- Instead of just the force applied, consider the **stress** on a material

$$\textbf{stress } (\sigma) = \frac{\textbf{force}}{\textbf{area}} \text{ unit N m}^{-2} \text{ or Pa}$$

$$\sigma = \frac{F}{A}$$

😐 $Pa = pascal$
$= pressure\ of\ 1\ newton\ per\ metre^2$

- Instead of the extension, consider the **strain** of a material because of the stress on it

$$\textbf{strain } (\varepsilon) = \frac{\textbf{extension}}{\textbf{original length}}$$

no units, this is a ratio

$$\varepsilon = \frac{e}{l}$$

- **Hooke's Law** can now be stated as

'The strain is proportional to the stress when elastic deformation is taking place'

The graph of a metal in the form of a wire undergoing stress looks like:

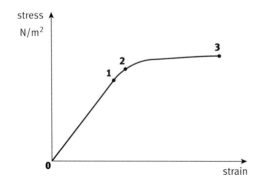

0–1 Here the wire obeys **Hooke's Law**. If the force is removed the wire will return to its original shape. This is **elastic deformation**

At 2 This is the **yield point**, and beyond this the wire will not return to its original shape when the force is removed. This is **plastic deformation**

At 3 Here the wire has broken

The Young Modulus (*E*)

- This is the ratio of stress to strain for a material. Within the limit of proportionality it is a constant It is a measure of a material's resistance to changing length (its strength really!)

$$E = \frac{\text{stress}}{\text{strain}}$$

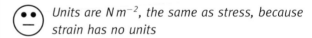

$$= \frac{F}{A} \div \frac{e}{l} = \frac{F}{A} \times \frac{l}{e}$$

$$E = \frac{Fl}{Ae}$$

😐 *Units are N m^{-2}, the same as stress, because strain has no units*

-
material	E/10^{10} N m^{-2}
steel	21
copper	13
glass	7

❄ EXPERIMENT

Find the Young Modulus for a length of copper

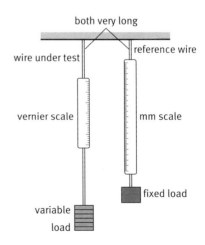

Both wires are made from the same material and initially of the same length

If the temperature changes, or the support yields, both wires are affected equally

- The diameter d of the test wire is measured in 3 places with a micrometer screw gauge and averaged. Cross-sectional area $A = \dfrac{\pi d^2}{4}$
- The length (l) of the wire is measured with a metre ruler
- The apparatus is set up and as successive weights (F) are placed on the test wire, the extensions (e) are measured with a vernier scale
- F and e are tabulated, and an F/e curve is plotted

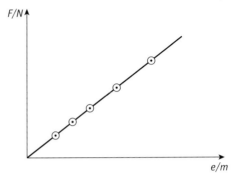

☹ *Watch your units*

$$E = \frac{Fl}{Ae} \therefore F = \frac{EAe}{l}$$

$\dfrac{EA}{l}$ is the gradient

The wire is long and thin to obtain as large an extension as possible

Assume the limit of proportionality of the wire is not exceeded

- **Typical stress/strain curves**

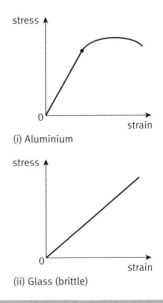

(i) Aluminium

(ii) Glass (brittle)

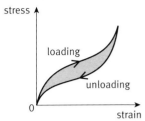

(iii) Rubber: Hysterisis loop

shaded area is the energy lost per unit volume.

It does not obey Hooke's Law

Strain energy

This is the work done in extending a wire

Consider a force/extension curve

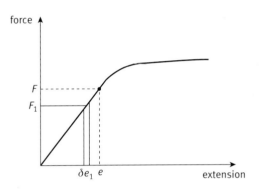

Work done = average force × distance = strain energy.

For an elastic change,

$$\boxed{\textbf{strain energy} = \tfrac{1}{2} \textbf{\textit{Fe}}}$$

which is the area under the curve

- According to Hooke's Law, force is proportional to extension, so

$F = ke$ k = spring constant for a wire

thus $\boxed{\textbf{strain energy} = \tfrac{1}{2} \textbf{\textit{ke}}^2}$

☹ *If Hooke's Law does not apply to a material this equation does not apply. However, the <u>work done</u> in stretching a material is always the area under the F/e curve*

Questions

1 The Young Modulus for copper is 13×10^{10} Pa, and for polythene is 30 MPa

a If the strain produced in the copper is 0.0003, what stress has it undergone?

b A strip of polythene has a cross-section of 40 mm by 0.3 mm, and is pulled down by a force. What value is the force if the strain is 0.0003?

In both cases, the elastic limit has not been exceeded.

Answers

a $E = \dfrac{\text{stress}}{\text{strain}} \rightarrow 13 \times 10^{10} = \dfrac{\text{stress}}{0.0003}$

stress $= 13 \times 10^{10} \times 0.0003 = 3.9 \times 10^7$ Pa

b $E = \dfrac{\text{stress}}{\text{strain}} \rightarrow 30 \times 10^6 = \dfrac{\text{stress}}{0.0003}$

stress $= 30 \times 10^6 \times 0.0003 = 9000$ Pa

stress $= \dfrac{F}{A}$ where $A = 40 \times 10^{-3} \times 0.3 \times 10^{-3}$

$9000 = \dfrac{F}{1.2 \times 10^{-5}} \rightarrow F = 0.11$ N

Questions

2 Here is a stress/strain curve for a steel wire

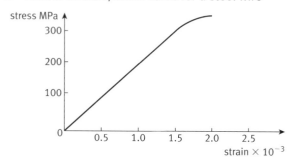

stress MPa

strain $\times 10^{-3}$

a Use the graph to find its Young Modulus

b Find the strain energy of the wire if its CSA is 0.2×10^{-6} m² and its original length is 3 m, when it has reached its limit of proportionality

 Make sure you use the information on the graph properly

Answers

a Take the gradient of the line, but watch your units

$E = \dfrac{\text{stress}}{\text{strain}} = \dfrac{300 \times 10^6}{1.5 \times 10^{-3}} = 2.0 \times 10^{11}$ Pa

b

Strain energy = area under an F/e curve $= \frac{1}{2}Fe$ not the area under a stress/strain curve

At the limit of proportionality

stress $= \dfrac{F}{0.2 \times 10^{-6}} = 300 \times 10^6 \therefore F = 60$ N

strain $= \dfrac{e}{3} = 1.5 \times 10^{-3} \therefore e = 4.5 \times 10^{-3}$ m

$\frac{1}{2}Fe = 0.5 \times 60 \times 4.5 \times 10^{-3} = 0.135$ J

Questions

3 Consider again the figure in Question **2**. Sketch the graph out again and draw new curves for

a A material, X, that has a smaller Young Modulus and is brittle

b A material, Y, that has a bigger Young Modulus, and that exhibits plastic behaviour at a lower value of strain

Answers

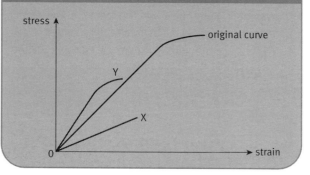

Question

4 An elastic band is cut, so it is one long strand with a CSA of 2 mm². It is stretched by 12% of its original length. Calculate the tension of the band.
Young Modulus of elastic band $= 4 \times 10^7$ Pa

Answer

$E = \dfrac{Fl}{Ae} = 4 \times 10^7$

$A = 2$ mm² $= 2 \times 10^{-6}$ m²

and $\therefore \dfrac{e}{l} = \dfrac{12}{100}$ since stretched by 12%

$\therefore 4 \times 10^7 = \dfrac{F}{2 \times 10^{-6}} \times \dfrac{100}{12}$

$F = 9.6$ N $=$ tension

Have assumed there were no changes in the CSA of the rubber band. If you'd needed it, they would have been *given to you*
Try not to overcomplicate questions,
YOU CAN DO THEM (it's only A Level!!!!!)

F32 Materials 2: Density and pressure

Beginner's box

- Density $= \dfrac{\text{mass}}{\text{volume}}$

- Pressure $= \dfrac{\text{force}}{\text{area}}$

Density

Question

1 Which has a greater mass, a pound of flour or a pound of feathers?

Answer

They are the same mass!

Have you ever been caught out on that one? A pound is a pound is a pound (unless you are trying to lose a pound in which case it seems like a stone!)

Perhaps the reason you might get caught out is that you visualise the same volume of flour and feathers, knowing that the flour is denser than the feathers

$$\text{Density, } \rho = \frac{M}{V}$$

unit of density is kg m^{-3}

Mass = Density × Volume

- You need to know how to find the **density of a solid and a liquid**. The following two questions will demonstrate simple methods

<u>Solid</u>

Question

2 You are given a lump of plasticine. Without using a balance briefly describe a way to measure its density

Answer

To find the volume, mould the plasticine into the shape of a cuboid
Using a millimetre ruler, measure the lengths of the sides
Volume = height × length × width

Alternatively place water in a Eureka can, so its level is just below the spout. Place a beaker underneath the spout and put the plasticine in the can. The volume of liquid displaced is equal to the volume of the plasticine

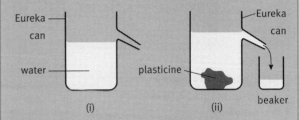

(i)   (ii)

To find the mass of the plasticine, use the concept of moments

 This is a favourite scenario in practical exams

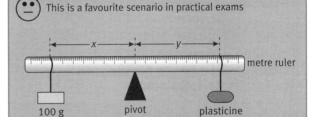

100 g   pivot   plasticine

Find the balance point of the ruler without any weights on.
Hang the known mass on one side and the plasticine on the other so that, again, the ruler balances
Both x and y can be directly measured to the nearest millimetre

known mass $\times x$ = plasticine mass $\times y$

There are errors in this experiment, eg, your plasticine cuboid will not have perfectly straight corners
Repeating measurements reduces errors

<u>Liquid</u>

This is easy, but just in case...

Question

3 How would you find the density of milk in a glass?

Answer

Find the mass of a clean, dry measuring cylinder
Pour the milk into it to establish the volume
Find the mass of the milk + measuring cylinder and simply substitute values into
$\rho_{\text{milk}} = \dfrac{\text{mass of milk}}{\text{volume of milk}}$

material	density (kg m^{-3})
nucleus of atom	10^{17}
metal	10^{4}
water	10^{3}
air	1

Question

4 Suggest why the air inside a balloon might have a greater density than the air outside it.

Answer

The air inside a balloon has been compressed

- **Archimedes' Principle**

 Greek Scientist, 3rd century BC

An object placed in a fluid causes some of the fluid to be displaced (your bath water rises when you sit in it) and. . .

The object experiences an upthrust equal to the weight of the fluid displaced

Hopefully you will agree that you feel lighter in the bath or swimming pool. This is because of the upthrust.

 __Upthrust__ is a force, and can be experienced by gases also, eg, air displaced around a parachutist causes an upthrust on him

Question

5 A body of volume 0.05 m³ and weight 550 N is completely immersed in water, suspended by a string. What is the tension in the supporting string?

$$\rho_{water} = 1000 \text{ kg m}^{-3} \qquad g = 10 \text{ m s}^{-2}$$

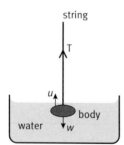

Answer

Step *1* The volume of water displaced = volume of object
$$= 0.05 \text{ m}^3$$
Using the density, we can calculate the mass of water
$$\rho = \frac{\text{mass}}{\text{volume}} \rightarrow 1000 = \frac{\text{mass}}{0.05} \therefore \text{mass} = 50 \text{ kg}$$
So the weight of water = mass × g = 500 N

Step *2* Using Archimedes' Principle
The upthrust on the object ⇑ = 500 N
The weight of the object ⇓ = 550 N
Tension of string = weight − upthrust = 50 N
It nearly floats!!

Questions

6 A disc, CSA 10 cm², floats in petrol with 2 cm of its body immersed

$$\rho_{petrol} = 710 \text{ kg m}^{-3}, g = 9.81 \text{ m s}^{-2}$$

a What weight of petrol does the disc replace?

b What is the weight of the disc?

Answers

a volume of disc immersed
$$= 2 \times 10 = 20 \text{ cm}^3 = 20 \times 10^{-6} \text{ m}^3$$
$$\therefore m_{petrol} = 0.0142 \text{ kg},$$
$$\therefore \text{ weight of petrol} = 0.0142 \times 9.81 = 0.14 \text{ N}$$
b As the disc is floating its weight is equal and opposite to the upthrust force acting on it

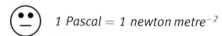 A metal ship floats because it has a shape that will cause the displacement of a lot of water, creating an upthrust *equal to its weight*

Pressure

- This is a **scalar** quantity measured in Pa or N m⁻²

 1 Pascal = 1 newton metre⁻²

- In a **liquid**, the pressure can be calculated by

$$p = h\rho g$$

where p is the pressure, at a depth, h, in liquid of density ρ

The pressure

— remains constant at the same horizontal level in a liquid

— is independent of the shape of the container

— acts in all directions

- **Manometers** are devices used to measure gas pressures

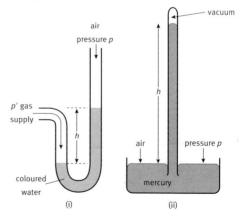

(i) This is a **U-tube manometer**

The gas of pressure p' pushes on the coloured water

The level stops rising when the pressure of the gas is balanced by the pressure of the liquid and the atmospheric pressure, p

$$p' = h\rho g + p$$

(ii) This is a **barometer**, and measures atmospheric pressure, if the tube is evacuated

Air pressure pushes down on the mercury causing it to rise up the tube

The vacuum has no pressure so does not push down

The liquid stops rising when its pressure balances the air pressure

$$p = h\rho g$$

• At **standard atmospheric pressure**, SAP, (at sea level) the barometer column is 760 mm long, so is described as 760 mm Hg

S.A.P = 760 mm Hg at sea level
   = 1.01325×10^5 Pa (used by chemists)

• Standard Unit of Pressure, for convenience

S.U.P = 10^5 Pa or N m^{-2}
   = 1 bar

 You have about 200,000 N of air acting over your body (body area = 2 m^2), but you don't feel it (phew). This is because our blood pressure is slightly greater than atmospheric and our lungs are full of air

Question

7 Calculate the standard atmospheric air pressure in SI units, given $\rho_{mercury} = 13.6 \times 10^3$ kg m^{-3} and $g = 9.81$ N kg^{-1}
Standard air pressure (SAP) = 760 mm Hg
Explain why nose bleeds are more common at high altitudes

Answer

Make sure all your units are SI

$p = h\rho g$
   $= 0.76 \times 13.6 \times 10^3 \times 9.81$
   $= 1.01 \times 10^5$ Pa or N m^{-2}

 This value is close to one bar ... so we live in a bar!!!

At high altitudes, the air pressure drops, but your blood pressure does not. The difference between them is more significant, and creates greater stresses on blood vessels

Question

8 A cylinder of gas is attached to a mercury manometer. The atmospheric pressure is 100 kPa. The mercury has a density of 1.36×10^4 kg m^{-3}. Calculate the pressure of the gas if the vertical distance between the two mercury surfaces is 37 cm

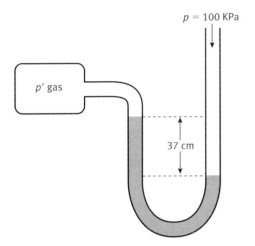

Answer

 Convert units

$p' = h\rho g + p$

but in this diagram the atmospheric pressure is balanced by the gas pressure and the 37 cm of liquid

$\therefore \quad p = h\rho g + p'$

$100\,000 = 0.37 \times 1.36 \times 10^4 \times 9.81 + p'$

$\therefore \quad p' = 100\,000 - 49\,364 = 50\,636$

gas pressure $\simeq 51$ kPa (gas pressure is less than atmospheric pressure)

- **Liquids transmit pressure**

- **Solids transmit force**

To understand this statement try this question

Questions

9 The piston arrangement below shows two cylinders with diameters of 15 and 7 mm. The piston X is pushed with a force of 100 N. F_Y is then the force exerted on the right by Y

Calculate F_Y if

a The cylinders contain a liquid

b The cylinders are wholly solid

Answers

a Liquids transmit pressure, so
Pressure exerted on face X = Pressure exerted on face Y

$$\frac{F_X}{A_X} = \frac{F_Y}{A_Y}$$

$A_X = \pi\, 3.5^2 = 38.5 \text{ mm}^2 \quad A_Y = \pi\, 7.5^2 = 176.7 \text{ mm}^2$

😐 Diameter units were not changed to SI as the units will become a ratio and cancel

$$\frac{100}{38.5} = \frac{F_Y}{176.7} \therefore F_Y = 459 \text{ N}$$

b Solids transmit force, so
Force exerted on face X = Force exerted on face Y

$$F_Y = 100 \text{ N}$$

G33 Probing matter and scattering

Beginner's box

- Know the nature of α and β particles and of γ radiation
- Be familiar with the atom model:

Nucleus consisting of neutrons and protons

surrounded by a cloud of electrons

- Know that:

particle	charge	mass
neutron	zero, neutral	1 unit
proton	unit, positive	similar, 1 unit
electron	unit, negative	tiny, $\frac{1}{2000}$ mass of proton $\frac{1}{2000}$ unit, approx

or

neutron is neutral, mass 1 unit

proton has positive charge, similar mass

electron has negative charge (same size as proton), tiny mass ($\frac{1}{2000}$ mass of proton)

- Know that
volume of sphere $= \frac{4}{3}\pi r^3$
volume of cylinder $= \pi r^2 h$

Get it in perspective

A tiny pencil dot (.) has about as many atoms in it as there are people in the world! The six billionth has now been born.

We're dealing with sub-microscopic sizes here and **enormous** or **mega** numbers.

 History...

Atomic theory goes back a long way ...

... Over 400 years BC (2400 years ago)
Democritus suggested there were open spaces between indivisible atoms/particles

... 200 years years ago
John Dalton published his atomic theory, that atoms of the same element are identical in weight

...In the last 100 years
Experiment and theory have developed ideas at an amazing pace, so that we now have antimatter, leptons, hadrons, quarks, etc

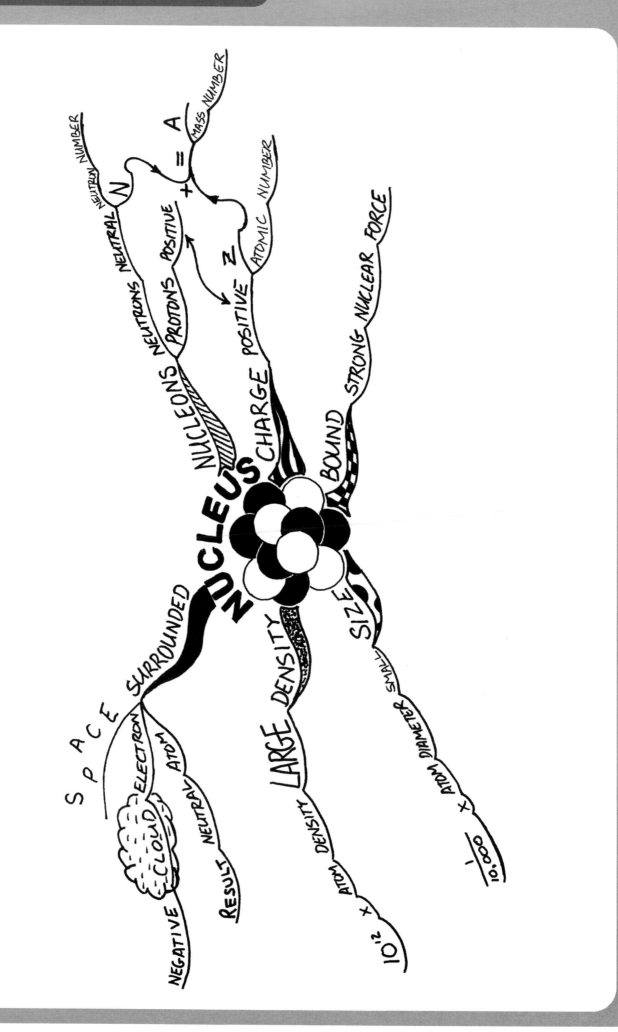

Inside the atom

 EXPERIMENT described in the following question:

Question

1 To measure the **size of an atom**, place a tiny drop of oleic acid, 0.63 mm in diameter, on a fine wire loop onto the surface of very clean water in a large waxed tray. The surface of the water is covered with fine powder. The oil immediately spreads out into a large circle pushing the powder aside. The diameter of this circle, D, is 24 cm

Assuming there are 20 atoms in the molecular chain of the oil, estimate the average diameter of an atom in the experiment above

Answer

The oil molecules act something like tadpoles with water-loving heads and water-hating tails
When dropped onto the clean surface of water, the heads dive into the water, while the tails stick up, keeping out of the water
So the oil molecules spread out to a single layer on the surface of the water *(you hope!)*

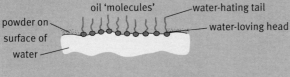

Step 1 Vol. of oil drop/sphere $= \frac{4}{3}\pi\left(\frac{d}{2}\right)^3$ where $d = 0.63$ mm

Step 2 Vol. of oil patch $= \pi\left(\frac{D}{2}\right)^2 h$ where $D = 24$ cm
$= 240$ mm
and $h =$ length of oil molecule

 *This is an example of an occasion when it is wise to work throughout in **mm***

Step 3 The oil patch came from the oil drop, so:

$$\frac{4}{3}\frac{d^3}{8} = \pi\frac{D^2}{4}h, \quad so, \quad \frac{2}{3}d^3 = D^2h$$

$$h = \frac{2}{3}\frac{d^3}{D^2}$$

$$h = \frac{2}{3}\frac{(0.63)^3}{(240)^2}\ mm$$

$$= \frac{2}{3}\frac{0.25}{57600} = 0.0000029$$

So: length of oil molecule, $h = 2.9 \times 10^{-6}$ mm (contains 20 atoms)

Atom diameter $= \frac{h}{20} = \frac{2.9 \times 10^{-6}}{20} = 0.14 \times 10^{-6}$ mm

Ans $= 0.14$ nm. This is an impressive result because...

- Diameter of an atom ~ 0.1 nm or 10^{-10} m

 Write this with all the noughts in it! Later we'll find the diameter of the nucleus $\sim 10^{-15}$ m (like a dot in the middle of the Albert Hall)

To probe the atom something very small and very energetic is needed

Rutherford, with Geiger and Marsden to take the measurements, used α-particles to bombard thin gold film

α-particle scattering by gold leaf

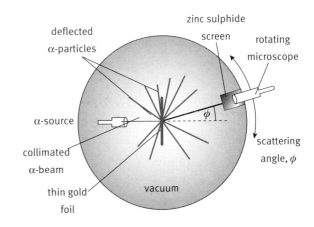

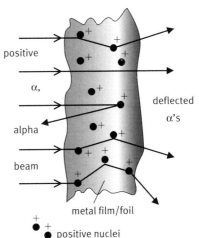

1 **Most** α's went straight through

2 A tiny number were strongly deflected

3 An even smaller number were fully deflected

- Why gold? Pure, doesn't tarnish, dense heavy atoms, can be beaten into very thin gold leaf

- Why a vacuum? α-particles are charged and relatively massive (2 protons and 2 neutrons), so relatively slow. So their energy is easily absorbed during numerous interactions. Range in air is only a few cm. The vacuum ensures that α-particles travel in straight lines and that their range is not limited

- Why collimated beam? This means a parallel beam made narrow so the scattering angle ϕ is known

- Why did **most** α's pass easily through the gold film? Rutherford suggested most of the gold was empty space

- Why were a few of the +vely charged α's detected on the source side of the film? Because the +ve α's were **strongly** deflected by the +vely charged nucleus when in a head-on collision

Result

Rutherford suggested each atom had a

tiny,

very dense,

+vely charged nucleus

surrounded by space

and a −ve electron cloud

to make the atom neutral

... the birth of the

nuclear model of the atom

The A-Z of the nucleus

No. of protons $= Z =$ Proton number

No. of neutrons $= N =$ neutron number

No. of nucleons $= Z + N = A =$ nucleon number

No. of electrons $=$ no. of protons (only in a neutral atom)

Atom — normally electrically neutral — about 10^{-10} m diameter

Nucleus — positively charged — massive — about 10^{-14} m diameter

The nucleus in an atom is like a dot in the Albert Hall to the same scale

Inverse Square Law, the atom and the nucleus

The Inverse Square Law can be used to calculate the size of the nucleus that an α-particle is approaching

Question

2 How close would a 6 MeV α-particle come to a gold nucleus in a head-on collision, given that, at a distance r, it will stop and have an

$$\text{electrical PE} = \frac{q_1 q_2}{4\pi\varepsilon_0 r} \qquad \text{(see E23)}$$

 *This assumes that the Inverse Square Law for electric fields holds even deep within the atom*

Gold nucleus charge $= +79\,e$ ($Z = 79$ for gold)

α-particle charge $= +2\,e$ ($Z = 2$ for helium)

$$\frac{1}{4\pi\varepsilon_0} = k = 9 \times 10^9 \, \text{N m}^2 \, \text{C}^{-2}$$

(from E23: $\varepsilon_0 = 8.85 \times 10^{-12} \, \text{C}^2 \, \text{N}^{-1} \, \text{m}^{-2}$)

1 ev $=$ energy $= 1.6 \times 10^{-19}$ J (energy gained by an electron when accelerated across 1 Volt)

Answer

Step 1 Initial KE of $\alpha = 6$ M eV $= 6 \times 10^6$ eV

$\qquad\qquad = 6 \times 10^6 \times 1.6 \times 10^{-19}$ J

$\qquad\qquad = 6 \times 10^6\, e$ $\qquad\qquad\qquad$ (1)

Step 2 It will decelerate as it approaches the gold nucleus head-on, stopping when this KE is converted to electrical PE, at distance r, where

$$\text{PE} = \frac{q_1 q_2}{4\pi\varepsilon_0 r}$$

$$= \frac{79\,e \times 2\,e \times 9 \times 10^9}{r} \qquad (2)$$

Step 3 At stopping distance, KE $=$ PE and

KE $= 6 \times 10^6\, e$ $\qquad\qquad\qquad$ from (1)

PE $= \dfrac{158 \times e^2 \times 9 \times 10^9}{r}$ $\qquad$ from (2)

So: $6 \times 10^6\, e = \dfrac{158 \times e^2 \times 9 \times 10^9}{r}$

$r = \dfrac{158 \times e \times 9 \times 10^9}{6 \times 10^6} = \dfrac{158 \times 1.6 \times 10^{-19} \times 9 \times 10^9}{6 \times 10^6}$

$\qquad = 380 \times 10^{-16} = 3.8 \times 10^{-14}$ m

 *This is where the alpha stops ... so ... The **nucleus** must be **smaller** than this!!!*

❄ EXPERIMENT

To see the **Inverse Square Law** in action

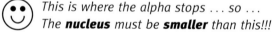

large ball-bearing

gravity PE $\alpha\ \dfrac{1}{r}$ dusted

launch ramp

hill with 'inverse square law' profile

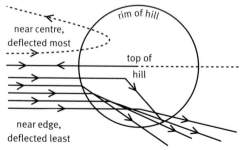

rim of hill

near centre, deflected most

top of hill

near edge, deflected least

1 Roll ball-bearings down a ramp at a hill. The hill should be modelled so that the PE, due to gravity on its slopes, varies as $\frac{1}{r}$, like the electrical PE around the nucleus.

[Both assume a force field that varies according to an Inverse Square Law]

2 If the hill and surrounding paper are dusted with powder, the tracks made by the ball-bearings will be similar in shape to those of α-particles approaching a nucleus.

affected by strong nuclear force		do not feel the strong nuclear force	
hadrons (heavy) } substructure **quarks**		**leptons** (small) } no substance fundamental	
mesons	*baryons*	include	
pions	*protons*, p$^+$	*electrons*	
kaons	*neutrons*, n	muons	
eta-	omega*	tauons	
	sigma*	*neutrinos*	
	lamda*	photons	
	(*particles)	gravitons (if they exist)	
All have antiparticles eg, antiproton p^- antineutrino $\bar{n}$			

Inside the nucleus

*Check that this section is included in **your** syllabus, as it is in only a few*
The neutrino and antineutrino are not always considered at this level

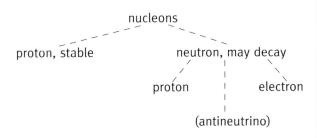

- The **strong nuclear force** operates within the nucleus to hold the positive protons together (in spite of their strong electrical repulsion) with the neutrons

- Since 1950, high-energy collision experiments, as a result of cosmic rays or accelerated particles, have produced evidence that the proton, neutron and electron are **not** 'fundamental' articles (ie, they are made up of smaller particles)
In fact, something like 30 new particles have been identified by analysing tracks in cloud chambers (p. 155), bubble chambers or by arrays of GM tubes or wires

Sorting out and classifying these is best left to recent textbooks or specialist lectures (eg, Royal Society, Royal Institution, Institute of Physics, etc)

The following is our attempt!

High-energy electrons were used to bombard individual protons
This showed that the proton density was not uniform
Perhaps the proton was made up of smaller masses?

- These are known as the **quarks**

A quark's charge

Apart from charge, quarks also have characteristics known as their *Baryon number* and their *strangeness*

Yes, you've guessed! Each quark has its *antiquark*

To satisfy the substructure of all **hadrons**, 3 further pairs of **quarks** are needed.

each with their antiquark partner

A top quark was predicted to be 20× the mass of a bottom quark. Experimental evidence was not found for it until a proton and an antiproton were made to collide in a new 1800 GeV Tevatron synchrotron in Fermilab (Chicago, USA) in the mid-1990s.

- To carry out interactions *between* particles **bosons** are needed, the most familiar one being the **photon**

G34 Nuclear radiation

Beginner's box

- Know the properties of alpha (α), beta (β) and gamma (γ) radiation from an unstable nucleus

property	α	β	γ
charge	$+2$	-1	0
absorption	thin paper	few mm of Al (Aluminium)	several cm of lead
range in air	fixed, up to 10 cm	variable, up to 1 m	spreads with almost no limit
ionising effect	strong	weak	very weak

- Know that there is *always* background radiation present
- Know that the half-life indicates the instability of a nucleus. It is the time taken for the number of undecayed atoms to halve

Unstable nuclei

Thinking again of the nucleus consisting of

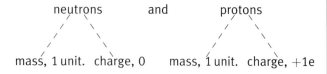

neutrons   and   protons

mass, 1 unit. charge, 0   mass, 1 unit. charge, $+1e$

 Putting it simply:
If the ratio of [neutrons:protons] becomes too large (ie, too many neutrons to protons), the nucleus becomes 'overweight' and unstable Instead of going to 'weight watchers' it can try to correct this imbalance in 2 ways:

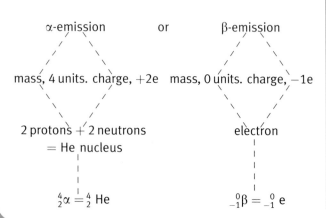

α-emission   or β-emission

mass, 4 units. charge, $+2e$ mass, 0 units. charge, $-1e$

2 protons + 2 neutrons   electron
= He nucleus

$^4_2\alpha = ^4_2\text{He}$ $^0_{-1}\beta = ^0_{-1}\text{e}$

Questions

1 In the Actinium series
a Protactinium, $^{231}_{91}\text{Pa}$, loses an α-particle to become actinium, Ac
b This in turn loses a β-particle to become thorium, Th
Show these decays as radioactive 'equations'

Answers

a $^{231}_{91}\text{Pa} \Rightarrow ^{227}_{89}\text{Ac} + ^4_2\alpha$ and γ radiation

b $^{227}_{89}\text{Ac} \Rightarrow ^{227}_{90}\text{Th} + ^0_{-1}\beta$

 b *There may be a neutrino produced, but since this has negligible mass and no charge it is usually neglected at this level*

In Question **1** above:

1 Check the **nucleon numbers**, **A**, equate:
a $231 = 227 + 4$
b $227 = 227 + 0$

2 Check the **proton numbers**, **Z**, equate:
a $91 = 89 + 2$
b $89 = 90 - 1$

3 The gamma and neutrino emission (with no charge or mass of significance) balance the energy of the decays, so that the principle of the conservation of energy holds.

Forces within the nucleus

 Again, check whether your syllabus requires this depth of study

1 Repulsion between protons ... electrical
2 Attraction acting on protons and neutrons ... short-range 'strong nuclear force'

For stability each nucleon (proton or neutron) must feel a net attractive force
Neutrons are useful because they add to the net attractive force without increasing the electrical repulsion
Extra neutrons help to increase the distance between protons and so reduce their repulsive electrostatic effect

The **balance** between the number of protons and the number of neutrons is critical. If there are too many neutrons compared with protons, instability and decay may result

Beta emission

Evidence has been found for both negative β's (electrons) and positive β's (positrons).

These emissions result from the following changes within the nucleus:

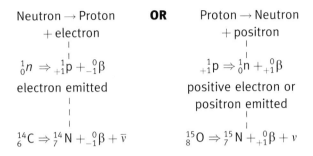

Neutron → Proton + electron   **OR**   Proton → Neutron + positron

$$^1_0n \Rightarrow {}^1_{+1}p + {}^0_{-1}\beta$$
electron emitted

$$^1_{+1}p \Rightarrow {}^1_0n + {}^0_{+1}\beta$$
positive electron or positron emitted

$$^{14}_6C \Rightarrow {}^{14}_7N + {}^0_{-1}\beta + \bar{v}$$

$$^{15}_8O \Rightarrow {}^{15}_7N + {}^0_{+1}\beta + v$$

($\bar{v}$ represents an antineutrino and v a neutrino)

😐 *Remember v's can usually be neglected at A Level*

- So β-decay results in either a neutron losing negative charge and becoming a proton, or a proton losing positive charge and becoming a neutron

Both change the delicate balance of:

neutron : proton ratio

Energy curve for β's

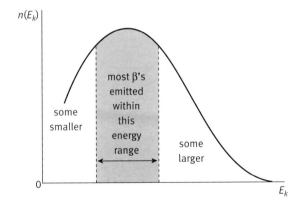

The graph plots the number of β's, $n(E_k)$, emitted with a certain energy, E_k, from a source. The graph shows the range of energies carried by β-particles when they are emitted from a nucleus

The rest of the available energy is carried by an antineutrino with an electron, or a neutrino with a positron (see above)

Radiation properties

nuclear radiation	alpha	beta	gamma
charge	$+2e$ $= 3.2 \times 10^{-19}$ C	$-e$ or $+e$ $= \pm 1.6 \times 10^{-19}$C	Zero
mass in a.m.u.	4u, large	0.0005u, negligible	Zero
composition	2p + 2n He nucleus	electron or positron	VHF photons (>X-rays) EM radiation, photon
symbol	He^{++}	e$^-$ or e$^+$	γ
ionisation caused	very high, 1	high, 1/100	low, 1/1000
range in air	about 3–5 cm	up to 100 cm+	very large obeys Inverse Square Law
stopped by	sheet of paper	1–3 mm Al sheet	several cm of lead
effect of EM fields	small deflection	larger and in opposite direction to α's	none
speed of emission	10^7m s^{-1} or $= 0.06$c	approaching 3×10^8 ms^{-1} or $= 0.99$c	3×10^8m s^{-1} $= c$ speed of light

Radiation detectors

alpha	beta	gamma
photographic film — for safety monitoring	photographic film — radiation badges	photographic film
gold-leaf electroscope		
spark counter		
cloud chamber bubble chamber	cloud chamber bubble chamber	bubble chamber by analysis of decay into charged particles
Geiger–Müller tube (thin window)	Geiger–Müller tube (G–M tube)	G–M tube (only 10% efficiency)
solid-state detector		solid-state detector
drift chamber	drift chamber	

Radiation detectors

To see how these are interlinked consider their Mind Map overleaf

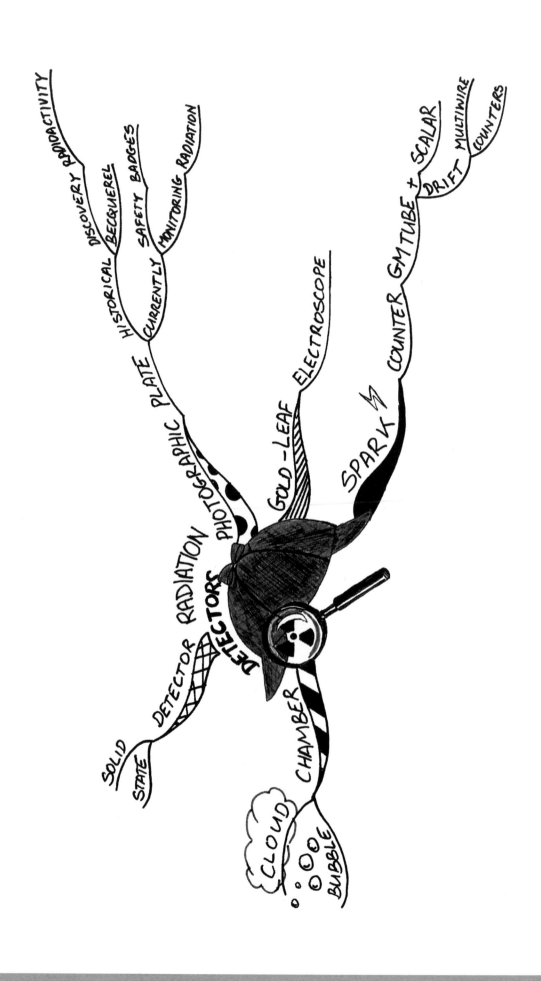

- Except for the photographic plate and the solid-state detector all of these rely on the ionising properties of the radiation so that they detect α's most easily, then β's, ie, the charged particles

- γ paths rarely show up directly as γ-ray photons are not charged and their presence is deduced as a result of analysing their decay into charged particles

- For details of the cloud chamber and GM tube refer to any advanced physics text

  Make sure you take the opportunity to set up and watch for several minutes the vapour tracks caused by α-particles and, if you are lucky, β-particles. These will convince you how unexpected or random the paths are

- Remember the radioactive (RA) source has been emitting particles *all the time* it has been in school, *and before*. Not just when you are watching the tracks in the cloud chamber

Natural or background radiation

Natural sources   **Man-made sources**
88%   12%

cosmic — Sun
10% — outer space

ground — rocks
and — soils, clay
— sand
buildings — brick
— concrete
14% — wood

air — radon
52% — thoron

food — plants — nuts
and drink — animals — bread
12% — tea, coffee

X rays
bone scans — medical
heart imaging — 11.4%
cancer
treatment

nuclear — power
stations
0.004%

luminous clocks
smoke detectors — misc
nuclear weapons — 0.6%
fallout
air travel

Measurement of range and penetration of radiations

(or 'Are they safe at arm's length?')

 EXPERIMENTS on radiation

During experiments on radiation, **background radiation** must be taken into account

1 Before starting such an experiment set the GM tube and scalar counting for 5 minutes

2 Note the counter reading, reset and repeat twice more

3 Background count rate = average of these three readings per minute

4 This must be subtracted from any later readings using an RA source

 SAFETY RULES

 Stick up 'RA danger' notices outside doors to the lab

Follow your teacher's instructions

Use only 'closed sources' where the RA material is inside a small protective can

Wear thin disposable gloves and use forceps to move the source

Always point the window of the source away from you and others

Work away from other students

APPARATUS

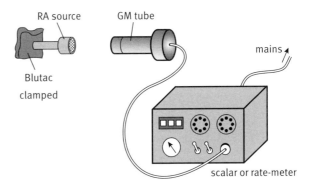

General apparatus for this group of experiments

 Before getting out the RA source take the background count rate

Pushing the stem of the source into blue-tac makes it easier and safer to clamp

EXPERIMENTS using the apparatus above.

a α-ray absorption/penetration

- Take the background count
  Suitable sources: americium, Am-241
  Detectors: thin window GM tube
          solid-state detector

  1. Increase the distance between the source and the detector taking 30-second counts, 3 times at each distance in air. Subtract the background count

  2. Note that this count-rate decreases rapidly after about 5 cm. This should be expected from your experiment with the cloud chamber

  3. With the source and detector close together (< 5 cm) insert thin paper between them

The drop in count-rate shows that the α's have been absorbed by the paper

α's are absorbed so easily because they are relatively massive (2 neutrons + 2 protons), and carry 2 positive charges

They cause frequent ionisations of molecules in their path and so lose energy rapidly as a result of all these collisions

When they have insufficient energy to ionise we say they have been absorbed

Paper is about 1000 times denser than air so only a very thin sheet is needed to absorb the α's compared with about 5 cm of air

 EXPERIMENT

b β-ray absorption

- Take the background count
  Suitable sources: strontium, Sr-90
  Detector: GM tube

  1. Remember to subtract the background count

  2. Sheets of Al between 1 and 4 mm are inserted before the β's are fully absorbed

As they are very fast electrons, β's penetrate matter much more easily than α's

They cause much less ionisation as shown by the few spidery tracks β's make in cloud chambers

 EXPERIMENT

c β-ray deflection by magnetic field

  1. To confirm the −ve charge on β's, a strong

horseshoe magnet can be placed between the source and detector

2. Offset the GM tube to one side as shown with magnetic field **down** from N–S

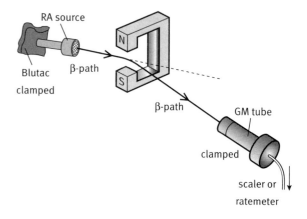

3. Take 30-second count readings 3 times. Average and subtract the background count

4. Turn the magnet upside down to make the magnetic field go **up** from N–S

5. Repeat the count readings

If this count-rate is lower than the one before, it shows that the β-rays are deflected out as shown in the diagram by the magnetic field

Use Fleming's left-hand rule to confirm that the β's must be **negative** to be deflected this way

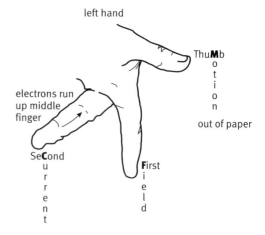

EXPERIMENT

d γ-ray penetration and the Inverse Square Law
- Take the background count
  Suitable sources: cobalt, Co-60
  radium, Ra-226
  Detector: GM tube

Add increasing thicknesses of Pb, noting the count-rate after subtracting the background count

Although the count-rate of γ-particles reduces they may not be completely absorbed even by several cm of lead

Remember γ-particles are pure energy radiation, so have no mass or charge

 EXPERIMENT

e To confirm that γ-intensity reduces according to the Inverse Square Law
- Take the background count
  Use the general apparatus arrangement on page 155

  1 Tape a metre-rule to the bench between the source and the detector

  2 Find the average count rate (less background count) for 5 to 10 different distances, r cm from the source to the detector

    The **Inverse Square Law** suggests that

    $$\text{Intensity} \propto \frac{1}{4\pi r^2}$$

    and the count-rate is a measure of the intensity of the γ-radiation

  3 Plot corrected average count-rate against $\frac{1}{r^2}$
    If this gives a straight line through the origin then γ-radiation obeys the Inverse Square Law

Question

2 Where else in physics does an Inverse Square Law hold?

Answer

light or solar radiation intensity
X-radiation
electric fields
gravitational fields
sound intensity

 SAFETY

RA sources are largely safe at arm's length since α- and β-particles will be absorbed by this distance of air

γ-particles are much more penetrating, but do not cause so much ionisation

Anyone working with these types of radiation will need protective clothing to absorb β-particles and will need to be monitored by film badges to detect any ionising radiation they are exposed to

Patients receiving such radiation also need protection and monitoring of the radiation dose they receive

Isotopes and their uses

Definition: Isotopes are nuclei of the same element with the same number of protons, but with different numbers of neutrons in their nuclei

- What is an **isotope**?

  Meaning: same — place in the periodic table
  same — Z-value, proton number
  same — number of protons in nucleus
  same — element
  same — chemical properties
  (same number of electrons)

- What is different?
  N, the number of neutrons in the nucleus
  $A = Z + N$, the nucleon number

- Z is the same for all isotopes of an element.

- $_Z^A X$ is the symbol used to show A and Z for any substance X

(remember $A \to Z$?)

Questions

3 **Radium** can exist as several isotopes

  $_{88}^{228}Ra$, $_{88}^{226}Ra$, $_{88}^{224}Ra$, $_{88}^{223}Ra$, etc

  a How many protons in each atom of the Ra isotope?
  b How many neutrons in each atom of the Ra isotope?

Answers

a 88 protons, proton no. $Z = 88$
b 140, 138, 136, 135 neutrons respectively
  All of these isotopes are unstable (with so many neutrons)
  some decay by α-decay, some by β-decay

Questions

4 Lead can exist with any nucleon number from

$$^{206}_{82}Pb - ^{214}_{82}Pb$$

a How many protons in each Pb nucleus?

b What is the range of numbers of neutrons in their nuclei?

Answers

a 82 protons, proton no. $Z = 82$

b 124 to 129 neutrons (no. of neutrons $= A-Z$)

The first three of these isotopes of lead are stable

Pb-206, end of uranium series (U-238)
Pb-207, end of actinium series (Pa-231)
Pb 208, end of thorium series (Th-232)

The heavier isotopes are unstable and several decay by β-decay

Questions

5

a Ra-224 decays by α-decay to form radon, Rn. Write the equation to show this decay (see Questions **1** and **3**)

b Bi-211 is formed when Pb, proton no. 82, loses a fast electron from its nucleus.
Represent this decay by an equation

Answers

a $^{224}_{88}Ra \Rightarrow ^{220}_{86}Rn + ^{4}_{2}He + \gamma$

b $^{211}_{82}Pb \Rightarrow ^{211}_{83}Bi + ^{0}_{-1}e + \gamma$

 In a β-decay, the proton no. Z goes up by 1, the nucleon no. A stays the same.

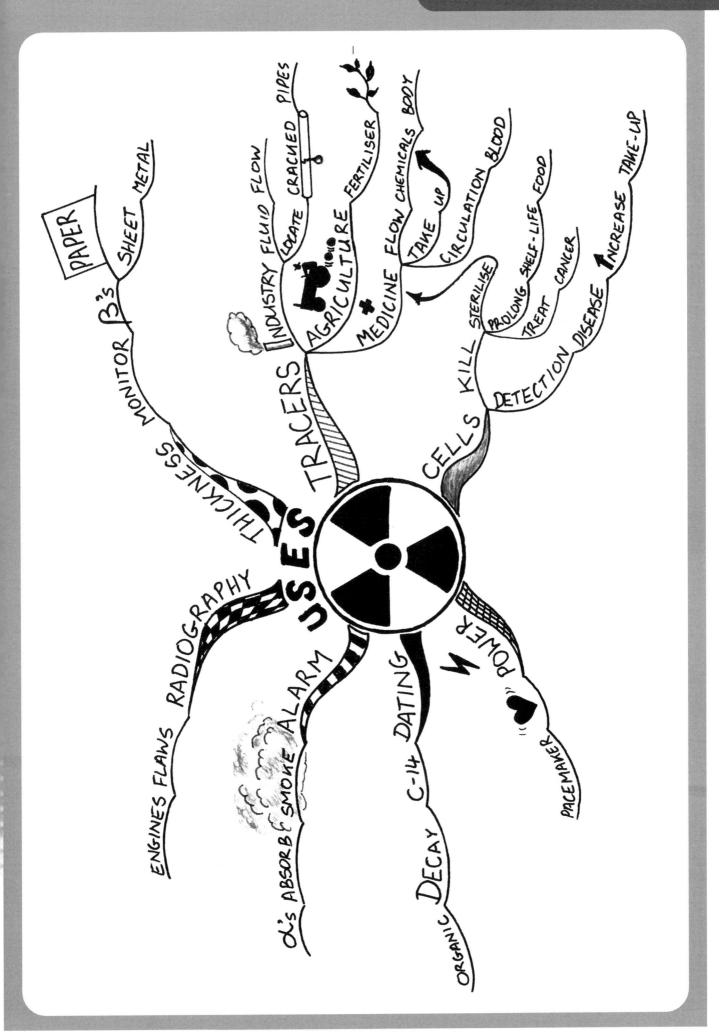

Use of radioisotopes

Radioactive tracer technique

To study the path of a chemical through a system, or to follow how it is being absorbed/taken up, a *very small* sample (tracer) of a radioactive isotope of the chemical can be introduced

This will be treated in exactly the same way by the system, but can be monitored by the RA radiations it emits

- GM tubes or other detectors can be used to follow the path of radioactive isotopes through a process as they emit ionising radiation

- The RA isotope will act in exactly the same way as the stable nuclide it is labelling (same *Z*)

- The one to be used is chosen so that its half-life is short and matched to the life of the process, and with due regard to patient safety

- The amount to be used can be very tiny because the detector can monitor very low numbers of β-particles or γ-rays emitted by the tracer. Gamma's are the most penetrating

 *α-emitters are **not suitable** as they are so heavily ionising and would damage the body or plant. They would also be absorbed before reaching the detector*

Examples of tracer techniques

1. Path and uptake of oxygen in the lungs
2. Uptake of phosphorus from fertilisers by different plants
3. Detection of underground leaks in pipes by adding RA tracer to the liquid flowing
4. Iodine, I-131, and technetium, Tc-99m, have a wide range of uses in medicine

Iodine for investigating the function of the thyroid
I-131 can also be used to treat cancerous thyroid
It can measure blood flow and volume
It can help diagnose heart disease

Technetium, Tc-99m, has a half-life of 6 hours and emits γ-rays of an energy that are easy to detect
It decays to an isotope that is virtually stable as it has a VERY long half-life
It can be used as a tracer instead of I-131
It can also be used to investigate bone disorders

G35 Radiation decay

Beginner's box

- Be familiar with the continuous presence of background radiation

- Know how to allow for this in any radiation experiment by taking a background count and subtracting it from experiment readings

- Revise the meaning of the half-life of a radioactive substance from your GCSE work

- Look again at the Questions in Book A, which show you how to deal with a term such as $e^{-\lambda t}$

Radioactive decay

Before we get involved in any equations or questions let's realise the *magic* of **radioactive decay**

In a radioactive substance *no-one* can tell which nucleus is going to be the next one to spit out an α- or β-particle. This is what's called the **randomness** of the decay.

But, in spite of this, each **sample** has its own particular:

> **activity**
> **rate of decay**
> **half-life**

 The **half-life** is the time it takes for half the original radioactive nuclei to decay

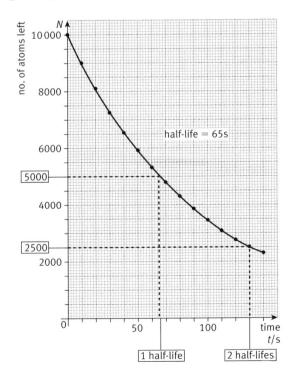

The graph of undecayed nuclei N, against time t, is **exponential**

There are always fewer nuclei, with a chance still to decay, as time goes on

What's more … the half-life can range from less than a millionth of a second:
polonium-220, 3×10^{-7} seconds
to more than a billion years:
thoron-232, 1.4×10^{10} years

Maths of radioactive decay

 *To save getting bogged down in pages of complex equations, etc, the **summary** is coming first!*

- **Avogadro's number [6.022×10^{23} per mol]** is the number of atoms in a **mole** of a substance

  If the **nucleon number** is *A*, then *A* **grams** of the substance will contain **Avogadro's number** of atoms

- The more atoms/nuclei there are to decay, the greater will be the rate of decay, so:

  The rate of decay is proportional to the number of atoms still to decay

  Rate of decay $\propto N$ where N is the number of undecayed nuclei

  > Rate of decay $= -\lambda N$
  > λ is called the decay constant

- The '−' sign comes in because it is *decay*, N is always decreasing.

  λ is also the *probability of decay per unit time*, so
  $\lambda N =$ no. of atoms that would decay per unit time

- **Rate of decay** is the number of nuclei that decay per unit time

  It is known mathematically as $\dfrac{\mathrm{d}N}{\mathrm{d}t}$

  [This value changes throughout the decay, because N changes]

  Rate of decay … $\dfrac{\mathrm{d}N}{\mathrm{d}t} = -\lambda N$

From this, integration can show that

> $N = N_0 e^{-\lambda t}$

where t is time
N_0 is the initial number of atoms/nuclei
$N = N_0$ at $t = 0$

• To find the half-life

$$N = N_0 e^{-\lambda t} \quad \text{so when} \quad N = \frac{N_0}{2}, \ t = t_{1/2}$$

$$\frac{N_0}{2} = N_0 e^{-\lambda t_{1/2}} \quad \text{or} \quad \frac{1}{2} = e^{-\lambda t_{1/2}} \Rightarrow 2 = e^{\lambda t_{1/2}}$$

taking natural logs of both sides:

$$\ln 2 = \lambda t_{1/2}$$

> **Half-life** ... $t_{1/2} = \dfrac{\ln 2}{\lambda} = \dfrac{0.693}{\lambda}$

ln 2 is a constant = 0.693

 Bonus *If either the half-life, $t_{1/2}$, or the decay constant, λ, is known, then the other can be found using this equation*

Activity, *A*

In practice it is easier to measure the number of radiations emitted per second from a sample, using a Geiger–Müller counter (G–M tube).

This will be proportional to the number of nuclei disintegrating per second, known as its **activity**, *A*

$$A = \frac{dN}{dt}$$

so ...
$$A = -\lambda N$$

A and A_0 can replace *N* and N_0 where convenient

$$A = A_0 e^{-\lambda t} \quad \textbf{and} \quad N = N_0 e^{-\lambda t}$$

The unit of **activity** or **decay rate** (rate of decay) is the **becquerel** where

1 becquerel, Bq = 1 decay per second

Questions

1 In an experiment to find the **half-life** of radon gas, using a ratemeter, the following results were obtained:

Background count = 108 min⁻¹

Counts per second, *n*, after time, *t* seconds:

n/s^{-1}	t/s	A/s^{-1}
29.8	0	28
26.3	10	24.5
23.6	20	
21.1	30	
18.8	40	
14.8	60	
11.8	80	
9.4	100	

a Why has a third column been drawn?

b Determine the half-life of the radioactive gas

Answers

a Correction needs to be made for the background radiation

Background count = 108 min⁻¹

$$= \frac{108}{60} = 1.8 \, s^{-1}$$

This must be subtracted from the count-rate, *n*, to find the activity, *A*. The first 2 readings have been entered

b Complete the column and plot activity, *A*, against time, *t*. Check with the figure above

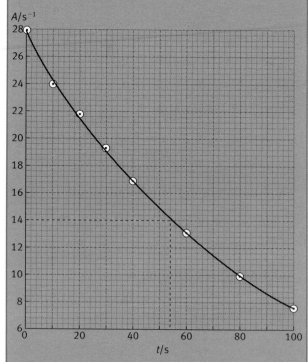

- To find the half-life, note the initial activity is 28.0 s⁻¹ The half-life is the time it takes for the activity to halve ... here to 14.0 s⁻¹

  Reading from the graph, this gives:

  Half-life of radon = 54 s

- Check that you get the same value for the half-life if you use a different starting activity, eg, $A = 20.0 \, s^{-1}$. How long until *A* halves?

We're not pretending decay questions are easy. We've tried to help by including lots of worked answers. Take a deep breath and take them slowly.

Question

2 The half-life of radium D $\left(^{210}_{82}\text{Pb}\right)$ is 20 years. Find its radioactive decay constant

Answer

$\frac{1}{2}$-life, $t_{1/2} = 20$ years $= 20 \times 365 \times 24 \times 60 \times 60$ s

$\qquad = 6.3 \times 10^8$ seconds

Decay constant, $\lambda = \frac{\ln 2}{t_{1/2}} = \frac{0.693}{6.3 \times 10^8}$

$\qquad = 1.1 \times 10^{-9}\,\text{s}^{-1}$

Question

3 The half-life of cobalt-60 is 5.3 years. How long does it take for the activity of a sample of this radioactive isotope to decrease to 70% of its initial value?

Answer

Step 1

So decay constant, $\lambda = \frac{\ln 2}{t_{1/2}} = \frac{0.693}{5.3} = 0.13\,\text{year}^{-1}$

Step 2 If the activity is to have reduced to 70% of its original value, then $A = 70\%$ of A_0

$\qquad$ or $A = \frac{70}{100}A_0 = 0.7\,A_0$

Step 3 To find the time for this reduction, use

$\qquad\qquad A = A_0\text{e}^{-\lambda t}$

here, $\qquad\qquad 0.7\,A_0 = A_0\text{e}^{-\lambda t}$

so, $\qquad\qquad 0.7 = \text{e}^{-\lambda t}$ $\quad\left(\text{and } \text{e}^{-\lambda t} = \frac{1}{\text{e}^{\lambda t}}\right)$

or, turning it upside down, $\frac{1}{0.7} = 1.428 = \text{e}^{\lambda t}$

Taking natural logs of both sides,

$\qquad\qquad \ln 1.428 = \lambda t$ $\qquad$ (see Section A1)

and $\lambda = 0.13\,\text{year}^{-1}$ from step 1

$\qquad t = \frac{\ln 1.428}{0.13} = \frac{0.3567}{0.13} = 2.7$ years

At 2.7 years the activity will have reduced to 70% of its original value

Question

4 The concentration of the radioisotope $^{14}_{6}\text{C}$ in living plants gives 16 000 disintegrations per min per kilogram of carbon

Estimate the age of a piece of timber, if 10.0 g of carbon extracted from it give 75 disintegrations per min

The half-life of carbon-14 is 5.57×10^3 years

 This questions needs a health warning. It is very nasty. Proceed at your peril!

Answer

Step 1 To find decay constant, λ:

$\lambda = \frac{\ln 2}{t_{1/2}} = \frac{0.693}{5.57 \times 10^3} = 0.124 \times 10^{-3}\,\text{year}^{-1}$

Step 2 To find the age of the timber, you need to find the time since it was living with the original activity, A_0

$\qquad A = A_0\text{e}^{-\lambda t}$

Calculate $\frac{A}{A_0}$ in disintegrations **per min per g** (Watch units)

where $A = 75/10\,\text{min}^{-1}\,\text{g}^{-1}$

and $A_0 = 16000/1000\,\text{min}^{-1}\,\text{g}^{-1}$

So

$7.5 = 16\text{e}^{-\lambda t}$

or $\frac{7.5}{16} = \text{e}^{-\lambda t}$, giving $\frac{16}{7.5} = \text{e}^{\lambda t} = 2.13$

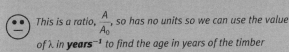 *This is a ratio, $\frac{A}{A_0}$, so has no units so we can use the value of λ in **years^{-1}** to find the age in years of the timber*

Step 3 $\lambda = 0.124 \times 10^{-3}\,\text{years}^{-1}$ from step 1

Taking ln $\quad \lambda t = \ln 2.13$ $\quad$ (see Section A 1)

$\qquad t = \frac{0.758}{0.124 \times 10^{-3}} = 6.1 \times 10^3$ years

The timber is over 6000 years old!

Question

5 In Question **2** above, the decay constant, $\lambda = 1.1 \times 10^{-9}$ s was found for radium D$\left(^{210}_{82}\text{Pb}\right)$.

If the original sample had a mass of 2 g, how many disintegrations per second would it have had initially?

Avogadro's number = 6.0×10^{23} per mol

 Easier question if you also study chemistry

Answer

Step 1 The isotope of lead $^{210}_{82}$Pb has a nucleon number = 210

This tells us that:

$$210\text{ g contain } 6 \times 10^{23}\text{ atoms}$$

$$\text{So 2 g contain } \frac{2 \times 6 \times 10^{23}}{210}\text{ atoms}$$

Giving an original number of lead atoms, N, as:

$$N = \frac{12 \times 10^{23}}{210} = 0.057 \times 10^{23}$$

Step 2 To find dN/d$t = A$, use

$$\frac{dN}{dt} = -\lambda N$$

$$= -1.1 \times 10^{-9} \times 0.057 \times 10^{23}$$

$$= -0.063 \times 10^{14}\text{ s}^{-1}$$

The minus sign shows this is a **decay**, with the isotope of lead having an activity of 6.3×10^{12} disintegrations every second = **6.3×10^{12} Bq**

Half-life, $t_{1/2}$

Question

6 Describe an experiment you could perform, with suitable supervision, in a school laboratory to find the half-life of radon-220.
It emits α-particles and has a half-life of just under a minute

 EXPERIMENT

Answer

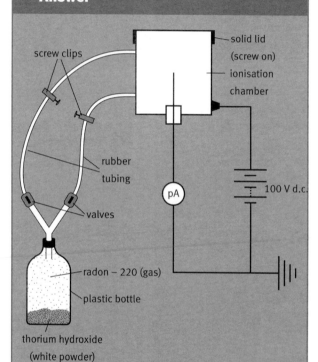

The screw clips should be closed initially and the centre disc removed from the ionisation chamber, if it has one, and the solid lid used to prevent thoron gas escaping

The dc voltage across the ionisation chamber allows the positively charged ions and electrons, produced by the alpha particles, to be collected

- These form the ionisation current $\sim 10^{-11}$ A

    1 picoAmp = 10^{-12} amp = 1 pA

    so a dc amplifier, or VERY sensitive ammeter, will be needed

1 Release the screw clips and squeeze the thoron bottle to puff radon gas into the ionisation chamber

2 Record the ionisation current every 15 s. The fluctuations in the values confirm the random nature of radioactive decay

3 Plot a graph of ionisation current, I in pA, against time, t in seconds

- A typical graph is shown:

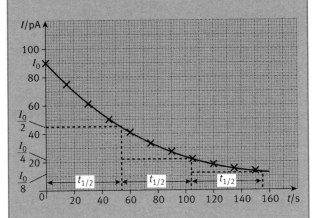

- Call the initial current I_0, at $t = 0$, then find the time it takes for the current to fall to $\frac{I_0}{2}$. This gives the **half-life** of the radon gas

Again, measure other values for the half-life by finding the time it takes for the current to halve. As the decay is exponential, these will give further half-lives and an average can be taken. This could be $\frac{I_0}{2}$ to $\frac{I_0}{4}$, $\frac{I_0}{4}$ to $\frac{I_0}{8}$ etc, each showing the same as $t_{1/2}$

- It should be noted that no allowance has been made for any *background radiation*.
  Before the radon gas was puffed in, the current reading could have been taken and subtracted from all following readings, for greater accuracy

Answer

Step 1 $A = A_0 e^{-\lambda t}$ $\dfrac{A}{A_0} = e^{-\lambda t}$ taking natural logs or ln

$\ln A - \ln A_0 = -\lambda t$, or

$$\ln A = -\lambda t + \ln A_0$$
$$\underset{y}{\uparrow} = \underset{m}{\uparrow}\;\underset{x}{\uparrow} + \underset{c}{\uparrow}$$

Step 2 Plot $\ln A$ as y against t as x, to give a linear graph with gradient $m = -\lambda$

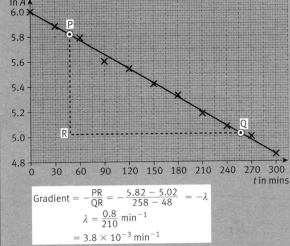

$$\text{Gradient} = -\frac{PR}{QR} = -\frac{5.82 - 5.02}{258 - 48} = -\lambda$$
$$\lambda = \frac{0.8}{210}\ \text{min}^{-1}$$
$$= 3.8 \times 10^{-3}\ \text{min}^{-1}$$

Step 3 Half-life, $t_{1/2} = \dfrac{0.693}{\lambda}$, so $t_{1/2} = \dfrac{0.693}{\text{gradient}}$

From the graph

$$\lambda = 3.8 \times 10^{-3}\ \text{min}^{-1}$$

Giving $t_{1/2} = \dfrac{0.693}{3.8 \times 10^{-3}}$

$$= 180\ \text{min}$$

So the half-life of silver-112 is 180 min

Question

7 A sample of silver contained a small amount of the radioactive isotope Ag-112. Counts were taken and corrected for the background count. Plot a **linear** graph to find the half-life of silver-112

time in min	counts per min	ln *A*
0	409	6.01
30	358	5.88
60	326	5.79
90	270	
120	254	
150	226	
180	206	
210	180	
240	163	
270	149	
300	129	

Variation of half-life for different isotopes

The value of half-lives varies more than any other physical quantity, from a millionth of a second to more than a billion *years*, and yet, it is unaffected by changes in temperature, electric fields, etc

For any use of an isotope, one with an appropriate length of half-life can be selected. (See **Uses of radioisotopes** p. 160)

Nuclide

- The term **nuclide** is often used. It simply refers to a nucleus with a particular number of protons, Z, and a particular number of neutrons, N
  i.e. a particular number of nucleons A

Remember: Nucleon number **A = Z + N**

So any symbol such as $^{\text{Nucleon no. A}}_{\text{Proton no. Z}}X$ is a **nuclide**

Examples: $^{1}_{1}H$, $^{4}_{2}He$, $^{12}_{6}C$, $^{208}_{82}Pb$, $^{226}_{88}Ra$, $^{235}_{92}U$

are all different **nuclides**

 *Nuclides have identical nuclei
Isotopes are different nuclides*

Radioactivity decay chain

A radioactive nuclide does not always decay to form a stable nuclide, it may still be unstable and decay again to form yet another unstable nuclide.
These may be called *parent* and *daughter* nuclides in turn, a parent decaying into a daughter nuclide

- Such a series of decay from one unstable nuclide to another is called a **decay chain** or a **radioactive series**

Question

8 Part of a decay chain can be shown as:

$^{238}_{92}U \Rightarrow {}^{234}_{90}Th \Rightarrow {}^{234}_{91}Pa \Rightarrow {}^{234}_{92}U \Rightarrow {}^{230}_{90}Th \Rightarrow {}^{226}_{88}Ra$

Which particles, in turn, are emitted during each of the 5 decays?

Answer

uranium-238 to thorium-234 = alpha

thorium-234 to protactinium-234 = beta

protactinium-234 to uranium-234 = beta

uranium-234 to thorium-230 = alpha

thorium-230 to radium-226 = alpha

Check that the changes in A and Z are satisfied

Refer to any standard physics text for further examples, such as the thorium series and the actinium series

All such **decay chains** will continue until a stable daughter (!) is reached. This is often a stable isotope of lead, eg,

Lead-206, 207, or 208,
proton no. = 82

 Take a break, if you haven't already!

G36 Energy for nuclear changes

Beginner's box

- Be familiar with the notation:
  $$_Z^A X$$
- where A = nucleon number
  and Z = proton number
  of a nuclide or nucleus X

Mass-energy equivalence

$E = mc^2$ has become the *logo* for physics

Einstein's Special Theory of Relativity [ESTOR] suggests that...

$$\Delta E = \Delta mc^2$$

where ΔE represents a *change* in energy and Δm the corresponding *change* in mass and c is the speed of light in a vacuum

$$c = 3 \times 10^8 \, m \, s^{-1}$$

 *What this actually means in practice is that if water is heated its mass should **increase**. On this scale, the mass increase is too small to be detected (c is so large). This equation has far more significance on an atomic scale*

To satisfy the law of conservation of energy:

- Energy **release** results in mass **decrease**
- Energy **put in** results in mass **increase**

Since $\Delta m = \dfrac{\Delta E}{c^2}$ and $c^2 = (3 \times 10^8)^2$
$$= 9 \times 10^{16} \, m^2 \, s^{-2}$$

Change in mass $= \dfrac{\text{Change in energy}}{9 \times 10^{16}} =$ very tiny

Questions

1

a In a nuclear reactor core uranium-235 is bombarded by slow neutrons, some of which are captured. The resulting fission releases 8×10^{13} J for every kilogram of uranium. Calculate the change in mass of the uranium

b During chemical reactions much smaller amounts of energy are released. For comparison, calculate the mass decrease brought about when 1 kilogram of petrol is burned, if the energy released is 5×10^7 J

Answers

a Energy released, $\Delta E = 8 \times 10^{13}$ J and $\Delta m = \dfrac{\Delta E}{c^2}$

Mass decrease, $\Delta m = \dfrac{8 \times 10^{13}}{9 \times 10^{16}} = 0.89 \times 10^{-3}$ kg
$$\simeq 0.9 \, g$$

This is roughly $\frac{1}{1000}$th of the original mass, which has been converted to energy

b Energy released, $\Delta E = 5 \times 10^7$ J and $\Delta m = \dfrac{\Delta E}{c^2}$

Mass decrease, $\Delta m = \dfrac{5 \times 10^7}{9 \times 10^{16}} = 0.55 \times 10^{-9}$ kg
$$= 0.55 \times 10^{-6} \, g$$

This is less than a *millionth* of the mass decrease for the nuclear reaction.

Question

2 A process similar to that of the fusion occurring in the Sun is when 2 deuterium ($_1^2 H$) nuclei fuse to form a helium-3 nucleus ($_2^3 He$) and a neutron ($_0^1 n$).

How much energy will be released by this reaction?

Mass of $_1^2 H = 3.344 \times 10^{-27}$ kg

Mass of $_2^3 He = 5.008 \times 10^{-27}$ kg

Mass of $_0^1 n = 1.675 \times 10^{-27}$ kg

Answer

Step 1 Write the equation:

$$_1^2 H + _1^2 H \Rightarrow _2^3 He + _0^1 n$$

Mass of LHS $= 2 \times 3.344 \times 10^{-27}$ kg $= 6.688 \times 10^{-27}$ kg

Mass of RHS $= (5.008 + 1.675) \times 10^{-27}$ kg
$$= 6.683 \times 10^{-27} \, kg$$

This represents a **decrease in mass** of:
$$(6.688 - 6.683) \times 10^{-27} = 0.005 \times 10^{-27} \, kg$$

Step 2
So **energy is released** by an amount, $\Delta E = \Delta mc^2$

Energy release $= 0.005 \times 10^{-27} \times (3 \times 10^8)^2$
$$= 0.005 \times 9 \times 10^{-27} \times 10^{16} = 0.045 \times 10^{-11}$$
$$= 4.5 \times 10^{-13} \, J$$

Did you know?

 It's hard to believe that the Sun is going to provide us with all our energy at that rate! In fact it needs to lose mass at a rate of 4 billion kg per second to burn as brightly as it does (nearly 4×10^{26} joules per second) A LOT of nuclear fusion going on!

Unified atomic mass constant, u

The previous questions have shown that the kilogram is *not* the most suitable unit of mass for calculations on the atomic or nuclear scale!

10^{-27} kg seems to feature frequently. Because such minute masses are involved, accuracy is *very* important

*   The isotope **carbon-12** has been chosen to act as the standard

? *Try to find out **why**. It is solid, fairly abundant and is the principal isotope????*

The nucleus of $^{12}_{6}C$ contains 6 protons and 6 neutrons, 12 nucleons in all

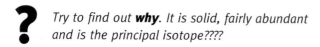

unified atomic mass constant, u, is defined as ...

$$u = \tfrac{1}{12} \text{ mass of } ^{12}_{6}C \text{ atom}$$

So, what is it in kilograms?

A **mole** of carbon contains **6.02×10^{23} atoms** and a mole of carbon has a mass of *exactly* **12 g**

$\therefore$ Mass of $1\ ^{12}_{6}C$ atom $= \dfrac{12 \times 10^{-3}}{6.02 \times 10^{23}}$

$= 1.993 \times 10^{-26}$ kg

$u = \tfrac{1}{12}$ mass of $^{12}_{6}C$ atom $= \dfrac{1.993 \times 10^{-26}}{12}$ kg

$= 1.66 \times 10^{-27}$ kg

the unified atomic mass constant:

$$u = 1.660 \times 10^{-27} \text{ kg}$$

☺ *Remember, we needed a unit of mass of around 10^{-27} kg, so there we have it, the '**u**'*

mass of proton = 1.00728 **u**

mass of neutron = 1.00867 **u**

mass of electron = 0.00055 **u** (often ignored)

mass of carbon atom = 12.00000 **u**

Electron-volt, eV

The other unit needed for this work is one for energy, called the **electron-volt, eV**.

1 joule is the energy gained by accelerating:
    1 coulomb across 1 volt
1 eV is the energy gained by accelerating:
    1 electron across 1 volt

1 electron has a charge of 1.602×10^{-19} coulomb

Energy gained = Charge × volts

So 1 electron-volt, $1\,eV = 1.602 \times 10^{-19} \times 1$ joules

$$1\,eV = 1.602 \times 10^{-19} \text{ J and } 1\,J = \dfrac{1}{1.602 \times 10^{-19}} \text{ eV}$$

☺ *HINT to get from:*
joules to electron-volts:
***divide** by 1.602×10^{-19}*
electron-volts to joules:
***multiply** by 1.602×10^{-19}*

☺ *Use the information given above in answering Questions **3–7**.*

Energy equivalence of 1 u

Questions

3

a Calculate the energy released in joules if a change in mass of just 1 unified atomic mass constant, 1 u, has occurred.
Is this the result of an increase or decrease in mass?

b What is this energy in electron-volts?

Answers

a Using $E = mc^2$
Energy equivalence of 1 u

$$= 1.660 \times 10^{-27} \times (2.998 \times 10^8)^2 \text{ J}$$
$$= 1.492 \times 10^{-10} \text{ J}$$

Because energy was *released*, this will mean a *decrease* in mass

☺ ***Energy release** rhymes with **mass decrease!***

b Energy equivalence of 1 u

$$= 1.492 \times 10^{-10} \text{ J}$$
$$= \dfrac{1.492 \times 10^{-10}}{1.602 \times 10^{-19}} \text{ eV (see } hint \text{ above)}$$
$$1\,u = 0.931 \times 10^9 \text{ eV}$$

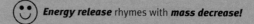

Energy equivalence of 1 **u** = 931 MeV

Mass defect

Question

4 Find the total mass of the particles making up an atom of $^{12}_{6}C$ and compare it with its atomic mass

Answer

carbon-12 atom

6 protons 6 neutrons 6 electrons

$[6 \times 1.00728\,u] + [6 \times 1.00867\,u] + [6 \times 0.00055\,u]$

$[6.04368\,u] \quad + \quad [6.05202\,u] \quad + \quad [0.0033\,u]$

Total mass of particles = 12.099 u

Atomic mass of carbon-12 = 12 u *(exactly)*

There is a **mass defect** between the mass of the particles and the mass of the atom

For $^{12}_{6}C$, mass defect = 0.099 u = Δm

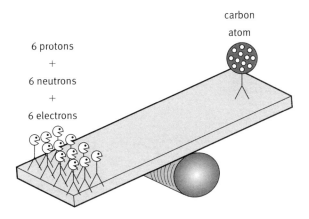

6 protons
+
6 neutrons
+
6 electrons

carbon atom

Mass of the particles > Mass of the atom
... *HELP!*

 EINSTEIN to the rescue!

When the particles **combine** to form an atom energy is released and:

> *energy release* means *mass decrease*

So a **mass defect** should be *expected* between the mass of the particles and the mass of the atom

Binding energy

If energy is *released on forming* an atom from its separate parts:

Energy is *required to separate* the atom into its constituent parts

This energy (which we can think of as holding the atom together) is known as the **binding energy** of the atom

- The **binding energy** is the energy equivalent to the **mass defect**

Question

5 What is the binding energy of carbon-12?

Answer

From the last question, **4**
Mass defect for $^{12}_{6}C$ = 0.099 u
also **energy equivalent of 1 u = 931 MeV**
giving **binding energy** of $^{12}_{6}C$ = 0.099 × 931 MeV
$\qquad\qquad\qquad\qquad = 92.2\,MeV$
Alternatively, $E = mc^2$ could have been used again

Binding energy per nucleon

To compare nuclei and to identify the most stable it is more useful to find the **binding energy per nucleon** for a nucleus

(The curve showing the change of binding energy per nucleon with nucleon number, A, is shown in figure (i), p. 170

Questions

6 What is the **binding energy per nucleon** for carbon-12

a in electron-volts

b in joules?

Answers

a Binding energy of an atom of $^{12}_{6}C$ = 92.2 MeV (Question **5**)
Each nucleus contains 6 protons, $Z = 6$
$\qquad\qquad\qquad\qquad$ and 6 neutrons, $N = 6$
$\qquad\qquad\qquad\qquad$ giving 12 nucleons, $A = 12$
So
Binding energy per nucleon

for $^{12}_{6}C = \dfrac{92.2 \times 10^6}{12}$ eV

$\qquad = 7.68 \times 10^6$ eV

$\qquad \textbf{= 7.68 MeV}$

b To convert this to joules, remember we found:
$1\,eV = 1.602 \times 10^{-19}$ J
So, $7.68\,MeV = 1.602 \times 10^{-19} \times 7.68 \times 10^6$ J
Binding energy per nucleon, $^{12}_{6}C$ = 12.3 × 10⁻¹³ J

$$\text{Binding energy per nucleon} = \frac{\text{binding energy}}{\text{nucleon number, } A}$$

The importance of the binding energy per nucleon lies in the fact that it determines the **stability** of a nucleus

The higher the value of the binding energy per nucleon, the more stable the element will be

The mass defect per nucleon is proportional to the binding energy per nucleon

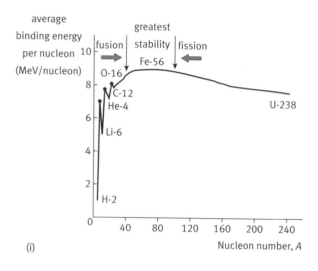

(i)

i The value of binding energy per nucleon starts very low for deuterium, $^{2}_{1}H$, rise sharply to a peak at iron, $^{56}_{26}Fe$, and then fall gradually towards uranium, $^{238}_{92}U$

ii Interestingly, $^{4}_{2}He$, $^{12}_{6}C$, and $^{16}_{8}O$, all multiples of the alpha particle, have stabilities that lie outside and *above* the general curve. They are unusually stable

iii Lead, $^{208}_{82}Pb$, often at the end of a radioactive chain, is to be found only just below the peak for iron

iv Nuclides of intermediate mass number are the most stable, with the greatest binding energy per nucleon

• So 2 light nuclides fuse to make a heavier one, releasing energy (**fusion**)

• And a heavy nucleus splits into 2 lighter ones, also emitting energy (**fission**)

In both cases, the resulting product has a greater binding energy/nucleon and so is more stable

Questions

7 nuclide	X	Y
Atomic mass	17.0049 u	15.9994 u
total mass of nucleons	17.1407 u	16.1320 u

a Calculate the mass defect in **u**'s of nuclei X and Y

b Which will be the more stable element, X or Y? Explain your answer

c Find the binding energy in joules of X and Y

d What assumption has been made about the nuclei of X and Y in answering part **b**?

Answers

a (1) Mass defect of X = (17.1407 − 17.0049) u
         = 0.1358 u
(2) Mass defect of Y = (16.1320 − 15.9994) u
         = 0.1326 u

b X will be more stable

Mass defect is proportional to binding energy; so X, needing more energy to disturb it, will be more stable

c

The symbol '≡' instead of '=' is used to mean 'equivalent to' instead of 'equal to'
*Mass is not **equal to** energy but **equivalent to** a certain amount of energy*

Step 1 Binding energy of 1 u ≡ 931 MeV
      and 1 eV = 1.602×10^{-19} J
so 1 u ≡ $931 \times 10^{6} \times 1.602 \times 10^{-19}$ J
giving 1 u ≡ 1491.5×10^{-13} J

$$1\,u \equiv 1.4915 \times 10^{-10}\ J$$

Step 2 (1) Binding energy of X = $0.1358 \times 1.4915 \times 10^{-10}$ J
         = 0.2025×10^{-10} J

(2) Binding energy of Y = $0.1326 \times 1.4915 \times 10^{-10}$ J
         = 0.1978×10^{-10} J

d It has been assumed that X and Y have the same number of nucleons, since the binding energy per nucleon should have been compared for stability

Nuclear stability

It is worth looking briefly at the chart showing **neutron number**, N, against **proton number**, Z, for stable nuclei

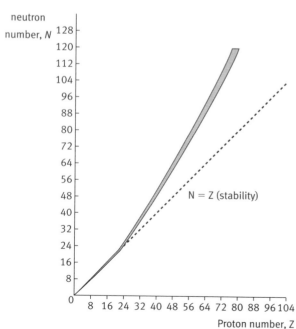

i The lightest nuclei lie close to the $N = Z$ line

ii The heavier nuclides have more neutrons than protons, so lie above the line. This follows from earlier study **G34** because the extra neutrons help to 'space out' the positive protons, overcoming their electrical repulsion

iii Radioactive nuclides that lie above the 'stable' curve decay by electron, β^- decay
Those that lie below the curve decay by positron, β^+ or alpha, α^{++} decay.
In these ways radioactive nuclides get nearer to stability

To find out how this energy is controlled and made to provide a useful supply of power refer to any 'A' level Physics text

Look for the meaning and purpose of the following:
slow neutron
fission fragments
fast neutron
stable chain reaction
fuel rods
moderator (graphite)
control rods (boron)
coolant (high-pressure carbon dioxide)
in a nuclear reactor

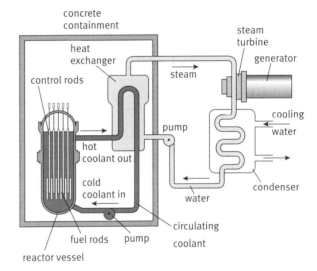

Nuclear reactor

Questions

8 The equation:

$$^{235}_{92}\text{U} + ^{1}_{0}\text{n} \Rightarrow ^{141}_{56}\text{Ba} + ^{92}_{36}\text{Kr} + 3^{1}_{0}\text{n} + \text{energy}$$

describes one possible reaction taking place in a thermal fission reactor, when a uranium-235 nucleus captures a slow neutron

To become more stable, it splits into 2 smaller nuclei and 3 fast neutrons are ejected

a Find the energy released by this reaction if the binding energies involved are:

uranium-235 . . . 1736.8 MeV
barium-141 . . . 1161.5 MeV
krypton-90 . . . 754.6 MeV

b Make an estimation of how much energy in joules would be released by 1 gram of uranium-235 in the reactor.
Avogadro's constant $= 6.022 \times 10^{23}$ per mole

 *In this section **G36** on nuclear changes, values used and answers given have all been given to more than 3 significant figures.*

The increased accuracy has demanded this.

Answers

a $1161.5 + 754.6 = 1916.1\,\text{MeV}$

$1916.1 - 1736.8 = 179.3\,\text{MeV}$

Each fission produces nearly 180 MeV of energy
Most of this energy is kinetic of the fission fragments, here barium and krypton, and the *fast* neutrons

b *Step 1*
235 grams of $^{235}_{92}\text{U}$ contain 6.022×10^{23} atoms,

so 1 gram . . . contains $\dfrac{6.022 \times 10^{23}}{235} = 0.0256 \times 10^{23}$

$\qquad\qquad\qquad\qquad\quad = 2.56 \times 10^{21}$ atoms

Step 2 1 reaction released 179.3 MeV, so
2.56×10^{21} atoms will release $2.56 \times 10^{21} \times 179.3$ MeV

1 gram of U-235 releases . . . 459.0×10^{27} eV

Step 3 Energy in joules $= 459.0 \times 10^{27} \times 1.602 \times 10^{-19}$

$\qquad$ 1 gram of U-235 releases $\sim 735 \times 10^{8}\,\text{J}$

H37 Photons

> ### Beginner's box
>
> - Know that the energy linked with electromagnetic radiation of frequency, f, is given by: $E = hf$
> - where h = Planck's constant = 6.63×10^{-34} J s

Photoelectric effect

When apple-bobbing, a minimum energy is needed to extract the apples from the water in the bucket ... overcoming the surface tension of the water, etc

- To emit an electron from a metal surface a minimum energy is needed.

  This is called the **work function**, ϕ, of the metal

Minimum energy for electron to escape = ϕ

 EXPERIMENT

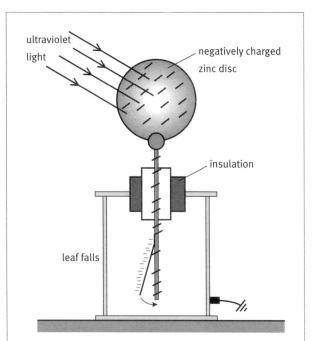

1 Clean a disc of zinc with emery paper and attach it to the top of a *positively* charged gold leaf electroscope

2 Shine ultraviolet radiation onto the clean zinc ... OK ... so nothing happens!

3 Now charge the electroscope *negatively* and illuminate it with ultraviolet light, as shown in the figure

4 The gold leaf immediately falls, showing that its charge has been carried away

5 Lennard showed that the particles emitted from the zinc plate, to carry the charge away, were electrons

6 Light of *longer* wavelength, however *intense*, could not produce this effect

Einstein's photoelectric equation

If light is to emit electrons from the surface of a metal, it must have a minimum frequency:

cut-off frequency = f_0

so that at least its electron's minimum escape energy is provided ... $hf_0 = \phi$

[now $E = hf$, where h is Planck's constant] see p. 175

Light of *higher* frequency, f, will give escaping electrons surplus energy as kinetic energy, where

> Light of energy, $E = hf$
> $$hf = \phi + \tfrac{1}{2} m_e v^2$$
> $$hf = hf_0 + \tfrac{1}{2} m_e v^2$$

m_e = mass of electron, v = maximum
                                    speed of electron

f_0 = cut-off frequency

Maximum kinetic energy of photoelectrons

$$\tfrac{1}{2} m_e v_{max}^2 = hf - \phi$$

v_{max} = maximum speed of photoelectrons
[because $\phi = hf_0$ is needed just to *emit* the electrons]

$$\tfrac{1}{2} m_e v_{max}^2 = hf - hf_0$$

KE_max of photoelectrons:

$$\boxed{\tfrac{1}{2} m_e v_{max}^2 = h(f - f_0)}$$

Work function, ϕ, is a constant for each metal and $\phi = hf_0$ where h = 6.63×10^{-34} J s

*Energy of emitted electrons $\propto$ **Frequency** of light wave*

*Current of photoelectrons $\propto$ **Intensity** of incident light*

Question

1 Light of wavelength less than 5.45×10^{-7} m produces a photoelectric effect with lithium. Find the minimum energy needed to remove an electron from a clean surface of lithium

 Remember ... if the wavelength goes down, $\Downarrow$, the frequency goes up, $\Uparrow$.

Answer

Step 1 $\lambda = 5.47 \times 10^{-7}$ m, and $v = f\lambda$

For light, $v = c = 3 \times 10^8$ m s^{-1}, so $f = \dfrac{c}{\lambda} = \dfrac{3 \times 10^8}{5.47 \times 10^{-7}}$

$= 0.548 \times 10^{15}$ Hz

Frequency of incident light $= 5.5 \times 10^{14}$ Hz

Only light of **higher** frequency than this will be sufficiently energetic to remove electrons from the lithium surface

Step 2 This minimum energy, at the cut-off frequency, is given by:

Minimum energy $= hf_0$ and $h = 6.6 \times 10^{-34}$ J s
$= 6.6 \times 10^{-34} \times 5.5 \times 10^{14}$ (J s $\times$ s^{-1})
$= 3.6 \times 10^{-20}$
$= 3.6 \times 10^{-19}$ J

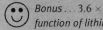 *Bonus ... 3.6×10^{-19} J is also the value of the work function of lithium, ϕ.*

In electron-volts $\left(= \dfrac{no.\ of\ Joules}{no.\ of\ Coulombs} \right)$

Work function $= \dfrac{3.63 \times 10^{-19}}{1.6 \times 10^{-19}}$

since 1.6×10^{-19} C is the charge on an electron.

Lithium work function, $\phi = 2.3$ eV

Question

2 When caesium is irradiated with light of a certain frequency, photoelectrons with maximum speed 4.0×10^5 m s^{-1} are emitted. If the work function of caesium is 3.04×10^{-19} J, what is the frequency of the incident light?
(mass of electron, $m_e = 9.0 \times 10^{-31}$ kg
$h = 6.6 \times 10^{-34}$ J s)

Answer

Max. KE of photoelectrons $= hf - \phi$

$\tfrac{1}{2} m_e v_{max}^2 = hf - \phi$

$hf = \tfrac{1}{2} m_e v_{max}^2 + \phi$

$hf = \dfrac{9.0 \times 10^{-31} \times (4 \times 10^5)^2}{2} + 3.04 \times 10^{-19}$

$= 72 \times 10^{-21} + 304 \times 10^{-21}$

$f = \dfrac{376 \times 10^{-21}}{6.6 \times 10^{-34}} = 57 \times 10^{13}$ Hz

Frequency of incident light $= 5.7 \times 10^{14}$ Hz

Questions

3 The work function of sodium, Na, is 2.3 eV. Find

a its threshold frequency

b the maximum speed of electrons produced when Na is irradiated with light of wavelength $\lambda = 5 \times 10^{-7}$ m

c the value of V required to just stop the photoelectrons

Given ... $h = 6.6 \times 10^{-34}$ J s
$c = 3 \times 10^8$ m s^{-1}
1 eV $= 1.6 \times 10^{-19}$ J
$m_e = 9.1 \times 10^{-31}$ kg

Answers

a $\phi = hf_0$
$2.3 \times 1.6 \times 10^{-19} = 6.6 \times 10^{-34} f_0$

$\therefore \quad f_0 = \dfrac{2.3 \times 1.6 \times 10^{-19}}{6.6 \times 10^{-34}} = 5.6 \times 10^{14}$ Hz

b *Step 1* $\lambda = 5 \times 10^{-7}$ m, $f = \dfrac{c}{\lambda} = \dfrac{3 \times 10^8}{5 \times 10^{-7}} = 6 \times 10^{14}$ Hz

$\tfrac{1}{2} m_e v_{max}^2 = h(f - f_0)$

$v_{max}^2 = \dfrac{2 \times 6.6 \times 10^{-34} \times 0.4 \times 10^{14}}{9.1 \times 10^{-31}} = 0.58 \times 10^{11}$

$= 5.8 \times 10^{10}$ m^2 s^{-2}

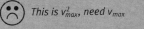 *This is v_{max}^2, need v_{max}*

$v_{max} = 2.4 \times 10^5$ m s$^{-1} = 240$ km s^{-1}!

c Stopping potential, V, can be found from:

$eV = \tfrac{1}{2} m_e v_{max}^2 = h(f - f_0) = 2.64 \times 10^{-20}$ [part **b**]

$V = \dfrac{2.64 \times 10^{-20}}{1.6 \times 10^{-19}} = 0.165$ V

or $\quad 1.6 \times 10^{-19} V = \tfrac{1}{2} \times 9.1 \times 10^{-31} \times 5.8 \times 10^{10}$

$V = 16.5 \times 10^{-2} = 0.165$ V

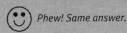 *Phew! Same answer.*

 EXPERIMENT

To find a value for **h**, **Planck's constant**, and to verify Einstein's photoelectric equation

$$\tfrac{1}{2} m_e v_{max}^2 = h(f - f_0)$$

 This experiment needs a health warning. It is very nasty. Only proceed if it is on your syllabus

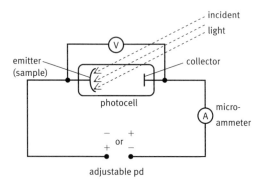

adjustable pd

The curved metal sample is contained in an evacuated bulb, partly surrounding a metal wire … known as a photocell

The photocell is illuminated by monochromatic light, often ultraviolet

If the light is of high enough frequency, −ve photoelectrons will be emitted from the metal surface and be collected by the +ve wire anode

Unless the wire is made **negative** with respect to the earthed metal sample (*sneaky*)

Here it is. The voltage is increased negatively until no more photoelectrons are received by the collector

- This reverse or **stopping potential**, V_s, means that no current will flow in the electrometer

- **All** of the electrons have been stopped, including those with maximum KE

  Electric energy = kinetic energy

  $$eV_s = \tfrac{1}{2} m_e v_{max}^2$$

  But $\tfrac{1}{2} m_e v_{max}^2 = hf - \phi$

  So $\ldots eV_s = hf - \phi$

  $$V_s = \frac{h}{e}f - \frac{\phi}{e}$$
  $$\uparrow \quad \uparrow\uparrow \quad \uparrow$$
  $$y = mx + c$$

- Plot V_s values against f-values

Sometimes a set of filters is used, giving light of known wavelength in the path of the incident light.
Their frequencies can be found using $c = f\lambda$

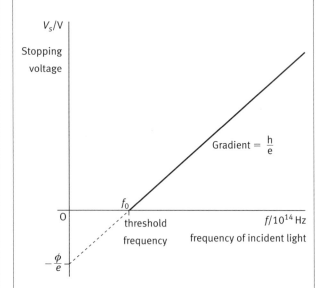

- If the graph is a straight line, then Einstein's photoelectric equation holds

- Planck's constant, h, can be found from the gradient $= \dfrac{h}{e}$

- Work function for the metal, ϕ, from the intercept $= -\dfrac{\phi}{e}$

Quantum theory

Early last century (1900–1910), physicists were struggling with a dilemma . . . *Light . . . is it a wave or is it a particle?*

Black body radiation and the photoelectric effect did not fit into the wave theory that had worked so well to explain diffraction and similar effects

The following chart summarises some of the arguments:

problem	wave theory says	particle theory says
1 energy carried:	by oscillations of electromagnetic fields	by stream of light particles (photons)
2 absorption of energy	causes oscillations of electrons in metals → electrons escaping from surface	as indivisible packets of energy called **quanta** with energy; $E = hf$, where h is Planck's constant
3 low intensities of light	no emission	even at lowest intensity, some emission
4 cut-off of emission due to	intensity	frequency
5 energy of emitted electrons	$\propto$ intensity of illumination of beam of light	$\propto$ depends on frequency of light wave
problems explained by	interference diffraction polarisation	Intensity of beam of light $\propto$ no. of particles/s $\propto$ no. of electrons emitted/s, (the current). One light particle, quantum, emits one electron **if** it carries enough energy (above cut-off frequency) i.e. **photoelectric effect**

Wave-particle duality
↓
Quantum theory

Light is emitted and absorbed in indivisible packets of energy called '**quanta**'. Einstein said:

Energy, $E \propto f$, frequency of light wave

 $E = hf$ **where h is the Planck constant** $= 6.6 \times 10^{-34}$ J s

emission of light by source . . .	light **travelling** from place to place . . .	**absorption** of light by metal, etc
↓	↓	↓
single electron emits single **quantum** or **PHOTON**	**WAVE** behaviour	single electron absorbs single **quantum** or **PHOTON**
↓		↓
PARTICLE behaviour		**PARTICLE** behaviour

Energy levels

- If a **pure** element is excited by burning or by electrical discharge, the spectrum from the E/M radiation it emits will contain only *certain* frequencies
  Seen through a diffraction grating or spectrometer, the radiation will appear as a series of coloured lines

- It is called a **line spectrum**. Each element has its own characteristic spectrum
  This suggests that each atom is only giving out a very particular set of frequencies

Quantum theory suggests that this radiation is the result of electrons in the atom jumping between a particular set of **energy levels/states**

 Think of a pine tree with its branches in layers, almost like an irregular ladder. Think of a flock of bad-tempered birds, who fly to the tree to perch, but want a branch each

The birds cannot perch between the branches

The birds at the top of the tree have the highest energy, with the ones below each having their own lower energy

- In an atom, each electron can only occupy one of a set of particular **energy levels/states**

- Electrons settle at the *lowest* energy level available ... **ground state**

  But atoms are constantly being bombarded by energy from outside, which knocks electrons up into higher empty energy levels
  This leaves an empty level below it

- An electron will drop into this, emitting its extra energy as a **photon** of light

- An atom above its ground state is said to be **excited**

Energy level changes

E_2 is the higher energy, E_1 is the lower energy

$$E_2 - E_1 = \text{energy of photon}$$
$$\Delta \boldsymbol{E} = \boldsymbol{hf}$$

Where:

ΔE = change in energy, in joules
f = frequency of emitted radiation, in Hz or s^{-1}
h = Planck's constant = 6.626×10^{-34} J s

- Frequency, $f = \dfrac{\Delta E}{h}$, and wavelength, $\lambda = \dfrac{hc}{\Delta E}$

ΔE is the **quantum** of energy emitted or absorbed as light, by a single electron, as it changes its energy state

Questions

4 The diagram below shows some of the energy levels of the mercury atom. When unexcited, the levels above the ground state are empty.

0	——————— Energy in eV
−1.6	———————
−3.7	———————
−5.5	———————
−10.4	———————

Decide whether the following statements are **True**, enter **(yes)** or **False**, enter **(no)**

statement	true
the ionisation energy of an electron in the ground state is 10.4 eV	a
1.66×10^{-18} J are needed to emit an electron from the unexcited atom	b
an electron moving from the −5.5 eV to the −1.6 eV level gives out a photon of energy 3.9 eV	c
radiation of wavelength 141×10^{-9} m is emitted when an electron jumps from the −1.6 eV to the −10.4 eV level	d

Answers

a It is common practice/convention to call the **energy levels** of an atom **negative**, because energy needs to be given to the atom to remove an electron from it.
Here it is *true* that 10.4 eV would be needed to ionise the mercury atom

b $10.4\,\text{eV} = 10.4 \times 1.6 \times 10^{-19}\,\text{J} = 16.6 \times 10^{-19}\,\text{J}$
$\qquad\quad = 1.66 \times 10^{-18}\,\text{J} \ldots \textit{true}$

c 5.5 eV is a *lower* energy level than −1.6 eV, so
$E_2 - E_1 = (-1.6 - -5.5) = (-1.6 + 5.5) = 3.9\,\text{eV}$ of energy would be *needed* to make this move. Statement is . . . *not true*

d $E_2 - E_1 = (-1.6 - -10.4) = (-1.6 + 10.4) = \textbf{8.8\,eV}$
Frequency of radiation of wavelength $141 \times 10^{-9}\,\text{m}$ is
$$f = \frac{c}{\lambda} = \frac{3 \times 10^8}{141 \times 10^{-9}} = 0.0213 \times 10^{17} = 2.13 \times 10^{15}\,\text{s}^{-1}$$

Now $E_2 - E_1 = hf$ if **d** is to be true
$\qquad hf = 6.6 \times 10^{-34} \times 2.13 \times 10^{15} = 14 \times 10^{-19}\,\text{J}$

in eV, $hf = \dfrac{14 \times 10^{-19}}{e} = \dfrac{14 \times 10^{-19}}{1.6 \times 10^{-19}} = \textbf{8.8\,eV}$

Statement is . . . *true* !!!!!!

 HINT! . . . It's always worth making a reasoned guess about questions like this. There's a 50% chance you'll be right

H38 Waves and/or particles?

Wave – particle duality of matter?

In Section **H37** the schizophrenic behaviour of light was dealt with by considering it to have wave properties when travelling, but to be emitted and absorbed as indivisible quanta or packets of energy (light photons)

Louis de Broglie (a prince and one-time historian) suggested, in 1924, that $E = hf$ should be applied to electrons as well as photons. In other words, to matter as well as to light. **Electrons** should have **wave properties** associated with them

Wavelength of an Electron?

Begin with ... $E = mc^2$ ... so ... $mc = \dfrac{E}{c}$

But ... mc = mass × velocity = momentum = p

So ... $p = \dfrac{E}{c}$

Now consider $E = hf$ ... and $c = f\lambda$, so $f = \dfrac{c}{\lambda}$

Giving ... $E = \dfrac{hc}{\lambda}$ ... or $\dfrac{E}{c} = \dfrac{h}{\lambda} = p$ from above

$$p = \dfrac{h}{\lambda}$$

de Broglie's wavelength

$$\lambda = \dfrac{h}{mv} \quad \text{... or, } mv = \dfrac{h}{\lambda}$$

$h = 6.63 \times 10^{-34}$ J s = Planck's constant

This means that $\lambda \propto \dfrac{1}{P}$ ... or $P\lambda$ = constant, for *any* particle. The greater its momentum, the shorter its de Broglie wavelength

 Check whether your syllabus requires this treatment
Since electrons are travelling at speeds approaching that of light, it is their relativistic

mass that should be considered. This takes account of their speed according to the special theory of relativity

If m_0 is the rest mass, and m *the mass when moving at speed,* v, *then:*

$$m = \dfrac{m_0}{\sqrt{1 - \dfrac{v^2}{c^2}}}$$

this is only important when $v \Rightarrow c$

unimportant if $v \ll c$, $\dfrac{v^2}{c^2} \Rightarrow 0$, *and* $m \Rightarrow m_0$

Questions

5

a Estimate the de Broglie wavelength for an electron with speed 10^7 m s^{-1} and mass of the order of 10^{-30} kg

b How many times slower would a neutron (mass $\sim 2000 \times$ electron mass) have to travel, to have the same wavelength as the electron?

Answers

a $\lambda = \dfrac{h}{mv} = \dfrac{6.63 \times 10^{-34}}{10^{-30} \times 10^7} = 6.63 \times 10^{-11}$ m

electron wavelength $\sim 10^{-10}$ m

For comparison, **wavelength of light $\sim 10^{-7}$ m**

b A neutron has a mass about 2000 times that of an electron, so for $\lambda = \dfrac{h}{mv}$ to be the same, its speed must be about 2000 times *smaller* than for the electron

electron momentum = $m_e v_e$

neutron momentum = $2000\,m_e \times \dfrac{v_e}{2000} = m_e v_e$

 Same momentum, same de Broglie wavelength

Question

6 Estimate the de Broglie wavelength of a tennis ball served at Wimbledon at nearly 120 mph (190 km h^{-1})
The mass of a tennis ball $\approx$ 55 g

Answer

Step 1 In m s^{-1}, 190 km h^{-1} = $\dfrac{190 \times 10^3 \text{ m}}{60 \times 60 \text{ s}}$

$\qquad\qquad\qquad = 53$ m s^{-1}

Step 2 $\lambda = \dfrac{h}{mv} = \dfrac{6.63 \times 10^{-34}}{55 \times 10^{-3} \times 53} = 0.002\,27 \times 10^{-31}$ m

Tennis ball wavelength $\sim 10^{-34}$ m, small enough to neglect!

 Don't even try at this stage to understand how a tennis ball has a wavelength

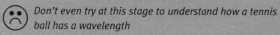

Question

7 Find the wavelength of an electron in a television tube that has been accelerated through 7 kV

Mass of electron $= 10^{-30}$ kg;
charge, $e = 1.6 \times 10^{-19}$ C

Answer

Step 1 To find speed of electron:
electrical energy $=$ KE, gained by electron
$$eV = \tfrac{1}{2} m_e v^2$$

So ... $v^2 = \dfrac{2eV}{m_e}$ ... and $v = \sqrt{\dfrac{2eV}{m_e}}$

$v = \sqrt{\dfrac{2 \times 1.6 \times 10^{-19} \times 7 \times 10^3}{10^{-30}}} = \sqrt{22.4 \times 10^{14}}$
$\quad = 4.7 \times 10^7 \,\mathrm{m\,s^{-1}}$

Step 2 To find wavelength of electron:
$\lambda = \dfrac{h}{mv} = \dfrac{6.63 \times 10^{-34}}{10^{-30} \times 4.7 \times 10^7} = 1.4 \times 10^{-11}$ m

- The higher the accelerating voltage, V, the smaller the de Broglie wavelength, λ (because the speed is higher)

☺ *Bonus question. Are there electrons in the nucleus? ... Fire an electron at a nucleus ... one of smaller and smaller wavelength would be needed to get close enough.*
So one of higher and higher energy would be needed.
At nuclear sizes, the electron's energy would be so great that even the attraction of the positive nucleus would not be able to hold the electron,
Answer ... No

Potential physics Profs only...
Are these matter waves? ... No!
The intensity of a wave at a point gives the probability of a particle being at that point
The probability of finding an electron at a given point $\propto$ (amplitude of the wave)^2 at that point

Electron diffraction

- If electrons have wave properties, it should be possible to see diffraction patterns, with the right conditions
  The main thing is to get the spacing of the 'grating' right

- Electron waves are so small ($\sim 10^{-10}$ m), similar to X-rays, that an atomic lattice was chosen ... a very thin sheet of graphite as a grating

- The electrons were accelerated by a pd of 3500–5000 V before hitting the graphite target. Electrons were diffracted from the carbon atoms to form concentric rings on a fluorescent screen

- As the voltage is increased, the energy and momentum of the electrons increases ...
  the diameter of the rings decreases ...
  de Broglie wavelength, λ, decreases.
  Confirming in practice what was expected from the theory

Playtime

Don't miss this ... **Experiment**

1 Set up a tiny bright bulb (compact light source) at the far end of the lab.

2 Powder a large sheet of glass (glass cupboard door) with lycopodium powder (or talc)

3 Look **through** the powdered glass at the light

4 Coloured rings will be seen surrounding the bright source

The two sets of rings are caused either by irregular spacing of dust,
or by carbon atoms in layers of graphite in the case of the electrons

INDEX

Index

Study and Revise AS and A2 Level Physics